# Service Quality Management
## In
## Hospitality & Tourism

# Service Quality Management

## In

## Hospitality & Tourism

Editors

Jay Kandampully, Ph.D., Connie Mok, Ph.D.
Beverley Sparks, Ph.D.

JAICO PUBLISHING HOUSE

Ahmedabad  Bangalore  Bhopal  Chennai
Delhi  Hyderabad  Kolkata  Mumbai

Published by Jaico Publishing House
A-2 Jash Chambers, 7-A Sir Phirozshah Mehta Road
Fort, Mumbai - 400 001
jaicopub@jaicobooks.com
www.jaicobooks.com

© The Haworth Press, Inc.

Published in arrangement with
The Haworth Hospitality Press®
an imprint of The Haworth Press, Inc.
10 Alice Street, Binghamton, NY 13904-1580, USA

SERVICE QUALITY MANAGEMENT IN HOSPITALITY & TOURISM

I! **ISBN** 81-7992-184-0

Fi

9 788179 921845

Printed by
Kumar Offset Printer
Delhi - 92

# CONTENTS

# ABOUT THE EDITORS

**Jay Kandampully, PhD,** is Associate Professor and Head of Services Management and Hospitality, Faculty of Business, Economics and Law, The University of Queensland, Ipswich, Australia. Dr. Kandampully has nine years of managerial experience in hotels in Austria, India, and the United States. He enjoys close alliances with leading service organizations in the United States, United Kingdom, Australia, New Zealand, Singapore, Malaysia, and India, where he is often invited to conduct management seminars to update managers with nascent strategies. He is the author of the book *Hotels As Integrated Services* scheduled for publication in 2000. He has published over fifty articles and has presented numerous papers at international conferences on issues relating to service quality, services marketing, and services management. His research publication on the concept of "Service Loyalty" earned him the prestigious "Literati Award" for the most outstanding paper of 1997, published in the journal *Managing Service Quality*. Dr. Kandampully's recent publication in the journal *Management Decision* received the "1999 Citation of Excellence Award." He was also recognized for "Excellence in Teaching" in 1997 and 1998. Dr. Kandampully serves on the editorial board of six refereed journals and is the editor of the journal *Managing Service Quality*. He holds a PhD in service quality management, and an MBA specializing in services marketing, both from the University of Exeter, England. His undergraduate qualification was in Hotel Management from Salzburg, Austria.

**Connie Mok, PhD,** is Associate Professor in the Conrad N. Hilton College of Hotel and Restaurant Management at the University of Houston in Texas. Dr. Mok has extensive teaching, industrial, and consulting experience in the hospitality and tourism fields. She is the author or co-author of over sixty-five published articles in academic journals, conference proceedings, books, and trade journals. Her research articles have been published in the United States, United Kingdom, India, Hong Kong, China, and Australia. She serves on the editorial boards of seven refereed academic journals. Dr. Mok received her PhD in Marketing from Murdoch University, her Masters degree from Iowa State University, and her undergraduate degree from the Conrad N. Hilton College of Hotel and Restaurant Management at the University of Houston.

**Beverley Sparks, PhD,** is Associate Professor in Hotel Management at the School of Tourism and Hotel Management, Griffith University, Gold Coast, Australia. Dr. Sparks has been involved in teaching and research at the tertiary level for over twelve years and maintains a close alliance with the hotel industry. Prior to entering tertiary teaching, Dr. Sparks ran her own restaurant in country Victoria, Australia. She has also worked in major hotels throughout Australia and New Zealand. Her research interests include service quality, customer satisfaction, and service recovery. She has several publications in top international hospitality journals. She serves on the editorial boards of numerous prestigious academic journals. Dr. Sparks is very active in presenting seminars and conference papers, both nationally and internationally. Her refereed paper won the Best Paper Award in Marketing at the 1996 CHRIE conference. Dr. Sparks is the president of the Australian and New Zealand Chapter of CHRIE.

# CONTRIBUTORS

**Jovo Ateljevic** is a PhD candidate at the School of Business and Public Management, Victoria University of Wellington, New Zealand. His thesis is focused on the role of information technology and its impact on both management practices and the competitiveness of small/micro tourism firms. Entrepreneurship, the general problems of smaller tourism businesses, and the role of local and central governments in assisting and supporting small tourism and hospitality businesses are his broader research interests. Prior work experience in the tourism and hospitality industry, mainly in hotel management, has helped him to better synthesize theory and practice.

**William N. Chernish, PhD,** is Associate Professor at the Conrad Hilton College of Hotel and Restaurant Management, University of Houston, Texas. His research interests are in management, human resources, and diversity.

**Bonnie J. Knutson, PhD,** is Professor in the School of Hospitality Business, Michigan State University. She is widely recognized as an authority on emerging lifestyle trends and creative marketing strategies. Her work has been featured in publications such as *The Wall Street Journal* and *USA Today* and on CNN. She has published numerous articles in prestigious journals and is the editor of the *Journal of Hospitality and Leisure Marketing*. Dr. Knutson is a frequent speaker at seminars, workshops, and industry meetings in both the United States and abroad. In 1991, Dr. Knutson was named a National Scholar by the Advertising Education Foundation. In 1996, she was awarded the prestigious Golden Key Teaching Excellence Award for outstanding instruction and dedication to students.

**Darren Lee-Ross, PhD,** is a Senior Lecturer in Management at the Business School, James Cook University, Australia. He has managed a variety of seasonal hotels in the U.K. over a number of years. His research interests are in human resource management, attitudes and work motivation, and service quality. He has been published in a variety of academic journals and authored or edited a number of textbooks, the most recent of which are *Research Methods for Service Industry Managers* and *HRM in Tourism and Hospitality*. Dr. Lee-Ross earned his PhD from Anglia Polytechnic University, United Kingdom.

**Gillian Maxwell** is a Senior Lecturer in Human Resource Management at Glasgow Caledonian University in Scotland. Her main research interest is in the operationalization of human resource management strategy and initiatives, particularly in the context of the service sector. Eight years' experience in line and personnel management in hotel and retail organizations informs her research activity. Her research focus is on areas such as: quality management, learning organizations, managing diversity, investors in people, employee commitment, and women in management. Ms. Maxwell has co-edited a book titled *Hospitality, Tourism and Leisure Management* and is currently co-editing another book, *International Human Resource Management in Tourism, Travel and Hospitality Organizations.* She has published numerous research papers in academic journals and conference proceedings.

**Simon Milne, PhD,** is Professor of Tourism and Associate Dean at the School of Management, Auckland University of Technology, Auckland, New Zealand. He also serves as Adjunct Professor, Department of Geography, McGill University, Montreal, Canada. His primary research interests lie in the links between tourism and regional economic development. In recent years he has been focusing on the ability of information technology to assist businesses and communities in developing more profitable and sustainable tourism products. Professor Milne is currently involved in research projects in Canada, the Caribbean, and New Zealand. Professor Milne received his PhD from Cambridge University, in the United Kingdom.

**Susan Ogden, PhD,** is a Lecturer in Management in the Department of Hospitality, Tourism, and Leisure Management at Glasgow Caledonian University, Scotland. Her current research interests center on service quality management and human resource management. Of particular interest is the impact of current U.K. government policy on the management of hospitality and leisure services provided within the public sector. Recent research includes benchmarking within the public leisure sector, a comparison of employee flexibility within public, private, and not-for-profit leisure organizations, and client-contractor relationships and service innovation in the contract-catering sector.

**Martin O'Neill** is currently a Lecturer and Head of the Department of Hospitality Management at Edith Cowan University, Western Australia. He has extensive experience within the hospitality industry. His research interests are in total quality management application in the hotel sector and measurement of service quality and customer satisfaction. He has published numerous articles in international journals and conference proceedings.

**Yvette Reisinger, PhD,** is a Senior Lecturer in Tourism and Tourism Coordinator in the Faculty of Business and Economics at Monash University, Australia. Formerly, she worked in the tourism industry for major tour operators in Europe, Asia, and Africa. Dr. Reisinger is the author of many articles and conference papers in tourism. Her research activities and publications have mainly focused on cross-cultural differences in tourist behavior and personal values, cross-cultural communication and interaction, and variations in perceptions of the tourism product by different tourist markets. Her PhD dissertation focused on the Asian tourist market. She serves on the editorial boards of *Journal of Vacation Marketing* and *An International Journal of Tourism.* She has been a visiting professor at the University of Colorado at Boulder, Colorado.

**Chris Roberts, PhD,** is Associate Professor of Strategic Management in the Department of Hotel, Restaurant, and Travel Administration at the University of Massachusetts, Amherst, Massachusetts. He has many years of industry experience in the hospitality and travel sectors, both as a manager and as an owner/operator. He also has eleven years of corporate marketing and sales experience with Bell Telephone Systems. His research focus is centered on the strategy decision-making process. Dr. Roberts has published numerous articles in prestigious academic journals. He received his doctorate in Management Strategy from the University of Massachusetts.

**Victoria Russell** is a Business Development Consultant working in the Moffat Centre for Travel and Tourism Business Development at Glasgow Caledonian University, Scotland. She undertakes consultancy and contract research on behalf of local economic development agencies, local authorities, and private clients across Scotland. Clients include the Glasgow Development Agency, Grampian Enterprise, Forth Valley Enterprise, and Stirling Council. The Moffat Centre manages and delivers the Tourism Partnership Programme for Renfrewshire Enterprise, an initiative that partners organizations such as the Scottish Tourist Board, Greater Glasgow, and Clyde Valley Tourist Board, and the three local authorities in this region. This program concentrates on business development support for tourism providers, including accommodation, visitor attractions, food and beverage providers, and travel operators.

**Linda J. Shea, PhD,** is Associate Professor of Marketing and Graduate Program Director in the Department of Hotel, Restaurant, and Travel Administration at the University of Massachusetts, Amherst, Massachusetts. Dr. Shea has worked with a wide range of hospitality and tourism businesses as a marketing research and training consultant. She has published numerous research articles in the area of strategic marketing and consumer behavior in a variety of books and prestigious hospitality journals. She received her doctorate in marketing from the University of Colorado, Boulder, and has been teaching marketing-related courses for nearly twenty-five years.

**Geoffrey N. Soutar, PhD,** is Professor of Marketing at the Graduate School of Management, University of Western Australia. He has many years of industry and university administrative experience. He is the editor of the *Journal of the Australian and New Zealand Academy of Management.* His areas of research and teaching are in marketing and consumer behavior. His numerous research findings have been published in many prestigious academic journals and he has been involved in many consulting projects in marketing and tourism. Dr. Soutar received his doctorate from Cornell University.

**Richard Teare, PhD, DLitt, FHCIMA,** is academic chairman of IMCA and Principal and Granada Professor of the Association's U.S.-based University of Action Learning. He has held professorial roles at three U.K. universities and worked for national and international hotel companies. Richard is a former chairman and nonexecutive director of the National Society for Quality through Teamwork in the United Kingdom, editor of the *International Journal of Contemporary Hospitality Management,* an associate editor of the *Journal of Workplace Learning,* and worldwide research director for the HCIMA's Worldwide Hospitality and Tourism Trends. He is a member of the editorial advisory boards of seven international journals and has co-authored and edited nineteen books and more than 100 articles and book chapters.

**Karl Titz, PhD,** is Assistant Professor at the Conrad N. Hilton College of Hotel and Restaurant Management, University of Houston, Texas. His experience in the industry ranges from business analyst to club management. Dr. Titz's areas of specialization are food production management, food and beverage management, casino, resort, and hotel management, and marketing. His research has been published in the *Journal of Hospitality and Tourism Research.* Dr. Titz earned his PhD from Kansas State University.

**Beth Schlagel Wuest, PhD,** is Assistant Professor in the Department of Family and Consumer Sciences, Southwest Texas State University, Texas. She gained her managerial experience at Ramada Inn Hotels in the United States. Her research interests include consumer behavior, customer services, and educational research. She has numerous publications in international research journals and in conference proceedings. Dr. Wuest earned her PhD from the University of Minnesota.

# Preface

Evidence suggests that, despite the continuous emphasis on "service quality" for more than a decade, there is still a lack of holistic understanding of what actually constitutes quality and how it can be nurtured and managed. The holistic understanding and interdisciplinary approach to service quality has become imperative for hospitality, tourism, and leisure services managers in their efforts to design and deliver a superior quality of service. The continued growth and maturation of hospitality, tourism, and leisure (HTL) has seen its transformation into a global industry. Moreover HTL service is no longer considered a luxury confined to economically developed countries; it has become an integral component of lifestyle, with producers and consumers spread throughout the world.

The hypercompetitive market of the new millennium will have a surplus of everything—a list encompassing products, services, employees, suppliers, retailers, etc.—thereby increasing customer choice in the marketplace. Moreover, as we approached the millennium, it became increasingly difficult for firms to assume that there exists an unlimited customer base prepared to maintain patronage. The increased competition is reflected in the ways that customers now critically assess the quality of service competing firms can provide. Thus the importance of managing service quality has never been greater. In the scheme of business process, it has become apparent that HTL organizations' ultimate goal of maintaining a loyal customer base, by offering superior quality of service, transcends the obvious primary functions of management confined within functional and organizational boundaries. Hence, this book has undertaken an interdisciplinary approach to service quality management within hospitality, tourism, and leisure.

Contributors to this book have drawn on their expertise from various disciplines and countries and, here, collectively examine nascent understanding, approaches, and strategies pertinent to the management of service quality in hospitality, tourism, and leisure organizations.

*xvii*

# Chapter 1

# Concepts of Tourism, Hospitality, and Leisure Services

Yvette Reisinger

## *INTRODUCTION*

In recent years, increasing attention has been paid to the management and marketing of tourism, hospitality, and leisure, which have been widely recognized as very important sectors of the service economy. However, a different approach to the management and marketing of tourism, hospitality, and leisure services than to that of physical goods is required. These services differ from physical goods in a number of unique characteristics, which have significant implications for management and marketing strategies.

This chapter covers three main issues:

1. It defines the phenomena of tourism, hospitality, and leisure and clarifies the relationships between these three areas.
2. It introduces the concepts of products, goods, and services in a marketing context.
3. It explains the concept of tourism products and tourism service.

## *WHAT ARE TOURISM, HOSPITALITY, AND LEISURE?*

Tourism has a number of different definitions. It is very difficult to pinpoint a definition that would give a meaningful and adequate explanation of tourism, because the concept is fragmented, wide-ranging, and multidimensional.

Historically, the concept of tourism was first developed in the period between the two world wars. Tourism was defined as a sum of relations and phenomena resulting from the travel and stay of non-residents, in so far as [travel] does not lead to permanent residence and is not connected with any permanent or temporary earning activity (Hunziker and Krapf in Burkart and Medlik, 1981). Since 1942, the concept of tourism has been broadened by including various forms of business and pleasure travel. McIntosh, Goeldner, and Ritchie (1995) defined tourism as a short-term movement of people to places other than their normal place of residence and work, including the activities of persons traveling to and staying in locations outside their places of residence and work for not more than twelve months, for the purpose of: (1) leisure (recreation, vacation, health, study, religion, and sport); and (2) business, family, mission, and meetings.

Several characteristics of tourism may be identified based on the analyzed definitions:

1. Two main elements: (a) movement, which refers to the journey (travel) to and from a destination (the dynamic element of tourism); and (b) the overnight stay outside the permanent residence in various destinations (the static element of tourism)
2. Movement to and from the destination is temporary (temporary change of residence), short-term, with intention to return
3. Destinations are visited for purposes other than taking up permanent residence or employment
4. The activities tourists engage in during their journey, and the stay outside the normal place of residence and work, are distinct from those of the local residents and working populations of the places visited

The review of various definitions also illustrates a number of conceptual problems in defining tourism. There is no agreement on how far an individual has to travel, how many nights the individual has to stay away from home, or what activities must be engaged in, etc. There are also cross-national differences in defining the concept of tourism.

Four groups of participants are involved and are influenced by tourism: (1) tourists, (2) businesses providing goods and services that the tourist market demands, (3) the government of the host community, and (4) the host community. McIntosh, Goeldner, and Ritchie (1995) defined tourism as the sum of the phenomena and relationships arising from the interaction of these four groups in the process of attracting and hosting tourists and other visitors. These groups cooperate to accomplish a set of goals at the micro and macro levels within constantly changing legal, political, economic, social, and technological environments. Tourism is very dynamic.

It is generally agreed that tourism is fragmented. It is made up of various sectors or subindustries such as transportation, accommodation, attractions, amenities, catering, entertainment, eating and drinking establishments, shops, activity facilities (leisure and recreation), and many others. These sectors provide products and services for individuals or groups of tourists who travel away from home. Consequently, tourism is an amalgam of the products and services that its various subsectors make available for tourists. The provision of these products and services depends on the linkages between various sectors and their mutual interactions.

Tourism is the most wide-ranging industry, in the sense that it demands products from many sectors of the economy (Edgell, 1990) and employs millions of people in different sectors. For example, airplanes and buses must be manufactured to transport tourists; computers must be produced to make hotel booking and airline reservations; steel, concrete, and glass are needed to build hotels and restaurants; fabrics are needed to make clothes; meat, wheat, and vegetables must be grown to feed visitors. No other industry has so many linkages and interactions with so many sectors of the economy (Edgell, 1990), and delivers so many different kinds of products and services to its consumers.

Tourism is multidimensional. McIntosh, Goeldner, and Ritchie (1995) noted that tourism embraces virtually all aspects of human life and society. Tourism is a major economic activity of the travel, lodging, retail, entertainment subsector, and many other subsectors that supply tourist needs. It is a major sociocultural activity that provides different tourist markets with cultural experiences. Tourism involves production, marketing, and consumption of numerous products such as car rentals, hotel rooms, meals, etc. It requires researching, planning, managing, and controlling tourist enterprises. It is about the location of tourist areas, their physical planning, and changes that tourism development brings to the landscape and community. The industry depends on various intermediaries and organizations that perform tourism activities. Tourism also involves a historical analysis of tourism activities and various institutions.

It is difficult to apply the concept of an industry to tourism in view of the special nature and complexity of the potential contributors to the tourism product. Tourism is about activities and services. It is about the buying, selling, managing, and marketing of numerous activities and services, which range from renting hotel rooms, selling souvenirs, and managing an airline (Edgell, 1990), to marketing special events. However, since these activities and services represent the supply in the market (tourists constitute the demand) and are part of the economy, they might be described as the tourism "industry."

There is a strong link between tourism and travel. *Travel* refers to the spatial displacement of people and the activities of people taking trips to places outside their residence for any purpose except daily commuting to and from work (McIntosh, Goeldner, and Ritchie, 1995). Travel may be undertaken for tourism purposes, or other purposes such as migration, commuting, or exploring. It includes both business and convention tourism as distinguished from "pure" pleasure tourism. Thus, travel has wider meaning and application than tourism.

*Hospitality* is concerned with the provision of accommodation and catering (food and beverage) services for guests. It also refers to the reception and entertainment of travelers, the way they are treated by industry employees (with empathy, kindness, and friendliness), and an overall concern for the traveler's well-being and satisfaction. Tourists are not the only consumers of hospitality services; local residents also use them.

*Leisure* is considered to be part of free time available to the individual after necessary work and duties are accomplished, to be spent at the discretion of the individual (Miller and Robinson in Mieczkowski, 1990). It refers to the time free from obligations, filled with specific activities, without pressure of necessity. The problem is, however, in distinguishing between work and leisure activities, and activities undertaken for the purpose of subsistence (e.g., eating). The same activities can be regarded as leisure and as obligations by different individuals. For instance, gardening can be regarded as a leisure activity by some people and as work by others. Eating, shopping, social activities, and even sleeping may be considered as leisure rather than necessity. The difficulties in categorizing leisure activities were illustrated by Cosgrove and Jackson in Mieczkowski (1990). Consequently, what is viewed as leisure or work depends upon personality, traditions, and/or education of an individual or, as Shaw and Williams (1994) noted, upon the individual's attitude of mind, feelings, perceptions, or social position.

Tourism activity is only possible during time available for leisure. However, much of leisure time is spent at home or close to the place of residence; therefore, it is beyond the scope of tourism. Tourism can also be substituted for leisure (e.g., swimming while on vacation can be substituted for swimming in the local sport and recreation center). Moreover, vacation experiences may affect the expectations of leisure experiences at home. For example, experiences of playing golf can create the expectation that golf courses should be provided in every local recreation and leisure center. Experiencing high-quality facilities in local recreation centers may create high expectations for vacation resorts.

Often, leisure is used synonymously with recreation. *Recreation* refers to the experiences and activities (or inactivities) undertaken during leisure time to recreate physically, psychologically, spiritually, and mentally after work in order to prepare the individual for future work (Mieczkowski, 1990). Recreation activities may include play, games, sports, cultural functions, informal education, sightseeing, entertainment, relaxation, and amusements, as well as travel and tourism. Clawson and Knetsch in Mieczkowski (1990) argued that recreation is the attitude toward activities. An activity is recreation when it involves no feeling of obligation. Recreation is only possible during leisure time. However, not all leisure can be regarded as recreation (e.g., studying, visiting parents). The same activities may be regarded as recreation by one individual yet work by another. The assessment of what activities are recreational depends on the individual's attitudes and feelings. For example, sport activities can be viewed as recreation, or as a job in professional sports (Mieczkowski, 1990).

Tourism is a form of recreation. Recreational tourism is the most significant part of tourism. However, tourism includes elements such as business tourism, which cannot be classified as recreation. Recreation also involves elements such as urban recreation, which cannot be classified as tourism. Further, tourism can occur within work time (business tourism) whereas recreation occurs during leisure time. Some forms of tourism, such as health tourism, pilgrimages, and visiting friends and relatives are often not associated with recreation. Also, tourism is always associated with temporary change of residence and overnight stay outside the permanent residence. In contrast, most recreation occurs at home within the local community. In addition, the purchase of recreation equipment often requires financial expenditures that otherwise could have been allocated to tourism and travel. Also, tourism has far more significant commercial implications for the economy than recreation, which is often provided for, free of charge, by the government or social organizations. Further, tourism does not require learning special skills, as opposed to recreation, which may require the acquisition of special skills (Mieczkowski, 1990) such as sport skills.

In summary, the concepts of tourism, hospitality, and leisure are different, although they are related. Tourism and hospitality are concerned with the provision of goods and services; leisure is a concept of time; and recreation is a concept of activity. Much tourism takes place during leisure time. Recreation is often the main purpose for participation in tourism. All these concepts are characterized by very complex relationships in the creation and delivery of their services to tourists.

## WHAT ARE PRODUCTS, GOODS, AND SERVICES?

In the marketing literature, goods and services are both described as products (Cowell, 1991). In simple terms, tangible products are often referred to as goods, while intangible products are often referred to as services. Services are a different type of product than goods (Foxall, 1985). Some products are a mixture of a tangible good and intangible service. For example, restaurants offer a tangible product in the form of food and an intangible product in the form of atmosphere, advice on food and beverage selection, and speed of meal preparation.

Kotler (1997) lists four distinct categories of products: (1) purely tangible goods, (2) tangible goods with accompanying intangible service, (3) a major intangible service with accompanying tangible goods, and (4) a pure intangible service. However, Levitt (1972) argued that there is no pure service industry because there are no pure intangible services, only industries with greater or smaller service components. It is very difficult to define a pure service and a pure good. A pure good implies that no element of intangible service is offered with the good the customer receives. A pure service implies that there is no element of physical goods in the service offered. However, Shostack (1977) went further in the analysis of the categories of products and described a product continuum, known as a tangibility spectrum, which ranges from tangible dominant goods to intangible dominant services. According to Shostack (1977), a key determinant of whether an offering is a service is the degree of intangibility. Services tend to be more intangible than manufactured products; manufactured products tend to be more tangible than services. For example: salt, soft drinks, detergents, or cars can be classified as very tangible products. On the other hand, education and consulting can be classified as very intangible products. However, tangible products such as cars also require many intangible service elements such as the transportation process itself. An intangible service such as education includes many tangible elements such as books. Consequently, all marketing products are mixtures of tangible goods and intangible services.

Services are provided in every sector of the economy: in retailing, wholesaling, transportation, telecommunication, finances, health, education, and many other sectors, including tourism, hospitality, and leisure. For example, renting a hotel room, depositing money in a bank, visiting a doctor, getting a haircut, or traveling on an airplane—all involve buying a service.

However, the theoretical concept of service is very complex and difficult to define. It consists of a set of different elements. Thus, it can be explained in several different ways. It has been agreed that service represents one of the main aspects of product delivery. Service has been defined as "any activity or benefit one party can offer to another that is essentially intangible and does not result in the ownership of anything. Production may or may not be tied to a physical product" (Kotler et al., 1998). The literature also refers to services as deeds, processes, and performances (Zeithaml and Bitner, 1996) and interactions or social events (Normann, 1991). The focus is on the service process or service encounter, which has been defined as the interaction between the customer and the firm or the dyadic interaction between customer and service provider (Czepiel, Solomon, and Surprenant, 1985; Shostack, 1985; Solomon et al., 1985; Surprenant and Solomon, 1987). Shostack (1985) defined this encounter as a period of time during which a provider and a customer confront each other, or a moment of truth. What happens between a customer and a provider during this encounter determines the quality of the services and a customer's satisfaction with service.

The extent of personal interaction between a provider and a customer and the length of this interaction vary among services. Mills (1986) divided services into three primary categories: maintenance-interactive, task-interactive, and personal-interactive. The first type is of a simple nature and is characterized by little uncertainty in transactions (e.g., fast-food restaurant services). The second type is characterized by greater risk in transactions and depends upon the service providers for information and expertise (e.g., banking services, brokerage firms) and is, consequently, an intense interaction between the service provider and the customer. The third type is the most complex. It depends upon a very intense interaction between the provider and the customer, the performance of the service providers, and their competence and personality. This type of service is very labor intensive and is characterized by the greatest risk in transactions (e.g., hospitality and tourism services).

The performances and activities of the providers during the service encounter create customers' experiences with service. When a customer "buys" a hotel room (tangible and visible goods such as bed or furniture) he or she also purchases a hotel experience (the hotel atmosphere, the way the customer is treated at the front desk, by a concierge or a waiter). The experiences purchased create certain real benefits for customers. Some of the benefits are physical, such as the comfort of a hotel bed, and others are psychological or emotional benefits such as enjoyment and happiness. Usually customers purchase a bundle of benefits that is a combination of physical and psychological benefits. During the interaction with a provider the customer evaluates whether the provider is able to fulfill the customer's expectations and deliver benefits that generate satisfaction. The provider's skills, motivations, and attitudes toward a customer greatly influence this evaluation. Bateson (1995) argued that services should be defined in terms of the extent to which the customer receives the intangible benefits of service during the service encounter.

The general consensus is that services could also be defined as satisfaction with interaction experiences. However, the services marketing literature indicates that there is a difference between these two concepts. Satisfaction is a psychological outcome deriving from an experience. Westbrook (1981) described it as an emotional state that occurs in response to an evaluation of the interactional experiences. Service and, in particular, service quality is concerned with the attributes of the service itself (Crompton and MacKay, 1989) and how to satisfy customers so that they develop positive perceptions of the service (Ostrowski, O'Brien, and Gordon, 1993). Satisfaction depends on the quality of service attributes (Crompton and MacKay, 1989). Usually a high quality of service attributes results in high satisfaction.

All services are characterized by intangibility, perishability, inseparability of production and consumption, and heterogeneity. These unique characteristics of services (which will be discussed later) are constantly acknowledged in the services marketing literature (e.g., Berry, 1980; Eiglier and Langeard, 1975; Lovelock, 1991). These characteristics make it difficult to evaluate services (Zeithaml, 1981). The criteria of service quality are still not adequately determined. Defining quality service and providing techniques for its measurement represent a major concern of service providers and researchers.

The difficulty of defining a service and its quality is also increased by its subjective nature. The perception of a service level varies according to an individual's sociodemographic and cultural grouping, needs and requirements, and previous service experiences. Parasuraman, Zeithaml, and Berry (1988) reported that service quality is determined by a subjective customer perception of service. Lewis and Booms (1983) highlighted the subjective nature of service quality by noting that there is an element of "appropriateness" about service quality. They noted that evaluation of service quality depends upon "what is acceptable and what is not" (p. 100).

In summary, the concept of service is multidimensional and difficult to define and evaluate. It becomes a particularly complex issue in high-contact service industries such as tourism, hospitality, or leisure, which by themselves are extremely difficult to define and explain.

## WHAT ARE TOURISM PRODUCTS AND SERVICES?

A tourism product is an amalgam of all goods, activities, and services offered to tourists by different sectors of the tourism industry in order to satisfy tourist needs while they are away from home. It includes the journey to and from a destination, transfer from and to an airport, accommodation, transportation while at the destination, and everything that a tourist does, sees, and uses on the way to and from the destination, including purchases of food and drinks, souvenirs, entertainment, amusement (French, Craig-Smith, and Collier, 1995), and a very wide range of other services such as financial, medical, insurance, etc.

A tourism product is often referred to as a tourism destination. However, a tourism destination is a geographical area or, as Burkart and Medlik (1981) noted, a geographical unit visited by a tourist, which may be a village, town, or city, a district or a region, an island, a country, or a continent. This geographical unit offers a number of different tourism products for purchase and consumption.

The major components of the tourism destination are:

1. accessibility, which is a function of distance from tourist markets, and external transport and communications, which enable a product to be reached;
2. amenities (e.g., catering, entertainment, internal transport, and communications, which enable the tourist to move around during his or her stay);
3. accommodation;
4. attractions, which may be site attractions (e.g., scenic, historical, natural wonders) or event attractions (e.g., exhibitions, sporting events, congresses); and
5. activities (e.g., outdoor and indoor recreation activities).

Tourist activities create demand for an extremely wide range of services in the course of the journey and stay at destination, classified as direct and indirect services. The direct services include transportation to and from the chosen destination (air, sea, land); transportation within a destination and between destinations; accommodation at the destination (hotels, motels, resorts, home and farm stays, RV parks, campgrounds, etc.); catering (food and beverage); sightseeing; shopping; entertainment; recreation; information; and many others. These services cater directly to tourist needs. The indirect services are financial, medical, insurance, retailing, wholesaling (travel agent, tour operator), cleaning, printing, telecommunication, good water, sewerage, or electricity. These services support the provision of direct services. Without indirect services the provision of direct services would be impossible. As a result, a tourism product is a service rather than a tangible product.

The tourism product is not only a collection of tangible products (hotel buildings) and intangible services (accommodation services) but also psychological experiences. It includes everything that tourists feel from the time they leave home until their return. Therefore, tourist perceptions form part of the tourism product and represent its psychological component. These perceptions are, however, very subjective. Different individuals seek different experiences from the same set of services and products. Consequently, they experience and perceive the same product differently. The demographic (e.g., age), socioeconomic (e.g., social class, income), geographic (e.g., place of origin), cultural (e.g., cultural values), and psychological (e.g., needs, motivations) makeup of travelers play an important role in creating these perceptions. Also, since individuals have diverse needs and try to obtain different benefits from the same product, the level of tourist satisfaction with the same product also differs.

Moreover, the tourism product also has a human component. The perceptions of this human component are particularly important. During their trips tourists come into direct and indirect contact with many people, such as motel staff, flight attendants, cashiers in shops, waitstaff, tour guides, and local residents. The tourist's perceptions of this contact and the services provided by industry personnel and the members of the host population determine the overall perceptions of tourism product quality and tourist satisfaction. The best quality of attractions, accommodation, transportation, amenities, and activities will not attract tourists if tourists feel unwelcomed by the host population, or if the service quality is poor. Consequently, in addition to the five major components of the tourism product, which are access, amenities, accommodation, attractions, and activities, a sixth component must be added—people.

Research shows that the tourism and hospitality industry relies very heavily on the development of positive perceptions of people providing services to tourists. For example, Pearce (1982) illustrated the role of many people associated with the travel and hospitality industry such as restaurateurs, salespeople, hoteliers, and others in contributing to tourists' overall perceptions of service. Sutton (1967) reported that competency in providing services is an important element influencing positive tourist perceptions of service. Pearce (1982) indicated variables that create tourists' negative perceptions of service such as the service providers' impoliteness or professional incompetence. Negative perceptions deter visitation and discourage repeat purchasing. Therefore, the way tourists perceive the service providers influences the success of a particular tourism product (destination).

In light of these perceptions, the tourism product is a combination of both tangible and intangible items that provide the tourist with total psychological experiences. The tangible items may be furniture in a hotel room or the food served in a restaurant. The intangible items include people and the services they provide, e.g., transportation or accommodation. The tangible and intangible items are offered by distinct sectors of the tourism industry as individual subproducts, which create the total tourism product. The individual subproducts may represent individual tourism products or one product. Individual subproducts are supplied by individual suppliers. They may be purchased separately or together with other subproducts as a package. Consequently, a tourism product is a combination of different subproducts and the total tourist experience and satisfaction with these subproducts (see Figure 1.1).

A tourism product may be developed with conscious effort to appeal to a specific market, e.g., theme parks or indoor entertainment. However, the

FIGURE 1.1. The Tourism Product—A Total Tourism Experience

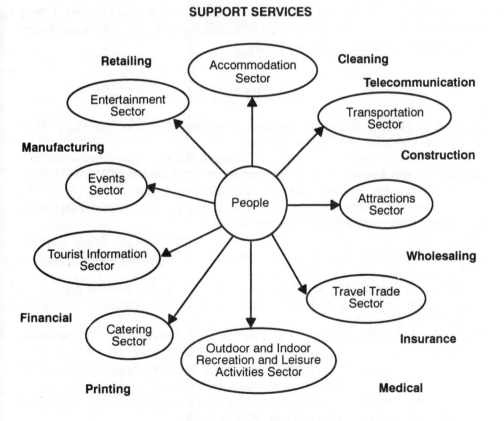

**SUPPORT SERVICES**

tourism product may also be developed without any conscious effort in the minds of potential tourists, through the creation of a particular image by promotion (Burkart and Medlik, 1981). The emphasis in the latter is on the psychological and experiential component of the tourism product rather than the tangible component.

The concept of the tourism product as a composite of various subproducts signifies the importance of the linkages and mutual dependence of all sectors. Unsatisfactory performance of one subproduct (sector) can reflect badly on the performance of the total product, and on overall tourist experience and satisfaction with the total product. The nature of the tourism product highlights the complexity and diversity of the tourism industry, which depends on the interrelationships among all the sectors delivering tourism products and services. The nature of the tourism product implies the importance of cooperation between all the sectors in order to achieve an integrated tourism product and accomplish a major goal, which is tourist satisfaction.

The concept of service has received substantial attention in the field of tourism (Fick and Ritchie, 1991; Ostrowski, O'Brien, and Gordon, 1993), hospitality (Lewis and Chambers, 1989; Saleh and Ryan, 1991) and recreation (MacKay and Crompton, 1988).

## REFERENCES

Bateson, J. (1995). *Managing Services Marketing: Text and Readings,* Third Edition. Orlando: The Dryden Press.

Berry, L. (1980). Services Marketing Is Different. *Business,* (May/June): 24-28.

Burkart, A. and Medlik, S. (1981). *Tourism: Past, Present and Future,* Second Edition. London: Heinemann Professional Publishing Ltd.

Cowell, D. (1991). Marketing Services. In M.J. Baker (Ed.), *The Marketing Book.* Oxford: Butterworth Heinemann, pp. 456-466.

Crompton, J. and MacKay, K. (1989). User's Perceptions of the Relative Importance of Service Quality Dimensions in Selected Public Recreation Programs. *Leisure Sciences,* 11(4): 367-375.

Czepiel, J., Solomon, M., and Surprenant, C. (1985). *The Service Encounter: Managing Employee/Customer Interaction in Service Business.* Lexington, MA: Lexington Books.

Edgell, D. Sr. (1990). *International Tourism Policy.* New York: Van Nostrand Reinhold.

Eiglier, P. and Langeard, E. (1975). Une Approache Nouvelle pour le Marketing de Services. *Revue Francaise de Gestion,* 2 (Spring): 97-114.

Fick, G. and Ritchie, J. (1991). Measuring Service Quality in the Travel and Tourism Industry. *Journal of Travel Research,* 30(2): 2-9.

Foxall, G. (1985). *Marketing in the Service Industries.* London: Frank Cass.

French, C., Craig-Smith, S., and Collier, A. (1995). *Principles of Tourism*. Melbourne: Longman Australia Ltd.

Kotler, P. (1997). *Marketing Management*. Englewood Cliffs, NJ: Prentice Hall.

Kotler, P., Chandler, P., Gibbs, R., and McColl, R. (1998). *Marketing in Australia, Fourth Edition*. New York: Prentice Hall.

Levitt, T. (1972). Production-Line Approach to Service. *Harvard Business Review*, (Sept.-Oct.): 41-52.

Lewis, R. and Booms, B. (1983). The Marketing Aspects of Service Quality. In Berry, L., Shostack, L., and Upah, G. (Eds.), *Emerging Perspectives on Services Marketing*. Chicago: American Marketing Association, pp. 99-107.

Lewis, R. and Chambers, R. (1989). *Marketing Leadership in Hospitality: Foundation Practices*. New York: Van Nostrand Reinhold.

Lovelock, C. (1991). *Services Marketing*, Second Edition. Englewood Cliffs, NJ: Prentice Hall.

MacKay, K. and Crompton, J. (1988). Conceptual Model of Consumer Evaluation of Recreation Service Quality. *Leisure Sciences*, 7: 41-49.

McIntosh, R., Goeldner, C., and Ritchie, J. (1995). *Tourism: Principles, Practices, Philosophies*, Seventh Edition. New York: John Wiley and Sons.

Mieczkowski, Z. (1990). *World Trends in Tourism and Recreation*, Volume 3. New York: Peter Lang Publishing.

Mills, P. (1986). *Managing Service Industries: Organizational Practices in a Post-Industrial Economy*. New York: Ballinger.

Normann, R. (1991). *Service Management Strategy and Leadership in Service Business*, Second Edition. Chichester: John Wiley and Sons.

Ostrowski, P., O'Brien, T., and Gordon, G. (1993). Service Quality and Customer Loyalty in the Commercial Airline Industry. *Journal of Travel Research*, 32(2): 16-24.

Parasuraman, A., Zeithaml, V., and Berry, L. (1988). SERVQUAL: A Multiple-Item Scale for Measuring Consumer Perceptions of Service Quality. *Journal of Retailing*, 64(1): 12-40.

Pearce, P. (1982). *The Social Psychology of Tourist Behavior*. International Series in Experimental Social Psychology, Volume 3. Oxford, New York: Pergamon Press.

Saleh, F. and Ryan, C. (1991). Analyzing Service Quality in the Hospitality Industry Using the SERVQUAL Model. *Service Industries Journal*, 11(3): 324-345.

Shaw, G. and Williams, A. (1994). *Critical Issues in Tourism: A Geographical Perspective*. Oxford: Blackwell.

Shostack, G. (1977). Breaking Free from Product Marketing. *Journal of Marketing*, 41(2): 73-80.

Shostack, G. (1985). Planning the Service Encounter. In Czepiel, J., Solomon, M., and Surprenant, C. (Eds.), *The Service Encounter*. Lexington, MA: Lexington Books, pp. 243-254.

Solomon, M., Surprenant, C., Czepiel, J., and Gutman, E. (1985). A Role Theory Perspective on Dyadic Interactions: The Service Encounter. *Journal of Marketing,* 49(1): 99-111.

Surprenant, C. and Solomon, M. (1987). Predictability and Personalization in the Service Encounter. *Journal of Marketing,* 51(2): 73-80.

Sutton, W. (1967). Travel and Understanding: Notes on the Social Structure of Touring. *International Journal of Comparative Sociology,* 8(2): 218-223.

Westbrook, R. (1981). Sources of Consumer Satisfaction with Retail Outlets. *Journal of Retailing,* 57(3): 68-85.

Zeithaml, V. (1981). How Consumer Evaluation Processes Differ Between Goods and Services. In Donnelly, J. and George, W. (Eds.), *Marketing of Services.* Chicago: American Marketing Association, pp. 186-190.

Zeithaml, V. and Bitner, M. (1996). *Services Marketing.* Singapore: McGraw-Hill.

Chapter 2

# Unique Characteristics of Tourism, Hospitality, and Leisure Services

Yvette Reisinger

This chapter presents the unique characteristics of tourism, hospitality, and leisure services, which distinguish them from physical goods, and very briefly outlines implications of the nature of these services for management and marketing strategies.

## HOW ARE TOURISM, HOSPITALITY, AND LEISURE SERVICES DIFFERENT FROM PHYSICAL GOODS?

It has been accepted that services have unique characteristics that distinguish them from goods and provide a ground for developing different marketing strategies for services and for goods (Lovelock, 1991; Booms and Bitner, 1981; Sasser, Olsen, and Wyckoff, 1978). It has also been recognized that tourism, hospitality, and leisure services have a number of characteristics that distinguish them from physical goods. These characteristics and their implications for managing and marketing strategies are identified in the following sections.

### Product

In a manufacturing sector, the physical good is the product. In a tourism service sector, the tourism service itself is the product. One part of this product is the service offering, which is visible to the customer; another part is invisible to the customer and consists of backstage activities. The backstage activities support the service offerings to tourists. They determine the visible performance of providers. For example, the visible in-

*15*

flight catering offerings have to be ordered and delivered to the plane. Computer systems have to be developed to ensure efficient baggage handling at the airport (Baron and Harris, 1995).

The tourism service offering can be viewed at several levels:

1. The core (basic) service (e.g., accommodation), which is the main reason for the service purchase
2. The expected (actual) service, which consists of the basic service and the tangible support service (e.g., accommodation services plus a comfortable bed, transportation services plus a relaxing waiting area, prompt in-flight service, good quality meals, clean lavatories, and on-time arrival)
3. The augmented product, which consists of the basic service, tangible support services, and added value in terms of reliability and responsiveness, service quality, price options, and supply of free travel brochures
4. The potential product, which consists of future service offerings such as all potential added features and benefits that might be of use to travelers (i.e., everything that professionally can be done to the product)

The core value of the physical good is produced in a manufacturing facility such as a factory. In contrast, the core value of a service is produced in buyer-seller interactions.

Some suppliers use services as a core product. These services are important and necessary to provide customers with the intangible benefits they are looking for. Other suppliers use services as an additional or peripheral element associated with the good. These services are needed to execute the core services or to improve the overall quality of the product (Gronroos, 1978). For example, the core service purchased can be a flight from New York to Chicago. The peripheral services can be meals, drinks, in-flight entertainment, pillows, and blankets. They are extra elements of the service that add to customer comfort and enjoyment. Unfortunately, the distinction between core and peripheral services is not always clear. It depends on what customers regard as a core or peripheral service, and what services are more or less important to them. When buying airline services, the actual transportation may be more important to the customer than the cleanliness of the airport. When buying travel agency services, the quality of the advice may be more important than the physical appearance of the travel consultants. Moreover, many tourism organizations compete on peripheral services by adding more of them to the core product to better satisfy customer needs. Unfortunately, many of these organizations cannot live up to the promises and the image they create, and fail to fulfill customer expectations. They lose their credibility and create customer dissatisfaction.

### Intangibility

Tourism services are primarily intangible. This means that tourism services do not have a physical dimension: they cannot be touched, seen, tasted, felt, heard, or smelled in the same way as goods before they are purchased (palpable intangibility). For example, a traveler cannot experience the tangible outcome of the holiday purchase in advance. However, since tourism services are activities and experiences of the service performance rather than physical objects, they can be perceived in the mind (mental intangibility). For example, the traveler can perceive intuitively whether his or her holiday experiences will be safe and enjoyable, prior to purchasing the trip. Consequently, tourism services represent a more abstract concept than physical goods.

However, very few tourism services are purely intangible (e.g., travel insurance) or purely tangible. Most tourism services offer a combination of intangible and tangible elements. For example, airlines offer intangible elements in the form of transportation, and tangible elements in the form of aircraft, food, seats, pillows, or blankets. Restaurants offer intangible elements such as catering, and tangible elements such as meals. Similarly, hotels offer intangible elements such as the atmosphere of a lobby, and tangible elements such as design and architecture. The amount of tangible and intangible elements involved determines the degree to which tourism services are tangible. For example, airline services are more tangible than tourism education services. On the other hand, airline services are more intangible than car rental services.

The implications of the intangibility of tourism services are that the tourism services cannot be displayed, sampled, tested, or evaluated before purchase. For example, the travel agency cannot display a trip to Hawaii, and a potential traveler cannot "try" the trip before purchase. This is in contrast to the purchase of physical goods such as shoes, which can be displayed and tried on before purchase.

To reduce some of the difficulties caused by the intangibility of tourism services, marketers often try to increase their tangibility. For example, potential travelers are shown pictures of the resort in promotional brochures. The benefits of the services offered (e.g., unforgettable memories) are explained to travelers. Brand names for tourism services such as the Qantas Frequent Flyer Program are developed. Also, celebrities are used in tourism promotion to create customer confidence and trust in the service. For example, the Australian-born actor Paul Hogan was used to promote Australia as a tourism destination for the American market.

## Inseparability of Production and Consumption

Production and consumption of tourism services are inseparable. Tourism services cannot be produced in one place, transported for sale in another, and sold and consumed again in another. Tourism services are sold first and then produced and consumed simultaneously at the same place and time. A passenger first purchases an airline ticket and then consumes the in-flight service as it is produced (Bateson, 1995). As a result of the inseparability of production and consumption, tourism services require simultaneous presence of the customer and service provider during their production and consumption. Also, the consumer must come to the place where the tourism services are "manufactured" (Coltmann, 1989) before they can be consumed. For example, a tourist who wishes to go on vacation must travel to the destination to consume the services offered at the destination (Fridgen, 1996). Production and consumption of these services begins upon the traveler's arrival at the destination. In addition, tourism services cannot be taken home because they cannot be separated from the place of production. In contrast, production, distribution, and consumption of physical goods are separated in both time and space (Bateson, 1995). Most manufactured physical goods are produced in one place, packaged and transported through wholesalers to retailers for sale in another location at a different time, sold somewhere else, and then consumed in another place. Thus, manufactured products can be produced at one time in one location and consumed at another time in a different location. Once purchased by consumers, they can be taken home (e.g., shoes).

The inseparability of the production and consumption of tourism services implies that the mass production of tourism services would be extremely difficult because it would require large numbers of tourists and producers at one time and place. This, of course, would have enormous environmental, social, cultural, and economic implications. Therefore, the scale of tourism operations must be limited to a manageable level.

In some instances, however, the production and consumption of hospitality services is not simultaneous, e.g., self-service options such as salad bars or smorgasbords.

## Heterogeneity

Tourism services are heterogeneous. They vary in standard and quality over time because they are delivered by people to people and are a function of human performance. Each service experience is different because it varies from producer to producer and from customer to customer. For example, services provided by the same travel agent vary on a daily, weekly, and even monthly basis, depending on the travel consultants' moods, feelings, attitudes, skills, and knowledge. Many travelers are aware of this fact and, as a result, they shop around before they select a provider. Similarly, customers differ in their needs and requirements. Since they are present at the service production, they influence the service output in a way similar to the providers. In contrast, physical goods such as cars or television sets are relatively homogeneous regardless of their brands. Their production does not depend so much on who produced them and where they are produced.

Further, providers are unable to maintain the same service performance because performance also depends on tourist demand for services. In the peak season, when there is great demand for tourism services, providers are unable to spend as much time with customers as in periods of low demand. Thus, quality of services may vary significantly.

Although tourism services are heterogeneous, they can be standardized. For example, one can replace the human voice with a computerized voice system at the front desk (Palmer and Cole, 1995).

## *Consistency*

Since employee performance fluctuates from day to day, it is difficult to achieve standardized tourism services. Consistency of service performance and uniformity in service quality depend on the consumers' and providers' demographic, socioeconomic, and psychological makeup and, in particular, the providers' skills and willingness to do a good job. Another factor is the consumers' ability and willingness to accurately communicate their needs and to participate in the service process. Problems of lack of consistency cannot be eliminated in tourism services, as they often can be with physical goods, because there is a lack of uniform objective standards according to which tourism service performance and quality can be assessed. Also, service performance often depends on external environmental factors such as climate, new technology, or political factors.

Consistency in services is critical for tourism business operations and success. Tourists who know that they will receive good quality service anytime they visit a business become repeat buyers. The heterogeneity of tourism services and their lack of consistency implies the need for quality personnel training and consumer management behavior. Many airlines, hotels, and hotel chains have spent substantial amounts of money training their employees. Only people with empathy and interpersonal skills should be employed in a people-oriented industry such as tourism and hospitality. Various learning techniques are used to facilitate consumer understanding of the service process and communication skills in receiving the required service.

### Perishability

Tourism services are perishable. They cannot be kept in stock or stored. For example, it is not possible to save the spare seat on a flight that is leaving today and move it to tomorrow if tomorrow's flight is overbooked. The unsold airline ticket cannot be stored and used at a later date. Similarly, the unsold hotel room cannot be stored and used one night later. Tourism services are short-lived. Airlines must try to fill all seats on all flights and hotels must fill all rooms each night because an empty seat or hotel room means that revenue is lost. To avoid loss, airlines and hotels charge travelers penalties for canceled tickets and rooms. The value of their services exists only at that point when they are used. In contrast, unsold physical goods can be stored, kept in stock for a period of time, and then sold without a loss of revenue.

Although most tourism and hospitality services cannot be stored and must be consumed at the point of production, some hospitality sectors can store part of their service process. For example, restaurants can store their ingredients for a limited period of time. However, they cannot store the entire dining experience by saving spare capacity on a Friday evening for the Saturday evening peak.

Also, unused tourism services cannot be returned, claimed, and resold (Fridgen, 1996). Passengers who did not use their airline tickets cannot return them to the airline after the departure day and claim a refund. Similarly, hotel or restaurant services of poor quality cannot be redone and resold. The restaurant manager cannot ask the guests to reenter the restaurant and start the whole experience from the beginning (Bateson, 1995). Consequently, perishability implies that tourism services must be consumed at the time of their production to avoid a loss.

### Ownership

The purchase and consumption of tourism services does not result in the transfer of ownership of these services. For example, the purchase and consumption of hotel or airline services does not result in ownership of airlines or hotel chains. An airline seat or a hotel room cannot be taken home either. When travelers purchase airline services they purchase a temporary right to a transportation service (service process), the access to it, the opportunity to use it (Palmer, 1994), and the transport process itself. However, when purchasing airline services, a customer does not purchase the right to own the service or the title to that service. The traveler can only own the benefits of the transportation service, not the service itself. In terms of a flight, the traveler can own the benefit of the flight experience, in-flight entertainment, the memory of the flight attendant's smile, or the opportunity to socialize with other travelers. But when the traveler arrives at the destination, he or she owns only an old ticket and boarding pass. In contrast, the purchase and consumption of physical goods such as cars or television sets results in the transfer of ownership. For example, buying shoes results in the transfer of ownership to the buyer.

### Benefits Purchased

The purchase of tourism services results in the purchase of a bundle of benefits through the experience that is created for the consumer (Bateson, 1995). In contrast, the purchase of a physical good results in the purchase of the benefits that are part of the actual good. Also, the ways in which consumers receive the benefits differ for tourism services and physical goods. In the case of tourism services, consumers experience different benefits during service consumption. These benefits are generated by a variety of sources at once:

1. visible to the consumer (front office);
2. invisible to the consumer (administration and maintenance of the physical facilities, e.g., the kitchen in a restaurant, housekeeping department in a hotel);
3. the inanimate physical environment in which the service encounter takes place;
4. interaction process and the contact personnel who actually provide the service; and
5. interaction with other customers who affect the customer who purchases the service (Bateson, 1995).

For example, a customer may find the dining-out experience pleasant if other customers in the restaurant are quiet and polite. Similarly, passengers on an airplane may develop very positive perceptions of the in-flight service if they sit next to interesting travelers with whom they can chat (Bateson, 1995). The benefits (if these experiences are positive) or dissatisfaction (if these experiences are negative) may last for a long time. In contrast, once physical goods have been consumed or are not being used, their benefits for consumers immediately disappear.

## More Difficult to Control Quality

It is more difficult to control the quality of tourism services than physical goods. The inability to store tourism services and their intangibility makes it difficult to select them for testing and evaluation. For example, when a tourist purchases a hotel room, he or she is not able to assess before purchase to what degree a room will satisfy his or her needs in terms of comfort. Also, because tourism services are heterogeneous and dependent on human performance, it is difficult to apply the standard specifications of quality and eliminate any deviations from the norms. In contrast, in the manufacturing sector, the quality of the product can be controlled before it reaches the consumer. The ability to store physical goods means that individual goods can be physically tested before they are released for distribution. They can be selected in shops to assess variability in their quality. For example, a customer who buys shoes can put them on and assess the shoes' fit and comfort.

The implication is that tourism services are usually purchased without prior testing of their quality. There are, however, a few exceptions to this rule, including home delivery of prepared food. Also, mistakes in the service process cannot be caught and corrected before their production and consumption. If something goes wrong with the service, it causes immediate damage and it is too late to implement quality control measures. Poor service quality cannot be rejected before it gets to the customer for consumption. Therefore, it is critically important for a service provider to perform perfectly all the time. However, many mistakes in the tourism and hospitality industry are accidental, unforeseen, and/or happen unexpectedly (e.g., the waiter drops a plate). These mistakes must be corrected by using specific recovery strategies (Bateson, 1995). In contrast, mistakes in manufactured products can be discovered and corrections made before they are purchased.

## Evaluation Process

The evaluation of tourism services occurs at three stages:

1. Preconsumption (consumer selects among alternatives)
2. Consumption (consumer compares experiences with expectations)
3. Postconsumption (consumer compares experiences with expectations formed at the preconsumption and consumption stage)

In the preconsumption stage, when consumers select among alternatives, there are not many cues that the consumer can identify from advertising to assess the service attributes prior to experiencing service. For most tourism services, the evoked set is limited (brands and alternatives that consumers consider before making a purchase decision). One of the reasons for the limited set of tourism services is that numerous travel retail establishments offer only a single "brand" for sale. Also, it is difficult to obtain adequate prepurchase information about tourism services. In contrast, the evoked set in physical goods is unlimited because consumers can see many competing brands of the same product as well as its alternatives. However, many travel agencies handle business for competing airlines, car rentals, and hotels.

Although the consumption of physical goods can be divided into three activities: buy, use, and dispose (Bateson, 1995) (the consumer buys a bottle of wine, drinks it at home, and disposes of the empty bottle), there are no clear boundaries between these stages in the consumption of tourism and hospitality services. The production/purchase/use of tourism services is a single process because of the prolonged interactions between the customer and the service provider. The whole process is evaluated rather than one single activity.

In the postconsumption stage consumers compare the service performance with expectations, which are developed on a basis of cognitive scripts (knowledge and understanding) that specify the actions and events that occur during service delivery. Since the consumers may not be familiar with the service prior to experiencing it, it is often difficult for them to develop cognitive scripts that show what should happen during the service offering. It is also difficult for advertising to reinforce the scripts in the consumers' memory. In contrast, consumers of physical goods can compare their experiences with expectations. They can form expectations at the preconsumption and consumption stages on the basis of many tangible cues identified from advertising prior to the purchase.

## Criteria for Evaluation

When tourism services are purchased, it is difficult for tourists to judge the quality of these services as they often involve very few tangible elements. The only reliable evaluation criteria are the price and the physical environment in which the service is offered (Zeithaml, 1991). However, even the price cannot always be used as a measure of evaluation as it is set by a producer and does not reflect the perceived value and benefits for individual consumers. In contrast, when physical goods are purchased, customers can use many factors such as color, size, weight, etc. to assess the product quality.

To facilitate the evaluation of service quality, Nelson (1974) and Darby and Karni (1973) distinguished three categories of properties of consumer goods, which determine consumer service quality and the degree of difficulty of service evaluation. These are: search properties, which can be evaluated prior to purchasing a product (size, color, feel); experience properties, which can be assessed only after purchase or during consumption (taste, wearability); and credence properties (competence, reputation, security), which often are impossible to evaluate even after purchase and consumption. Tangible goods are high in search attributes and thus can be easily evaluated before purchase. Many tourism services are also high in search properties (retailing) and are easy to evaluate. However, most tourism services are high in experience attributes (taste, credibility, atmosphere, friendliness, catering meals, vacation) and can only be evaluated after a service has been received or during its consumption. Tourism services are also high in credence attributes and cannot be assessed confidently even after purchase and/or when the service is completed (recreational, medical benefits of vacation, rental services). These tourism services are, therefore, the hardest to evaluate or even impossible to evaluate after purchase. Since most tourism services contain a high percentage of experience and credence properties, tourism service quality is more difficult to evaluate than the quality of goods that contain a high percentage of search properties.

## Process As Service Quality Evaluation Criteria

The final assessment of tourism service quality does not rely solely on the outcome of service, but also on the service process, that is, the quality of the interpersonal interaction between a tourist and a provider. In contrast, the final assessment of physical goods depends on the outcome of the offering: whether the purchased product satisfied the consumer's needs in terms of speed, weight, size, or color.

## Dimensions of Quality Evaluation

There are many dimensions of service quality as opposed to goods quality. According to Lehtinen and Lehtinen (1982), the three distinct quality dimensions are: physical (includes the physical aspects of the service); corporate (involves the service organization's image or profile); and interactive (derives from the interaction between contact personnel and the customer). This interaction is central to service, and the quality of this interaction is vital to the assessment of the overall quality of service (Crosby and Stephens, 1987; Parasuraman, Zeithaml, and Berry, 1985, 1988; Solomon et al., 1985; Urry, 1991). Martin (1987) distinguished procedural (mechanistic in nature, system of selling and distributing a product to a customer) and convivial dimension (interpersonal in nature, emphasizes the service providers' positive attitudes to customers, behavior, and appropriate verbal and nonverbal skills). Gronroos (1984) distinguished technical (what the consumer actually receives from the service as a result of the interaction with the service provider) and functional dimensions (the manner in which the service provider delivers the service to a customer). The interactive, convivial, and functional dimensions are interpersonal in nature. They are important for the evaluation of the quality of the interpersonal interaction between a tourist and a provider, and they are important for the evaluation of tourism services rather than physical goods.

### No Warranties or Guarantees

It is rare for tourism services to carry any warranties or guarantees because they are performances rather than tangible items, and because their production depends not only on the providers' but also on the customers' involvement. The dissatisfied customer often cannot claim any refund for wrong service or compensation because he or she is part of the service process and together with providers determines its final outcome. However, there are exceptions; for example, an unhappy customer can be served another meal, or be offered a cheaper holiday package during the rainy season. On the other hand, physical goods usually carry warranties and guarantees, which show that it is the fault of the producer if the product fails.

### Easy Imitation

The intangibility of tourism services makes them relatively easy for competitors to copy (Coltman, 1989). It is impossible to keep competitors away from the location of tourism services production. The competitors can visit these places and consume them. Most tourism and hospitality services cannot be patented either. These services are provided by people and for people; thus, people can imitate them (Morrison, 1996). Also, since the tourism and hospitality industry is very labor intensive and the cost of entering the tourism services market is low, anyone can enter it and potentially offer the same type of service. In contrast, in the manufacturing sector the physical products cannot be as easily copied by competitors, because various copyrights and legislation prevent it.

### People Based and Personality Intensive

Tourism, hospitality, and leisure services are provided by people (providers) for people (customers) who share these services with other people (other customers). People are part of the total tourism product offered, as much as any other attribute of the product (Bateson, 1995). People can enhance the quality of the tourism product or destroy it. For example, tourists may decide not to purchase a package tour if the travel consultants are rude and unwelcoming. Similarly, front-office employees may not be able to guarantee their guests a hotel room with an ocean view if the guests are unable to communicate their needs adequately. Since tourism and hospitality services are very labor intensive and characterized by a very high level of personal contact between service providers and customers, and between customers themselves, the quality of their social interactions influences the service perceptions. In particular, peoples' behavior, their attitudes toward each other, willingness to anticipate and fulfill one another's needs, motivation, and personal characteristics are all of great importance to the production and consumption of tourism services, and the development of perceptions of the overall tourism product. As a result, tourism, hospitality, and leisure marketers must be very selective in terms of whom they hire (employees-providers). Employees should have suitable interpersonal skills to avoid human conflicts. Consequently, staff recruitment, selection, orientation, training, supervision, and motivation play an extremely important role in the tourism, hospitality, and leisure industry (Morrison, 1996). Tourism and hospitality managers and marketers should also be selective in terms of who their customers are. Matching customers and service offerings and managing customers are equally important. In contrast, the production and consumption of physical goods are less people oriented.

Low-contact tourism and hospitality services also exist, which rely on selling tickets and keeping clear records rather than intensive contact between a provider and a customer; and capital-intensive and equipment-based tourism services such as airline services. Very often customers do not have face-to-face contact with the people providing the service. For example, travelers may never see the airline pilot when they fly in an airplane.

## Service Providers Are Products

Service providers are part of the service process and experience (Bateson, 1995). They are present at service production and consumption. They check in tourists, prepare and serve food, organize activities, seek payments, etc. (Fridgen, 1996). The providers' behavior, emotions, skills, knowledge, and the way they perform service, regardless of whether they are backed up by a large amount of equipment, is part of the service experience, which determines consumer evaluation and satisfaction with the service. The behavior of providers can ruin or enhance the experience. Martin (1987) emphasized the role of service providers in fulfilling customers' psychological needs and meeting their expectations. He highlighted the importance of the providers' personal interest in the customer, being friendly, appreciative of the customer, gracious, tactful, courteous, and attentive. Callan (1990) stressed the importance of "a responsive, caring and attentive staff," who "get things done promptly and provide honest answers to problems," who "treat others in a kindly fashion," making the recipient "feel thoughtful, efficient, correct, and magnanimous" (p. 48). Knutson (1988) indicated the importance of prompt and courteous service as important for clients' satisfaction. Saleh and Ryan (1992) noted that staff appearance is even more important than the range of facilities being offered. Many varied cognitive, emotional, and physiological factors influence providers' behavior and have a significant impact on customer service experiences.

The providers are also a source of tourism product differentiation. This is particularly true in airline services, where many airlines offer similar bundles of benefits and fly the same aircraft type from the same airport, and the only element of competitive advantage is at the service level (Bateson, 1995). In contrast, the manufacturing-based services are more standardized and less labor intensive.

The importance of service providers indicates the necessity of developing internal marketing: attracting, motivating, and training quality employees, developing jobs that satisfy the employees' needs, and encouraging staff to behave in a manner that attracts customers' attention. For example, British Airways trained its employees to understand that the aim of their jobs is to deliver to the travelers satisfying flight experiences. British Airways adopted the philosophy that employees who are looked after well will pass on the caring attitude to their own customers (Payne, 1993). Thus, the employees of service organizations are also seen as part of the product.

One implication is that the quality of providers is the key element in the provision of services in tourism and hospitality. Consequently, the success of tourism and hospitality businesses depends upon the right selection, training, motivation, management, and control of employees. However, the ability to control and manage employees requires special skills and techniques.

### Consumers Are Products

Consumers are also an integral part of service provision in tourism and hospitality. Although they are the recipients of services, they are a very important component of the tourism product. Because of the inseparability of production and consumption, consumers can observe the service process, participate in it, and influence its outcome. The consumer's character, personality, motivations, and overall behavior may determine the final outcome of the service provision and the level of satisfaction with service. In contrast, manufacturers of physical goods keep customers away from production for safety and propriety reasons (Morrison, 1996).

Consumers are also a source of tourism product differentiation. Tourism services are customized and differentiated depending on the consumers' requirements. Providers must adequately identify these needs and adequately segment the total tourist market.

Further, since the consumers are part of the tourism service production, they need to be managed as carefully as providers. The customers' perceptions of the tourism and hospitality service quality determine repeat purchase or visitation and customer retention.

Moreover, many tourism services are customer-to-customer interactions. Consequently, the other customers are also products (Bateson, 1995). For example, interactions with other travelers can influence the assessment of service quality. A pleasant conversation with other travelers may enhance the service experience.

### Greater Customer Participation in the Service Process

Tourists as consumers are involved to a greater extent in the production of tourism services than of physical goods. Their participation may be very active (explorers) or passive (mass-organized packaged tour), complete (leisure and recreation services in resorts) or partial (when service is performed on a tourist's possession such as a car). The producer of tourism services has constant contact with a customer because tourists are present in the service production. For example, tourists must travel to a chosen holiday destination, check into a hotel, order food, participate in activities, and pay for services (Fridgen, 1996). In contrast, the producer of the physical good has little or no contact with the customer. Thus, consumers do not (normally) participate in the production of physical goods.

Because customers participate to a greater extent in production of tourism services, they may be more responsible for their dissatisfaction with the tourism experience than with physical goods. Customers need to communicate their needs and requirements adequately. In contrast, when purchasing physical goods, the main form of consumer participation in the service provision is the act of purchase (Zeithaml, 1991). Although the consumers can be blamed for a wrong decision and buying a faulty product, the producer is responsible for poor product performance.

### Brand Loyalty

Many buyers of a tourism product may have little or no brand loyalty (Coltman, 1989); they often choose different products (destinations) for their vacations. However, many tourists are more brand loyal with tourism services than with physical goods, for several reasons:

1. It might be more expensive to change brands of a tourism product/ service (e.g., airlines)
2. It might be more difficult to obtain effective information about the availability of a substitute tourism product with the same attributes
3. It might be more difficult to assess a new product before purchase
4. It might be more difficult to find alternative tourism products with similar attributes and which offer similar benefits
5. The risk of purchasing an intangible new tourism product is higher

As a result, consumers of tourism services may show greater brand loyalty to specific tourism products/services in order to achieve guaranteed satisfaction. They develop trustful social relationships with a chosen provider, rely on his or her advice and information, and become repeat customers. This also allows the provider to gain better knowledge and understanding of the customer's preferences and tastes, and often a better product match.

### Supply Dependence

Tourism services are more supply dependent than demand dependent (Seaton and Bennett, 1996). Their purchase and consumption depend upon the places of their availability and production. For example, accommodation services are provided along major highways, in downtown areas, and near airports. Similarly, catering and dining services are provided in areas of high population density, city centers, and shopping centers. Consequently, the physical location of tourism services determines where their purchase and consumption will take place. Also, the physical location of tourism services determines the location of their distribution. Consumers have to be brought to points of sale (intermediaries) and locations of production (e.g., resorts). In contrast, manufactured products may be produced and consumed in different locations. For example, refrigerators can be produced in one city and sold and consumed in another.

The supply of tourism product is fixed in the short term. For example, a hotel has only a specific number of rooms and an aircraft has a specific number of seats (Coltman, 1989; Holloway, 1986). In the long term, the supply can be changed by building new hotels, planes, attractions, etc. Usually only a few financially strong companies are able to afford to develop new products in the short term. In contrast, the supply of physical goods typically can be changed within a shorter time. For example, depending on demand, more refrigerators and microwaves can be produced.

## More Dependence on Complementary Sectors

The tourist's experiences and satisfaction with services depend on mutual cooperation of various sectors (e.g., transportation, accommodation, attractions) and organizations (e.g., travel agents, shopping centers, car rentals, or food stores) which deliver tourism products and services and generate tourist experiences. Without this cooperation and complementary performance these sectors and organizations will not achieve an integrated total product and accomplish a major goal, which is tourist satisfaction. The poor performance of one sector or organization always reflects badly on the performance of others.

## Dispersed Control and Responsibility

Since the tourism product is an amalgam of products offered by various suppliers in different subsectors, and control of the service provision is dispersed over the several suppliers (Seaton and Bennett, 1996), the failure of one subsector affects the reputation of the total product. In contrast, the production of physical goods depends on one sector, and control over production belongs to the producer.

## Demand

### Customer Demand Dependence

Tourism services are offered where the customer is and where demand for the services exists. Restaurants cook meals when customers order them. Although restaurants can precook meals, they cannot serve them ahead of time. The provider of tourism services has to ensure that service offerings are widespread enough to cover the areas where there is demand for them (Bateson, 1995). Consequently, tourism and hospitality services are provided across a variety of locations. For example, McDonald's has to offer its services in a variety of locations such as in downtown areas, in airports, or along major highways. In contrast, physical goods can be manufactured even when customers do not ask for them. They can be stored and distributed for sale at times of high demand.

### Seasonality of Demand

The consumption of tourism services varies over time because the tourism product is consumed and in demand more at certain times of the year than others. Most tourism services are consumed and produced during prime vacation months (annual summer or winter vacations, school holidays, Easter and Christmas) than during off-peak seasons, and, for example, during weekends rather than weekdays. As a result, the demand for tourism services is seasonal. In contrast, the consumption of physical goods is usually more stable through the entire year. The demand for manufactured goods is less seasonal.

### Demand Fluctuations

Demand for tourism services constantly fluctuates depending on external forces beyond the control of suppliers, such as economic (fluctuations in currency exchange rates), political (wars, terrorist attacks, instability), and physical conditions (weather, hurricanes, droughts) (Coltman, 1989; Seaton and Bennett, 1996). Tourism demand also depends on economic and cultural distance. Economic distance refers to the distance the customer has to travel in terms of time and cost. The longer the travel time, the higher the resistance to travel to that destination and the lower the demand. Cultural distance refers to the cultural differences between a tourist's country of origin and the destination visited. The greater the difference between the culture of the destination and the culture of origin, the lower the demand for visiting that particular destination (McIntosh, Goeldner, and Ritchie, 1995). Tourism demand also fluctuates depending on consumers' health considerations, facility standards, and service quality. The perceptions of service quality are very subjective and depend on previous tourist experiences and perceptions. Tourism demand is very competitive, subject to fashion and changes in the level of individuals' motivations.

The fluctuations in demand for tourism services can be temporal or cyclical. In contrast, demand for physical goods is more stable and relatively less dependent upon weather conditions, political instability, economic and cultural distance, consumers' health, and facility standards. A more stable demand for physical goods also allows building inventories and storing unsold items. In contrast, since the demand for tourism services fluctuates, one cannot build inventories and save unsold services, consequently experiencing loss. If demand is lost, the tourism industry needs to develop strong recovery strategies to regain travelers.

One implication of demand fluctuation is that it is important to accurately forecast tourism demand to match tourism supply. However, it is extremely difficult to predict and accurately forecast demand for tourism services. The in and out flows of intangible and perishable tourism services cannot be measured. On the other hand, it is relatively easy to forecast demand for physical goods. The in and out flow of physical goods can be easily assessed using objective yardsticks of measurement.

## Time Dependence of Quality

The quality of tourism services depends on timely provision. At peak times and high vacation season (summer) hotels are usually fully booked and then stand empty for the rest of the year. Similarly, some restaurants can experience a rush of customers at Christmas and New Year and then can be nearly empty for the rest of the year. When airlines work at full capacity during annual holidays, delays are often caused by overcrowding. When restaurants work at full capacity, the waiting time for meals is prolonged. At a time of high demand, providers have to be quick in responding to customers' demands and spend less time serving each customer. They are unable to be as attentive to the customer's well-being and satisfaction as during a time of low demand. The stress on service providers and resources creates many human errors and may result in very poor customer experiences. Consequently, excessive demand is disadvantageous for service providers and for customers. On the other hand, when demand is too low, service quality also falls because of underutilized infrastructure and personnel boredom and demotivation (Rust, Zahorik, and Keiningham, 1996). Thus, the time at which the consumer chooses to use a tourism service is critical to its performance and quality, and therefore, the consumer's experience and satisfaction.

## Managing Demand

To stop service quality from declining it is advisable that tourism organizations do not work at full capacity. However, in some organizations it is desirable to work at full capacity, e.g., sporting events and music concerts. Unfortunately, most tourism/hospitality organizations experience operational problems when demand exceeds supply or when more than 75 percent of capacity is used (Rust, Zahorik, and Kleiningham, 1996). The inability to store intangible and perishable tourism services creates the need to manage demand in low and peak seasons. To manage demand for tourism services one must manage the marketing mix, e.g., hotels must raise room rates during the peak season and lower rates in off-peak seasons.

## Moving Demand

There are many advantages for both suppliers and customers if they are able to move demand, e.g., from the peak to the slack times. For example, many airlines and hotels offer discounted airfares and lower room rates in the off-peak seasons. In addition to better rates, service quality is enhanced and customers receive better attention. Providers can spend more time serving each customer. They are less stressed and make fewer errors. Consequently, the image of the services is enhanced, demand for services increases, and extra profit can be earned. In the case of physical goods, there is no need to move demand from peak to off-peak times. The existence of inventory prepares producers for times of higher consumption.

## Demand Elasticity

Demand for tourism services is highly elastic. Tourists are very responsive to changes in price. An increase in price brings a proportional decrease in the demand for tourism services and the volume of tourist arrivals. However, an increase in price for very elite tourism services such as luxury hotels or yacht cruises may also generate a higher demand from the status and prestige-oriented market. This is the Veblen effect, which sets up the demand curve based on exclusivity and prestige. The higher the cost of an experience or product, the more desirable it becomes—up to a point. Decreasing the price causes only a small increase in the amount purchased. Increasing the price actually causes the demand to increase, instead of decreasing. On the other hand, a decrease in price brings a proportional increase in tourism demand. The demand for business travel is inelastic. Business travelers are less responsive to changes in price than are holidaymakers. For physical goods, the demand for luxury goods such as cars or houses is elastic. The demand for necessities such as food or medicine is price inelastic.

## Changes in Tourism Supply Bring Changes in Tourist Demand

Changes in the supply and production of tourism services lead to changes in tourist behavior. For example, changes in the layout of a restaurant, its furniture, and atmosphere can affect the demand for services and lead to tourists having new expectations of service quality and availability. In contrast, changes in the supply of physical goods often do not create any changes in consumer behavior.

## Changes in the Benefits to Tourists Lead to Changes in Tourism Supply

Changes in the benefits offered to tourists mean that a new product is offered and a new market is tapped. For example, upgrading the take-out shop to the upmarket silver service restaurant may result in the alienation of its family consumers, repositioning the service operations in a new segment (Bateson, 1995) and changing consumers' expectations and service evaluation criteria. If fewer benefits are offered, the consumer's perceptions of service quality change, and the consumer goes somewhere else. If more benefits are offered, the perceptions of service quality are enhanced and the consumer may become a repeat buyer. Consequently, if the benefits change then the total product has to be changed into a new one. Changes in benefits have far greater implications in tourism service organizations than in manufacturing firms. Many changes made to services are usually visible to the consumer.

## Customers Have Different Demands for Tourism Services

Various individuals demand different types of tourism services depending on their lifestyle, motivation, and sociodemographic, economic, and psychological makeup. For example, the psychocentric type of tourist, who is concerned with small problem areas of his or her life, usually likes to spend vacation in nearby destinations and participate in familiar activities. The allocentric type of tourist, who is outgoing, self-confident, and willing to experiment with life, prefers to travel to destinations such as Africa or Asia to experience adventure and satisfy curiosity.

## Market Segments Have Different Demands for Tourism Services

Business travelers spend more than vacationers on a daily basis, as they demand specific facilities and flexible arrangements, which are more expensive to maintain. They also need year-round travel and reliable and convenient transportation. They are prepared to pay more for the availability of timely airline services, work stations, computer data ports, and fax and phone facilities in a hotel room. On the other hand, vacationers are more interested in easy access to sports facilities and recreation activities. Families are inclined to rent accommodations with fully equipped kitchens, irons and ironing boards, weekly housekeeping, laundry facilities, and easy access to playgrounds. First-class airline passengers demand additional value and add-ons in the form of a wider range and better quality of food or more comfortable seats. Students and retirees, however, often demand good-quality services at lower prices.

## More Emotional and Nonrational Appeal

The tourism product has more emotional and nonrational appeal than physical goods, depending partly upon the customer's dreams and fantasies (Seaton and Bennett, 1996). Customers frequently have emotional reasons for buying tourism, hospitality, and leisure services (e.g., to feel beautiful, to feel like a TV star) which are about making their dreams come true. Emotions and feelings are generated by experiencing different physical environments, the culture and heritage of the visited region, and the atmosphere of friendliness, hospitality, empathy, and safety. Therefore, the product is largely psychological rather than just physical in its attractiveness (Holloway, 1986). In contrast, consumers buy physical products for rational reasons (specific functions) rather than emotional. However, very often they are also influenced in their purchases by the status image and sex appeal that are used by advertisers of products such as cars, clothing, or alcohol in commercial campaigns.

## Difficult Positioning and Marketing

The successful positioning of tourism services is more difficult than that of physical goods because it is more difficult to promote abstract concepts such as experiences, benefits, or values than the tangible elements of physical goods such as size, color, or weight. These intangible elements of service, including staff competence, reputation, expertise, and skills form the basis for positioning of tourism services.

### Greater Emphasis on Image and Perceptions

Image and perceptions are more important tools in marketing and positioning tourism services than physical products. This is because the former lack tangible cues, which could be used to present them to consumers as objects rather than performances and which could make them more easily evaluated by consumers. Advertisers put a lot of effort into creating the desired mental image. The entire process of service evaluation takes place in the mind of the customer. It is the image or perception of the service, rather than the actual service, which is being sold to the customer. The images are used to create the consumer's desired "dreamed reality." Tourism services are often presented in a more positive way to generate quick sales. As a result, the image of tourism services often deviates from the reality. The larger the gap between image and reality, the more likely it is that the tourist will be dissatisfied. In addition, consumers often tend to buy tourism, hospitality, and leisure services that match their self-image. They fly first-class and stay at luxury hotels because this fits their mental picture of successful people (Morrison, 1996). In contrast, sales of physical goods depend more often on the real product (and its performance) than on its image.

In addition, environmental dimensions such as noise, music, temperature, or space utilization such as equipment, layout, and furnishings affect tourists' perceptions of the service experience. For example, the lack of signs on the street or at an airport may significantly decrease travelers' perceptions of the destination's accessibility and safety. Similarly, lack of space inside the overhead locker can affect passengers' perceptions of the comfort of their travel (Baron and Harris, 1995).

### Higher Perceived Risk of Purchase

The risk of buying intangible tourism services is higher than the risk of buying physical goods.

Various types of risk are associated with the purchase of tourism services:

1. Financial (there may be financial cost if the service goes wrong)
2. Performance (providers will not perform and deliver benefits to customers)

3. Physical (the injury may be inflicted on the purchaser)
4. Social (a loss of personal social status might be associated with a purchase) (Bateson, 1995)

The risk of purchasing tourism services is higher for several reasons:

1. Tourism services are difficult to standardize (there is no guarantee whether the providers will perform according to customers' expectations and deliver service quality)
2. Tourism services cannot be easily evaluated and assessed before purchase (because there are no measurable and objective criteria for their evaluation)
3. Tourism services are experiences (they are sold without guarantees and warranties, they cannot be returned, resold, and reclaimed since they have been consumed, and the opportunity cost of a failed holiday is irreversible)
4. It is difficult to replicate exactly the same service experience
5. The tourism product is partly composed of dreams and fantasies rather than assessable objects
6. Consumers are not aware of what to expect (many suppliers are involved in service provision and, therefore, the failure of one supplier may change the perceptions of the total product)
7. Tourism services involve highly complex human interactions (the perceptions of service quality depend on the quality of these interactions and human performance, in particular, the interpersonal skills of the interactants and their backgrounds)
8. Because of their intangibility and a high level of experience qualities tourism services must be selected on the basis of less pre-purchase information than is the case for physical goods (customers must rely on the advice of travel agents and other intermediaries who are motivated for quick sales and profit)
9. There is uncertainty about the outcome of the services even though the same service may be purchased
10. The dreams and image are sold at risk of selling image instead of reality
11. Many customers do not have the knowledge and experience to evaluate whether they are satisfied, even after they have consumed the service

In contrast, the risk of buying physical goods is smaller because physical goods are more standardized, more easily evaluated on the basis of objective and measurable criteria, and can be experienced before purchase. Consumers know in advance what product performance to expect. Goods can also be returned if their performance fails.

The perception of high risk in purchasing tourism services may be reduced in the following ways:

1. Seeking out additional information about the product before purchase
2. Developing customers' high-brand and high-service loyalty to preclude them from trying a new product
3. Focusing on personal recommendations and opinions of those whose judgment consumers trust (e.g., relatives) and who have good knowledge of the service (e.g., frequent buyers)
4. Developing the consumer's perceptions of a greater control over the service process and responsibility for service quality (informing potential buyers about the importance of communicating their needs and requirements adequately
5. Providing consumers with more and better information about services (e.g., informing passengers about delayed flights or changes in the service process
6. Communicating to customers about the role and responsibilities of the providers in fulfilling the customers' needs
7. Informing customers about their needs that cannot be fulfilled

### Shorter Exposure to Services

Customers' exposure to tourism, hospitality, and leisure services is usually shorter than to physical goods. These services in many cases are individual trips to restaurants, fast-food establishments, short flights, visits to travel agents, or relatively short annual vacations. There is also less time for providers to make a good or bad impression on customers (Morrison, 1996) and prove the quality of the product offered. In contrast, customers' exposure to physical products such as cars and refrigerators is longer. Many physical products can be stored for years; even food can be stored for a long time in freezers.

### Cost Determination

The cost structure of service production is also different. In the manufacturing sector, fixed costs (e.g., building, manufacturing machinery, tax on land, interest payments) and variable costs (e.g., gas, fuel, electricity, labor) can be precisely estimated. The production output can also be estimated. The fixed costs do not change over time, as opposed to variable costs. The fixed costs represent a relatively smaller percentage of total costs. In the tourism and hospitality sector, fixed and variable costs of intangible tourism services may not always be known exactly. The volume sold of tourism services cannot be estimated. The fixed costs (cost of promotion, cost of flight) represent a high percentage of total costs. These costs do not change over time. In the long run all variable costs become fixed costs. For example, in the long run all variable costs of one extra meal for one extra passenger, which are borne by many extra single passengers, become fixed costs (Palmer and Cole, 1995). Unfortunately, it is difficult to estimate how much these variable costs change over time. It is also difficult to assess the basis on which to calculate fixed costs: on the basis of the percentage of seats occupied, staff time used, or total turnover? Moreover, it is not easy to predict what these costs will be at different times (e.g., gasoline and aviation fuel costs are volatile).

## Price

It is more difficult to estimate price for tourism services than for physical goods since the cost of tourism services production and volume sold cannot be precisely estimated as they can with physical goods. Tourism services typically consist of much abstract input such as knowledge, skills, and effort, which cannot be evaluated objectively. Thus, pricing takes into account an intrinsic value (perceived benefits) for the customer, rather than the cost of performing the service. In tourism, price is the only concrete information available for evaluation of the service quality in the absence of other tangible criteria such as weight or size. Price indicates value and benefits to customers. It is also used as a positioning tool. Since tourism products cannot be displayed (except in promotional brochures) and their attributes demonstrated, their values can only be shown by displaying their price. For example, very often restaurants place their menus in their windows to show what they offer in terms of food and value (Payne, 1993). In contrast, the value of physical goods is determined by the total cost of their production.

Tourism services are also priced differently depending on the type of customer, different locations (luxury hotels on French Riviera), buying behavior of different market segments at different locations (consumers in New York and consumers in Moscow), and different types of use at different times (on a daily basis, weekly, annually), depending on the strength of the demand, capacity, and existence of alternatives. A very common strategy is to use price bundling, that is, to make the price of a total package lower than the price of individual components of the package (Palmer and Cole, 1995).

## More Variety and Types of Distribution Channels

The channels of distribution for most manufactured products consist of three locations: a producer, a retail store, and a place of consumption. In hospitality there is often one location where services are bought. For example: customers come to a restaurant (producer), where food and beverage are produced and sold (retail store), and consume their purchases (place of consumption) (Morrison, 1996). However, since tourism and leisure products are often located a long way from the customers, tourism requires a more complex distribution system through the use of many intermediaries such as travel agents, tour wholesalers, corporate travel managers, convention planners, conference and meeting planners, and many other specialty channels. They represent suppliers that not only influence the potential tourists in terms of purchase but also make the purchase of the tourism product easier, quicker, and more informative in terms of such issues as hotel location, transportation availability, etc. In contrast, intermediaries in the manufacturing sector seldom influence customers' purchase decisions and do not influence which products customers select in retail stores. There are several types of distribution channels in tourism and hospitality, depending on the number of channel levels, which aim to bring the product closer to the final buyer.

### Direct Distribution

Channel 1, called the direct marketing channel, has no intermediary level. It consists of a provider who is a retailer and sells directly to the consumer. The consumer goes directly to the provider to buy a product (e.g., a tourist goes to the hotel to book a room). The consumer may also stay at home and purchase a product from the supplier (retailer) via a reservation system (e.g., hotels, airlines). The location of the provider in the direct distribution process is very important because it determines the number of clients and competitors.

Service transactions, such as banking services, can also occur at locations separate from the provider's premises (Payne, 1993). In this case, the location is irrelevant. New technologies (e.g., reservation systems, electronic communication, telephone, and fax facilities) all play an important role in tourism service offerings. The reservation systems inform potential tourists about the availability of the product in terms of transportation, accommodation, etc. Most airlines and hotels operate room and flight reservation systems. In some cases, however, a customer's presence at the provider's location is important. For example, a travel agent can sell travel insurance or banking services (money exchange) if a customer wishes to buy these services in person at the premises of a travel agent.

Due to the inseparability of production and consumption, direct sales of tourism services are more convenient. Further, service operations must be decentralized; services must be delivered at a convenient location depending on the availability of consumers.

A less common form of direct distribution occurs when a service provider goes to the customer's location (e.g., home pizza delivery). In this case, the provider's location is less important, as long as it is close to the customer.

### Indirect Distribution

The consumer goes to the provider indirectly through an intermediary (travel agent, tour wholesaler, or specialty channel). In this case, location, number, and expertise of the intermediaries are also very important because they determine the number of customers and sales. There are three types of indirect marketing channels, depending on the number of channel levels used:

- The first type, Channel 2, uses one channel level, which is a single middleman (travel agent) who buys travel services from a provider and sells them to a client. The consumer goes directly either to the retailer owned by the provider (e.g., car rental company, airlines, hotels) or the individual travel agent who is paid a commission by the provider for the performed services (hotel centers, airlines).
- The second type, Channel 3, uses two channel levels or two middlemen (travel agent and wholesaler). The consumer purchases a product from an individual travel agent who purchases a product from a wholesaler. In this case, a provider negotiates bulk sales with the wholesaler.
- The third type, Channel 4, uses three channel levels or three middlemen (travel agent, wholesaler, and specialty channel). The consumer goes to the specialty channel that purchases a product from a travel agent who, in turn, negotiates sales with a wholesaler. The specialty channel is involved in selling tour packages that are designed for target markets with particular needs (e.g., educational study, conference tours).

From the traveler's point of view, one of the most important advantages of having two channel levels in the distribution process is that travel services purchased by wholesalers in large quantities at discounted prices allow the traveler to obtain cheaper travel packages.

From the producer's point of view, having more intermediaries in the channel means less control and more complexity of operations.

### Promotion

It is more difficult to promote tourism services than physical goods. The main objective of tourism promotion is to present service as a tangible object rather than an intangible performance in order to make the services better understood and their evaluation easier. This is usually done by advertising the tangible features of the services, developing symbols that better describe them, and consistently using the same symbols, logos, and themes symbolizing a product (e.g., McDonald's "M" logo).

### Importance of Word-of-Mouth and Personal Sources of Information

The most effective communication means for the tourism industry is word of mouth. It has a more significant impact on tourist perceptions than any other form of mass communication. Since experiencing and assessing the tourism product is impossible before its purchase, potential tourists seek and rely mostly on advice from friends and relatives. Consumers believe that personal sources provide the most adequate and up-to-date information (Bateson, 1995). As customers purchase more diverse and complex products, consisting of more subproducts, personal sources of information become increasingly important. Similarly, subjective rather than objective criteria of product evaluation also become increasingly important (Robertson, 1971). In addition, word-of-mouth techniques are perceived as more credible and less biased (Lovelock, 1991) and can reach more potential customers than any other promotional technique because it has a multiple effect. Dissatisfied customers tell more than two times as many people about their poor experiences than those who are satisfied (Payne, 1993). In the manufacturing sector, personal sources of information are less important because physical goods can be easily assessed using tangible criteria rather than subjective advice.

### Emphasis on Emotional Appeal

Because tourism and leisure services have more emotional and non-rational appeal than physical goods, promotional campaigns aim to appeal to customers' feelings by showing the distinct personality and features of the tourism product. Therefore, for example, in promotional advertising for an airline, there is little focus on aircraft types and more focus on the comfort of the seats and welcoming attitudes of the cabin crew.

## Emphasis on Off-Peak Promotion

In tourism, hospitality, and leisure, off-peak promotion is emphasized when customers are at the initial stage of the decision-making process about their vacations. Also, since the supply components of restaurants, hotels, or airports are fixed, customer demand needs to be regulated. In most cases, demand needs to be moved from the peak to the off-peak season (Morrison, 1996). In addition, pressure on the infrastructure and human resources (providers) in peak seasons also has to be regulated (usually shifted to the off-peak season) to maintain quality of service. The ability to produce more goods in times of high demand, and the ability to store these goods in off-peak seasons, indicates that there is little need to promote physical goods in a specific period of time.

## Misleading Advertising

Marketers often adopt advertising practices that are misleading. For example, promotional brochures often include untrue statements about a destination. They exaggerate the standard of facilities or quality of attractions to encourage tourists to visit them. They use superlatives such as "tropical and exotic" instead of "rainy," "outstanding and superior" instead of "standard," etc. These statements are known as double talk. They are used to generate customers' interest, emotional appeal, and quick sales. However, they also create very high customer expectations that often cannot be fulfilled. Such statements can even lead to legal action. Consequently, consumer protection has become an extremely important issue. Misleading advertising practices, however, have a very short life. Negative word-of-mouth publicity spreads very quickly and discourages tourists from using the advertised service. The loss in consumer demand causes a loss of revenue for the providers.

## Greater Importance of Physical Evidence

When customers purchase tourism services they need more tangible evidence of the service quality than in the manufacturing sector. This physical evidence helps customers to make the right decision when choosing a tourism product. Physical evidence includes the environment where the service is created and the service provider and customer interact. The physical environment also includes tangible elements that are used to communicate or support the role of the service.

There are two types of physical evidence: essential and peripheral. Essential evidence (design and layout of the hotel and its furniture, carpets, wall coverings, staff uniforms) is subject to key decisions by the providers. Peripheral evidence has little value on its own. For example, the essential physical evidence is represented by airline transportation, the peripheral by an airline ticket. The airline ticket has no independent value. However, it represents a right to experience the service. Similarly, the peripheral physical evidence represented by quality of food, cold course options, or free bottle of champagne have little value on their own. However, they add value to the essential services and help to better position service. The physical evidence must be managed to ensure that it is matched by the quality of personal service.

### Greater Emphasis on Process

Emphasis on the service process is greater in tourism and hospitality than in the manufacturing sector. The process involves procedures, tasks, schedules, activities, and routines by which a service is delivered to the customer (Payne, 1993) as well as how it is delivered. For example, the amount of attention and effort that the staff put into servicing the customer can disappoint or satisfy the customer. Providing a meal on time can make a customer happy. Upgrading an economy class traveler to business class on a low-capacity flight can create a positive customer experience and gain a favorable reputation for the airline. The ability to provide a low-fat meal on request can differentiate restaurant services and give a competitive advantage over restaurants with fixed menus (Payne, 1993). Consequently, process in tourism and hospitality is a very significant source of competitive advantage. It also helps to develop the right positioning strategy.

### Greater Emphasis on Customer Service

Tourism and hospitality requires a greater emphasis on customer service than the manufacturing sector. The provision of high-quality customer service depends upon understanding why and what the customer buys and determining what additional value can be added to the offer to better satisfy the customer's needs. Tourism includes a wider variety of activities intended to ensure that customers receive the best possible service which matches their requirements in the most effective and efficient manner (e.g., free advice, service quality audit, complaints handling). Tourism and hospitality services are characterized by close personal contact between the service provider and customer. This represents an advantage and an opportunity to provide excellent customer service. However, it also allows poorly trained employees to destroy the service experience. High-quality customer service is a major source of competitive advantage and a major differentiating element in tourism positioning (Payne, 1993).

## *Importance of Packaging and Programming*

Packaging is used in tourism, hospitality, and leisure to sell services when demand for them is lowest. Packaging refers to combining a range of services and programs in one package for one price (Fridgen, 1996). The combinations may include, e.g., fly-drive and fly-cruise packages, or accommodation, meal, and event packages. Programming refers to special activities, new events, and programs that add appeal to a package. Guided nature tours or tourist information centers are examples of such programming. Packaging and programming play a key role in selling travel and hospitality services that are perishable and are lost forever if not sold when they are offered. Packaging and programming are very popular with customers because they make travel and travel planning easier, less time consuming, more affordable, and offer greater assurance of consistent quality. They are tailored to the individual consumer's needs (Morrison, 1996). Also, packaging and programming help to match demand with supply. In particular, they help to increase business in off-peak periods by motivating customers to purchase services. For example, many hotels offer lower room rates and weekend packages in off-peak seasons. Restaurants offer early-bird discounts for senior citizens (Morrison, 1996). The packaging of travel and hospitality services is different from the packaging of physical goods. Tourism and hospitality packages usually involve some combination of services from principals, carriers, and intermediaries, and they require cooperation of numerous industry groups.

## *Importance of Partnership and Cooperation*

Because of the interdependent nature of tourism, hospitality, and leisure, various sectors such as transportation, accommodation, or food and beverage, and their organizations such as travel agents, motels, or bus companies need to cooperate to deliver a total integrated product to a customer in order to achieve customer satisfaction. Partnership is also formed to share the costs of promotion (Fridgen, 1996). This cooperation is very important and unique in tourism and hospitality.

### Importance of the Relationship Between Customers and Providers

Positive relationships between customers and providers are advantageous for the tourism, hospitality, and leisure industry. The positive attitudes of customers and providers toward each other can enhance the overall quality of the tourism product by developing a satisfying social interaction during the service process. It is more important to enhance these relationships in the tourism sector than in the manufacturing sector, as these relationships have a direct impact on customer satisfaction and retention.

### Difficulty in Analyzing International Tourism Services

It is difficult to analyze international tourism services. Although services can be exported and imported similarly to physical goods, the flow of payments and commodities versus the flow of tourism services are different.

In tourism export, the flow of tourism services and payments are in the same direction. When Australia exports tourism services to Bali, the Balinese tourists have to travel to Australia to experience these services in Australia. The Australian tourism producers cannot take the product to tourists in Bali. Tourists also pay for the services in Australia (see Figure 2.1).

FIGURE 2.1. Export of Tourism Services

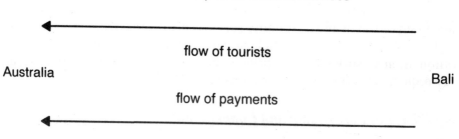

In tourism import, services and payments move in the same direction. When Australia imports tourism services from Bali, the Australian tourists must travel to Bali to receive these services. Australian tourists also pay for these services in Bali (see Figure 2.2).

FIGURE 2.2. Import of Tourism Services

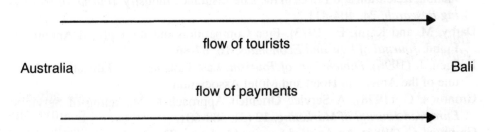

Because international tourism services are intangible and perishable, one cannot easily measure a physical flow of these services passing through countries, in contrast with tangible goods.

## CONCLUSION

There is a growing recognition that tourism, hospitality, and leisure services require different marketing and management approaches than physical goods. These services share many common features that make them quite different from manufactured goods. They have unique characteristics and different evaluation criteria, distribution processes, pricing, promotional focus, and cost structures. They include a high risk of purchase, are people oriented, and are very much concerned with customer satisfaction. Tourism and hospitality services differ from manufactured goods in many other specific features. To be successful and develop effective tourism strategies, marketers and managers must understand these features.

## REFERENCES

Baron, S. and Harris, K. (1995). *Services Marketing: Text and Cases.* London: Macmillan Press Ltd.

Bateson, J. (1995). *Managing Services Marketing: Text and Readings,* Third Edition. Orlando: The Dryden Press.

Booms, B. and Bitner, M. (1981). Marketing Strategies and Organizational Structures for Service Firms. In J.H. Donnelly and W. George (Eds.), *Marketing of Services.* Chicago: American Marketing Association, pp. 47-51.

Callan, R. (1990). Hotel Award Schemes As a Measurement of Service Quality— An Assessment by Travel Industry Journalists As Surrogate Consumers. *International Journal of Hospitality Management,* 9 (1): 45-58.

Coltman, M. (1989). *Tourism Marketing.* New York: Van Nostrand Reinhold.

Crosby, L. and Stephens, N. (1987). Effects of Relationship Marketing on Satisfaction, Retention and Prices in the Life Insurance Industry. *Journal of Marketing Research,* 24: 404-411.

Darby, M. and Karni, E. (1973). Free Competition and the Optimal Amount of Fraud. *Journal of Law and Economics,* 16: 67-86.

Fridgen, J. (1996). *Dimensions of Tourism.* East Lansing, MI: Educational Institute of the American Hotel and Motel Association.

Gronroos, C. (1978). A Service Oriented Approach to Marketing of Services. *European Journal of Marketing,* 12 (3): 588-601.

Gronroos, C. (1984). An Applied Service Marketing Theory. *European Journal of Marketing,* 16 (17): 30-41.

Holloway, J. (1986). *The Business of Tourism,* Second Edition. London: Pitman Publishing Ltd.

Knutson, B. (1988). Ten Laws of Customer Satisfaction. *Cornell Hotel and Restaurant Administration Quarterly,* 29 (3): 14-17.

Lehtinen, U. and Lehtinen, J. (1982). *Service Quality: A Study of Quality Dimensions.* Working Paper, Service Management, Institute of Helsinki, Finland.

Lovelock, C. (1991). *Services Marketing,* Second Edition. Englewood Cliffs, NJ: Prentice Hall.

Martin, W. (1987). A New Approach to the Understanding and Teaching of Service Behavior. *Hospitality Education and Research Journal,* 11 (2): 255-262.

McIntosh, R., Goeldner, C., and Ritchie, J. (1995). *Tourism: Principles, Practices, Philosophies,* Seventh Edition. New York: John Wiley and Sons.

Morrison, A. (1996). *Hospitality and Travel Marketing,* Second Edition. New York: Delmar Publishers.

Nelson, P. (1974). Advertising As Information. *The Journal of Political Economy,* 82 (4): 729-754.

Palmer, A. (1994). *Principles of Services Marketing.* Berkshire: McGraw-Hill Book Company.

Palmer, A. and Cole, C. (1995). *Services Marketing: Principles and Practice.* Englewood Cliffs, NJ: Prentice Hall.

Parasuraman, A., Zeithaml, V., and Berry, L. (1985). A Conceptual Model of Service Quality and Its Implications for Future Research. *Journal of Marketing,* 49 (4): 41-50.

Parasuraman, A., Zeithaml, V., and Berry, L. (1988). SERVQUAL: A Multiple-Item Scale for Measuring Consumer Perceptions of Service Quality. *Journal of Retailing,* 64 (1): 12-40.

Payne, A. (1993). *The Essence of Services Marketing.* New York: Prentice Hall.

Robertson, T. (1971). *Innovative Behavior and Communication.* New York: Holt, Rinehart and Winston.

Rust, R., Zahorik, A., and Keiningham, T. (1996). *Service Marketing.* New York: Harper Collins College Publishers.

Saleh, F. and Ryan, C. (1992). Client Perceptions of Hotels: A Multi-Attribute Approach. *Tourism Management,* 13 (2): 163-168.

Sasser, W., Olsen, R., and Wyckoff, D. (1978). *The Management of Service Operations.* Boston: Allyn and Bacon.

Seaton, A. and Bennett, M. (1996). *Marketing Tourism Products: Concepts, Issues, Cases.* Oxford, England: Thompson Business Press.

Solomon, M., Surprenant, C., Czepiel, J., and Gutman, E. (1985). A Role Theory Perspective on Dyadic Interactions: The Service Encounter. *Journal of Marketing,* 49 (1): 99-111.

Urry, J. (1991). The Sociology of Tourism. In Cooper, C. (Ed.), *Progress in Tourism, Recreation and Hospitality Management 3.* Surrey, England: The University of Surrey, pp. 48-57.

Zeithaml, V. (1991). How Consumer Evaluation Processes Differ Between Goods and Services. In Lovelock, C. (Ed.), *Services Marketing,* Second Edition. Englewood Cliffs, NJ: Prentice Hall, pp. 39-47.

Chapter 3

# Service Quality Concepts and Dimensions Pertinent to Tourism, Hospitality, and Leisure Services

Beth Schlagel Wuest

## *PERCEPTIONS OF SERVICE QUALITY*

Guests' perceptions of service quality vary widely. Likewise, guests' perceived satisfaction with performed services also varies widely. Two distinct variables influence their perceptions: customer expectations and service standards. The gap between expectations and service standards/performance is the primary indicator of overall service quality (Parasuraman, Zeithaml, and Leonard, 1994b).

### *Customer Expectations*

Guests are the judges of service quality (Berry and Parasuraman, 1991). Their expectations of services greatly influence their resulting level of satisfaction. It is far easier to please guests with lower expectations than those with higher expectations. Consequently, an understanding of guests' expectations is critical. Lewison (1997) categorizes service expectations in three levels: essential, expected, and optional. Zeithaml, Berry, and Parasuraman (1993) include three similar levels in their conceptual model of customer service expectations: predicted, adequate, and desired.

Essential services are those which are the essence of the service business. These services meet the fundamental requirements to continue operations. For example, tourism, hospitality, and leisure service providers must maintain reasonable business hours, admit or check-in guests, inform guests of service details, and acknowledge complaints. Guests predict or believe these services will be performed.

Expected services are those which guests assume the service provider should offer in order to provide adequate service. Expected services go beyond the essential services required for the company to stay in business. However, because of guests' expectations, such services need to be offered in order to be competitive. Services such as convenient operating hours, payment options, reservations, and reasonable information pertaining to the services, facilities, and locale are expected by most guests. It is also important to note that as guests are provided with additional services, these services soon become commonplace. Over the years, expected services increase. Guests become more demanding, requiring the service provider to move beyond what is commonplace.

Other services are considered optional or desired. Guests consider these services an added bonus that enhances the value of their visit. Optional services express the uniqueness of the service provider and contribute to its competitive edge. Today, the trend in optional services is toward indulgence, including ambiance, convenience, and unobtrusive service ("Indulgence Rules," 1998). However, because guests generally do not expect optional services, they ordinarily will not fault the service provider if such services are not available. To effectively provide optional services, it becomes essential for the service provider to recognize the true desires of the targeted guests.

### Service Standards

Tourism, hospitality, and leisure service providers establish service standards. Standards, however, are "changing benchmarks as customer's [sic] expectations increase and the organisation responds to such changes" (Callan, 1994, p. 482). Appropriate service standards depend on the mission of the organization. Standards achieved, however, further depend on two basic factors: the service policies of the organization and the actual performance of the service procedures.

Service providers establish policies that are deemed comparable to their image and appropriate to their target market. Such policies may be initiated by management or a service team. They may be developed through a formalized process or may simply evolve from experience and preferences. Policies may be elaborated in company documents or merely spread by word of mouth throughout the organization. Regardless of the system, service policies set the standards for the provision of guest services in the company.

Service standards are only as good as the resultant performance. Although service policies may establish guidelines and performance standards, personnel may not perform adequately. Some companies develop extensive service policies only to have staff fall short in performance. After all, why would a recent survey (Dailey, 1997) find that respondents were more satisfied with their experience of facing a drill in the dentist's office than ordering a meal at a fast-food restaurant? Consequently, service managers who successfully set an example, relay procedures, and motivate employees are more likely to capture the essence of a quality service plan. Starbucks is a case in point. Their early goal of providing excellent service has led to considerable success in a pricey coffee market (Dailey, 1997).

### Perceived Service Performance

Perceived service quality reflects the difference between guests' expectations and the actual services performed (Parasuraman, Zeithaml, and Berry, 1994a). The extent to which expectations and service performance are similar or different influence the extent to which guests are satisfied or dissatisfied. Although varying approaches have been taken to study these differences, the subjective disconfirmation conceptual model has been cited as most influential in determining customer satisfaction (Dion, DiLorenzo-Aiss, and Javalgi, 1998; Oliver, 1993). In this model, a "better-than/worse-than" comparison between expectations and actual services results in a positive or negative outcome. Interestingly, it has been noted that disconfirmation may explain the perceived variance in service quality more than mere performance (Parasuraman, Zeithaml, and Berry, 1994b). For example, disconfirmation helps to explain the variance in guests' perceptions of service quality in situations when similar services were rendered.

Typically, guests consider services performed to be exceptional when the expected services have been surpassed in quality and quantity. If guests are pleasantly surprised by a host of unexpected optional services, their level of satisfaction and rating of service performance will be considerably higher. As an added bonus, a highly satisfied guest is one of the best forms of advertisement.

If guests' expectations are sufficiently met with the services provided, they will assess the services as adequate. Unfortunately, what is adequate today may not be adequate tomorrow. Further, mediocrity is not a standard by which companies will excel.

The worst-case scenario occurs when service performed does not measure up to guests' expectations. Poor service leaves a guest unimpressed, discouraged, and unsatisfied. Although, in some instances, the dissatisfied guest represents an opportunity for the service provider to rectify the unpleasant experience and correct service policies and performance, in too many instances the service provider is completely unaware of the guest's displeasure. Although many guests let their dissatisfaction be known by telling the front desk staff or the manager, according to a recent American Express Travel Index, 14 percent of leisure travelers do nothing and 4 percent never return ("Handling Bad Hotel Service," 1998). In another study conducted by the Technical Assistance Research Corporation, dissatisfied customers told nine or ten people about their unpleasant experience, while satisfied customers told only four to five people (Vanderleest and Borna, 1988). Just as a highly satisfied customer can be a major asset, a dissatisfied guest can be a liability.

## DIMENSIONS OF SERVICE QUALITY

Service quality is the result of a complex network of several dimensions. Through the years, researchers have been on a quest to identify the most significant components of service quality. A variety of factors have been identified as contributing to service quality.

Parasuraman, Zeithaml, and Berry (1988, 1994a) are among the most recognized researchers in the area of service quality. Their development and refinement of the SERVQUAL battery has produced a generic measure of service quality through the examination of twenty-two service items, which factor into five basic service dimensions (Parasuraman, Zeithaml, and Berry, 1988, 1994a; Parasuraman, Berry, and Zeithaml, 1991). The service dimensions consist of reliability, tangibles, responsiveness, assurance, and empathy.

Reliability reflects the service provider's "ability to perform service dependably and accurately" (Parsuraman, Zeithaml, and Berry, 1988, p. 23). Reliability includes "doing it right the first time," which is one of the most important service components for customers (Berry and Parasuraman, 1991). Reliability also extends to providing services as and when promised and maintaining error-free records. Thus, the penchant to over-promise services and lead guests toward unrealistic expectations only serves to undermine guests' tolerance and trust.

Tangibles consist of the "appearance of physical facilities, equipment, personnel, and communications materials" (Berry and Parasuraman, 1991, p. 16). Although typically rated the least important of the five services, tangibles are still considered a core service component. The importance of tangibles can be illustrated by Holiday Inn's recent endeavor to evaluate and redefine their image after customers told them they were "looking a little old" (Wagner, 1998).

Responsiveness represents the "willingness to help customers and provide prompt service" (Parasuraman, Zeithaml, and Berry, 1988, p. 23). It has been said that "today luxury is time" (Watkins, 1998, p. 26). Consequently, service providers' ability to provide services in a timely manner is a critical component of service quality for many guests.

Assurance reflects the "knowledge and courtesy of employees and their ability to inspire trust and confidence" (Parasuraman, Zeithaml, and Berry, 1988, p. 23). Guests expect to feel safe in their transactions with employees. Situations in which employees enter guest rooms without knocking, confront guests without appropriate identification, or misguide guests with inaccurate information discredit the staff's ability to reassure the guest.

Empathy involves the "caring, individualized attention the firm provides its customers" (Parasuraman, Zeithaml, and Berry, 1988, p. 23). The importance of empathy may be the root of the statement, "If one looks at who is winning, it tends to be companies that see the guest as an individual" (Watkins, 1998, p. 26). Due to guests' desires that employees see things from their point of view, Holiday Inn, Holiday Inn Select, and Holiday Inn Sunspree properties are piloting an empathy training program intended to help employees relate to their guests in a more empathic manner (Wagner, 1998).

Numerous researchers have adapted the SERVQUAL battery to specific industries, products, and target markets. Saleh and Ryan (1991) were among the first to analyze service quality in the hospitality industry using SERVQUAL dimensions. More recently, Baker and Fesenmaier (1997) effectively used the SERVQUAL model to study service quality expectation differences among three groups (visitors, employees, and managers) involved in a tourism service encounter. Wuest, Emenheiser, and Tas (1996) also used SERVQUAL as a basis for examining mature travelers' perceptions of lodging service quality. Some researchers, however, have questioned the effectiveness of SERVQUAL for the hospitality industry (Fick and Ritchie, 1991; Johns, 1993). Webster and Hung (1994) adapted and condensed SERVQUAL in an attempt to make it more manageable for the hospitality industry. Similarly, Knutson and colleagues (1991) developed LODGSERV, a modified version of SERVQUAL, which measures the expectations of guests in the lodging industry and which substantiates the earlier works on SERVQUAL. Stevens, Knutson, and Patton (1995) also devised DINESERV, yet another take on SERVQUAL, intended to measure guests' expectations in the restaurant industry. Although scale items measuring hospitality service quality may vary depending on the specific end use, the same five service dimensions remain constant. Regardless of the version or adaptation of SERVQUAL that is used, the five dimensions (reliability, tangibles, responsiveness, assurance, and empathy) clearly appear to be the best and most consistent measure of service quality.

## OBJECTIVES OF SERVICE

Why is customer service so important to tourism, hospitality, and leisure service providers? Customer service has a direct impact on the customer's level of satisfaction, which, in turn, ultimately reflects on the service provider's bottom line. Although it is difficult to measure the true impact of customer service, quality customer service has been cited as a means for improving a variety of aspects of a business. The following discussion focuses on several objectives of services.

### Improve Guest Convenience

Many services contribute to the guest's sense of convenience, comfort, and well-being. Services such as accessible rest rooms, refreshment vending, shuttle service, and comfortable seating add to guest convenience, enjoyment, and satisfaction and indirectly encourage guests to extend their stay. The key to getting closer to one's customers is making it easier for them to do business with the service provider, better known as convenience (Anton, 1996).

### Enhance Service Provider's Image

The number and quality of services offered establishes the image of the service provider. For example, no-frills motels offer limited services in order to reduce overall costs. Full-service hotels, on the other hand, provide almost every imaginable service to their guests. Although the price paid by the guest may vary, the greater difference may be in the perceived image of each of these properties.

### Ensure Customer Security

Multiple services reinforce guests' sense of security. Protective services such as adequate lighting, security staff, emergency medical facilities, guest room locks, sprinklers, and clearly marked exits instill confidence. Conversely, in a study commissioned by *Lodging Hospitality*, questionable neighborhoods and lack of deadbolt locks were cited as the primary reasons for guests to avoid lodging at a hotel (Wagner and Watkins, 1994).

### Generate Traffic

Quality customer service has the potential to generate increased traffic for the service provider. Satisfied guests will be more likely to extend their stay, return to the destination, and recommend the property to other potential guests. Further, the delivery of quality service and customer satisfaction has been clearly linked with profits, cost savings, and market share (Sager, 1994). As a result, a satisfied guest is a key element in improving traffic and creating repeat business.

### Establish a Competitive Edge

Tourism, hospitality, and leisure service providers, as members of the service industry, are expected by the great majority of potential guests to provide a set of baseline services. However, service providers who extend their services beyond minimal expectations have a far better chance of satisfying their guests. With creative ideas and a strong understanding of the needs and desires of their guests, hospitality service providers are developing innovative, extensive service strategies. The "critical differences in customer/guest service are what often separate hospitality industry leaders from industry followers" ("The New Imperative," 1998, p. 54).

### Customer Demand

By providing specific services, businesses can generate demand among certain target markets. Business travelers, family vacationers, and conventioneers have been among the most frequently targeted groups. Each group requires a series of customized services that can be promoted as a special package in order to attract greater guest demand. According to a survey conducted by *Lodging Hospitality,* topflight businesspeople use and expect the amenities of home including such services as basic cable television, newspaper delivery, coffee, room service, fitness facilities, and laundry/dry cleaning (Wolff, 1998). The quality-conscious service manager should provide these services if vying for travel dollars and attempting to generate customer demand among business travelers.

## CONTINUUM OF SERVICE

When looking for ways to improve service quality, hospitality industry service providers often focus on the face-to-face encounter with guests. It seems only natural to assume that the guest will remember and be influenced by a positive, personable experience with staff. However, the guest's overall perception of service quality results from a variety of experiences with the service provider over a period of time. Therefore, it is important to encourage service providers to look not only at the on-site personal experience of the guest, but also at events that precede and follow. To provide effective services throughout the service continuum, consultants such as KPMG's Customer Centric Management have broadened their scope to enable companies in the hospitality industry to provide adequate services from the initial reservation through checkout and marketing follow-up ("The New Imperative," 1998). A service continuum illustrates how a guest encounters the services provided over a period of time. On the continuum, services are described as those the guest experiences before entering the facilities of the service provider, those the guest encounters while the service is actually being performed, and those that occur after the guest has departed (see Figure 3.1).

### Before

Information about hospitality, tourism, and leisure services is marketed in a variety of ways—television and radio spots, newspaper and magazine advertisements, pamphlets, direct mail flyers, Web pages, and billboards,

FIGURE 3.1. Continuum of Service: Before, During, and After the Customer Encounter with the Hospitality Service Provider

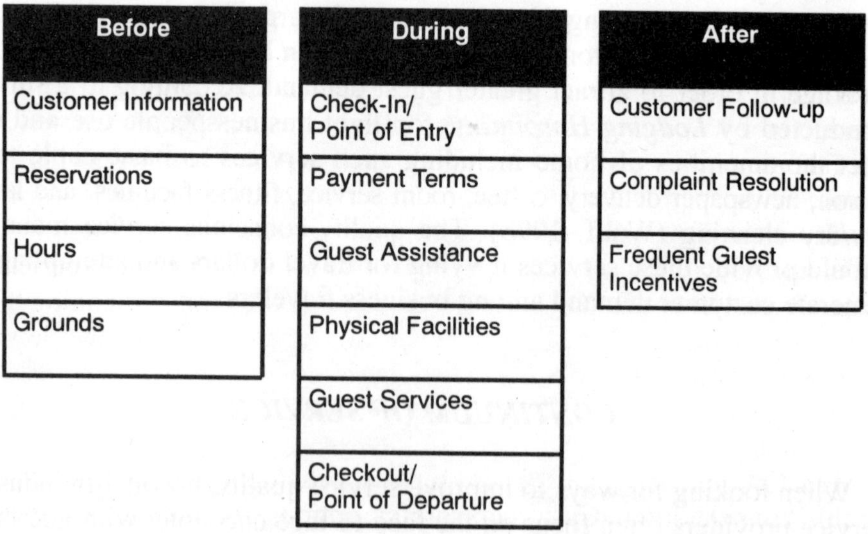

| Before | During | After |
|---|---|---|
| Customer Information | Check-In/ Point of Entry | Customer Follow-up |
| Reservations | Payment Terms | Complaint Resolution |
| Hours | Guest Assistance | Frequent Guest Incentives |
| Grounds | Physical Facilities | |
| | Guest Services | |
| | Checkout/ Point of Departure | |

to name a few. Such information gives potential guests their first perception of the services provided and contributes to the establishment of their expectations. Consequently, if the services are marketed in a straightforward, honest format, they will be more apt to measure up to guests' expectations. Information must also provide sufficient detail to answer potential guests' basic questions, and if possible, a means for acquiring additional information. For example, the guest will need clear directions, operating hours, and other essential details to be able to successfully utilize the services.

Many tourism, hospitality, and leisure service providers encourage guests to make advance reservations. For many guests, this is their first encounter with the service provider. Whether reservations are made directly with staff on the property, or through a central reservation center, reservationists must convey a sincere desire to assist the guest and enable the guest to access the facilities with ease.

Customers have become accustomed to convenient hours of operation. Service providers must establish convenient hours of operation and maintain them in accordance with those posted. Offering consistent services without unexpected interruptions will go a long way in establishing a loyal customer base.

The old adage "first impressions are lasting impressions" seems equally true among tourism and hospitality facilities. Upon entering the grounds of the hotel, restaurant, or other tourist facility, customers gain their first impression. Design, maintenance, and aesthetics of parking areas, grounds, and facilities, appropriateness of signs, and adequate lighting and security all add to the quality of the impressions generated.

### During

When the guest arrives, the service provider has the opportunity to interact face-to-face with the guest. Because guests experience services and facilities in a variety of ways and because many guests feel that any contact with employees is a service experience, all employees must be considered as part of the service equation.

As guests arrive, they typically anticipate a most pleasant experience. After all, isn't that why they spend more than a little time in planning their travel or recreation? Guests want their first encounter with the service provider to be consistent with their expectations. Pleasant and efficient service at the point of entry or check-in must be consistent with guest expectations.

Monetary exchanges between service providers and guests require careful consideration. Customers prefer options for making payments, such as cash, checks, traveler's checks, and a variety of credit cards. Service providers, on the other hand, have to weigh the profitability, efficiency, and security of providing an array of alternatives. Guests also expect efficiency and security, as well as accuracy, in their transactions with the service provider.

Of all services, guest assistance typifies what is thought of as "pure" customer service. The elements of human interaction, personalized service, and responsiveness to guest needs are the essence of guest assistance and service. Without acceptable provision of these core services, service providers will have difficulty earning the guest's vote of confidence. Although it is common to associate quality guest services with "high-end luxury properties," even budget properties are able to meet their guests' needs through creative solutions. For example, some budget hotels that are economically unable to provide room service have developed partnerships with nearby restaurants. Hospitality Franchise Systems, with their 4,200 franchised hotels under the Days Inn, Howard Johnson, Park Inn, Ramada, Super 8, and Villager motel chains, has partnered with Pizza Hut to deliver to over 900 of its hotels (Rubel, 1995). Such ideas prove to be win-win solutions for everyone involved: guests, property managers, and outside service providers.

Physical facilities reflect the policies of management and signify the quality of guest service. Properties that have been maintained and appropriately updated give the guest a feeling of cleanliness, security, and safety. Overall, the condition of the property suggests a level of value (or lack thereof) to the guest. Even simple tasks such as replacing light bulbs, maintaining parking areas, and checking rest rooms for cleanliness contribute to the guest's perception of the property. Obviously, remodeling and redecorating spaces, which is a costly undertaking, should be included in long-range plans. Staybridge Suites by Holiday Inn has gone so far in providing satisfactory facilities that they adopted an interactive television system whereby extended-stay guests can select from alternate floor plans and have their suite rearranged for them while they are out (Staybridge Suites by Holiday Inn, 1998).

Target markets ordinarily require targeted services. Guest services focus on the special needs and desires of the anticipated guests. For example, family-focused tourism destinations provide specialized services for all members of the family. Business-centered properties, on the other hand, narrow their offering of services to the needs of the business traveler. Walt Disney World Resorts attempts to meet its varied target markets through six resorts, each with a distinctive combination of space, facilities, themes, and entertainment options ("Walt Disney World Resorts," 1998).

Guest checkout/point of departure signals the last chance for personal, face-to-face contact with the guest. Not only does this experience contribute to the guest's lasting impressions, but it is also the property's last chance to inspire the guest. Ideally, if any problems have surfaced, this is a perfect time for resolution. At the point of departure guests are somewhat sensitive and require special care. After all, their vacations are coming to an end, they are going back to work, they may be tired, their schedules may have been disrupted, or they may have spent more than they had planned. Regardless of reasons, a host of situations preoccupy their thoughts, making friendliness and efficiency an important part of departure procedures.

## After

After leaving the premises of the service provider, the service experience is not yet complete. Many opportunities remain for the continued provision of quality service.

Guest follow-up allows evaluation of the types and quality of services provided. Tourism, hospitality, or leisure service providers have responsibility for assessing as well as developing and delivering their service programs. Surveys provided near the time of departure that can be completed and returned at a later date, follow-up telephone interviews, and mailed questionnaires have been used by hospitality service providers to evaluate their service plans. Assessments enable the service provider to identify whether the appropriate services were provided, if other pertinent services were overlooked, and if customers perceive services in the same manner as the service provider. Most important, however, is the fact that assessment results indicate appropriate modifications for service policies.

In some cases, guests depart the premises before their concerns or complaints are fully resolved. In these instances, service providers still have an opportunity to convert the guest's experience into a positive one. Studies show that customers who express concerns and have their problems effectively resolved are often more loyal than customers who never faced undesirable experiences. However, studies also show that every complaint that is voiced represents about 2,000 that are left unvoiced (Plymire, 1991). An effective customer complaint resolution procedure and a vehicle allowing easy guest access to staff when problems occur are simply mandatory customer service components in today's competitive environment.

Frequent guest incentive programs are another means of promoting customer service and repeat business. Through correspondence and other marketing techniques associated with frequent guest incentive programs, guests can be made aware of specific services and recent developments.

The incentive program also provides an opportunity to maintain contact with guests.

## TOTAL SERVICE COMMITMENT

Quality service emanates from a total service commitment. Tourism, hospitality, and leisure service providers must address service issues by first developing appropriate policies and procedures, by attaining a firm commitment from service employees, and by measuring the ongoing effectiveness of their service plan.

### Development of Service Policies and Procedures

Service commitment begins with the establishment of service policies and procedures. Policies must be developed that are in line with the desired service image and target market. Managers generally have a strong sense of the desired service image. Many also believe they have an equally good understanding of what services their target market wants and at what price. However, many managers miss the mark when it comes to profiling their customers' needs. Likewise, employees will likely have a different perspective than their managers with respect to the feasibility and effectiveness of service polices and procedures. Heymann (1992) encourages the development of customer-driven policies and procedures with input from customers as well as from employees who have regular contact with guests. The opinions of guests and employees should be incorporated into the policymaking process in order for the resulting policies and procedures to be rooted in reality. In all cases, policies and procedures must be consistent, effective, and efficient and must address all of the important dimensions of service quality.

### Commitment from Service Provider's Employees

Quality service requires a commitment on several levels. Whether it is the manager making policy decisions or an employee addressing guests' concerns, service must be projected from a unified front. The only true means of providing seamless service is through a team approach, with management guiding and ensuring full implementation of the process.

Service providers must involve all of their staff in each department in an effort to provide quality service. Everyone in the organization should work together toward the common goal of delivering quality service. The staff must fully comprehend the significance of providing quality service; they must truly understand and respect the essential roles that other departments play in the delivery of quality service (Heymann, 1992). Recognition of the integration of departmental functions enables employees to see greater value in their own roles as component providers of quality service.

Empowerment is critical if the team approach is to function properly. Numerous organizations tout the value of the team approach. Yet many of these same organizations fail to empower their employees to be effective service providers. A commitment to service means everyone in the organization must have the power to serve the needs and problems of guests (Kirwin, 1992). Consequently, frontline employees must be given the credibility and granted the authority to resolve guest problems without constant approval from a manager or other higher authority.

Management plays a vital role in the delivery of quality service. Management guides the tourism, hospitality, and leisure organization toward the achievement of quality service. The leadership, guidance, and actions of managers set the stage for effective service delivery. One successful hotel manager stressed the importance of management's actions when he indicated that a manager cannot teach values. Instead, he believes that employees learn by observing the behavior and values of the manager ("Robert Small," 1987). Heymann (1992) recommends transformational leadership, managers who "communicate high expectations and promote intelligence, rationality, and careful problem solving" and who "treat employees as individuals and give personal attention" (p. 55). Essentially, the promotion of quality service internally to employees goes a long way toward effectuating quality service to guests (Lewis, 1989).

Much of management's role in serving guests lies in the development of a service-oriented staff. Managers' ability to hire, train, motivate, and reward service-oriented employees greatly influences the organization's ability to provide quality service. It is often said that the key to quality service is hiring the right employees. One restaurant executive said it was far more important to him to hire a good, friendly person than merely a competent one, because he could more easily train the person to do the job (Dailey, 1997). Country Hospitality evaluates potential employees according to what they call "PICI"—passion, intelligence, compassion, and intensity (Kirwin, 1992). After hiring quality employees, regular staff training must emphasize the value of the service program, incorporate the dimensions and continuum of quality customer service, and develop techniques for effective achievement of service quality. Continual motivation, performance assessment, and reward are essential ingredients in maintaining positive, productive employees. Regular and consistent feedback on job-specific responsibilities followed by fair and meaningful reward and recognition helps to motivate employees toward the provision of enhanced service quality (Heymann, 1992).

### Assessment of Effectiveness

A total service commitment requires regular and continual assessment. Reasonable standards and effective measures of performance must be developed to ensure quality service. Currently, many tourism, hospitality, and leisure service providers have assessment systems in place. Some service providers seem to feel that they are overburdened with assessment. However, many of these systems need to be reexamined. For example, measuring service quality solely through guest comment cards cannot be termed a reasonable assessment of performance, since only 2 to 3 percent of guests respond to the request ("Handling Bad Hotel Service," 1998). Systems of assessment must be devised with an intent to improve performance (Heymann, 1992). Effective measurement must be broad based and focused on the dimensions of service quality.

## SUMMARY

A foundation of concepts and dimensions of service quality will guide the tourism, hospitality, and leisure service provider in the development of a quality service strategy. Understanding the factors influencing guests' perceptions of service quality—such as expectations and service standards—illustrates the importance of ongoing assessment and revision of service plans. Knowledge of the dimensions and continuum of service is essential for the service provider to develop a comprehensive and truly effective service strategy. Finally, recognizing the objectives of quality service and the need for a total service commitment will encourage managers to view quality service as their priority and enable them to take the necessary steps to ensure its success.

## REFERENCES

Anton, J. (1996). *Customer Relationship Management: Making Hard Decisions with Soft Numbers.* New York: Prentice Hall.

Baker, D. and Fesenmaier, D. (1997). Effects of service climate on managers' and employees' rating of visitors' service quality expectations. *Journal of Travel Research, 36* (1), 15-22.

Berry, L. and Parasuraman, A. (1991). *Marketing Services: Competing Through Quality.* New York: The Free Press.

Callan, R. (1994). Quality assurance certification for hospitality marketing, sales and customer services. *The Services Industries Journal, 14* (4), 482-499.

Dailey, P. (1997). The drill on customer service. *Restaurants and Institutions, 107* (18), 20.

Dion, P., DiLorenzo-Aiss, J., and Javalgi, R. (1998). An empirical assessment of the Zeithaml, Berry and Parasuraman service expections model. *Service Industries Journal, 18* (4), 66-86.

Fick, G. and Ritchie, J. (1991). Measuring service quality in the travel and tourism industry. *Journal of Travel Research, 30* (2), 2-9.

Handling bad hotel service. (1998, July 27). *USA Today,* 1D.

Heymann, K. (1992). Quality management: A ten-point model. *Cornell Hotel and Restaurant Administration Quarterly, 33* (5), 50-60.

Indulgence rules. (1998). *Institutional Investor, 32* (1), W2-W3.

Johns, N. (1993). Quality management in the hospitality industry: Part 3—Recent developments. *International Journal of Contemporary Hospitality Management, 5* (1), 10-15.

Kirwin, P. (1992). Increasing sales and profits through guest satisfaction. *Cornell Hotel and Restaurant Administration Quarterly, 33* (5), 38-39.

Knutson, B., Stevens, P., Wullaert, C., Patton, M., and Yokoyama, F. (1991). LODGSERV: A service quality index for the lodging industry. *Hospitality Research Journal, 14* (2), 277-284.

Lewis, R.C. (1989). Hospitality marketing: The internal approach. *Cornell Hotel and Restaurant Administration Quarterly, 30* (3), 41-45.

Lewison, D.M. (1997). *Retailing,* Sixth Edition. Upper Saddle River, NJ: Prentice Hall.

The new imperative: Customer centric management. (1998). *Lodging Hospitality, 54* (5), R6-R7.

Oliver, R. (1993). A conceptual model of service quality and service satisfaction: Compatible goals, different concepts. In T. Swartz and S. Brown (Eds.), *Advances in Services Marketing and Management,* Volume 2. Westport, CT: JAI Press, pp. 65-85.

Parasuraman, A., Berry, L., and Zeithaml, V. (1991). Refinement and reassessment of the SERVQUAL Scale. *Journal of Retailing, 76* (4), 420-450.

Parasuraman, A., Zeithaml, V., and Berry, L. (1988). SERVQUAL: A multiple-item scale for measuring consumer perceptions of service quality. *Journal of Retailing, 64* (1), 12-40.

Parasuraman, A., Zeithaml, V., and Berry, L. (1994a). Alternative scales for measuring service quality: A comparative assessment based on psychometric and diagnostic criteria. *Journal of Retailing, 70* (3), 201-230.

Parasuraman, A., Zeithaml, V., and Berry, L. (1994b). Reassessment of expectations as a comparison standard in measuring service quality: Implications for further research. *Journal of Marketing, 58* (1), 111-124.

Plymire, J. (1991, March/April). Complaints as opportunities. *Business Horizons,* 80.

Robert Small: Excellence and employees. (1987). *Cornell Hotel and Restaurant Administration Quarterly, 28* (2), 73-76.

Rubel, C. (1995). Hotels help lodgers who help themselves. *Marketing News, 29* (10), 6.

Sager, I. (1994, May 30). The few, the true, the blue. *Business Week,* 124.

Saleh, F. and Ryan, C. (1991). Analyzing service quality in the hospitality industry using the SERVQUAL model. *Services Industries Journal, 11* (3), 324-345.

Staybridge Suites by Holiday Inn. (1998). *Hotel and Motel Management, 213* (9), 40.

Stevens, P., Knutson, B., and Patton, M. (1995). DINESERV: A tool for measuring service quality in restaurants. *Cornell Hotel and Restaurant Administration Quarterly, 36* (2), 56-60.

Swan, J. and Oliver, R. (1989). Postpurchase communications by consumers. *Journal of Retailing, 65* (4), 419-420.

Vanderleest, H. and Borna, S. (1988). A structured approach to handling customer complaints. *Retail Control, 56* (8), 14-19.

Wagner, G. (1998). In the driver's seat. *Lodging Hospitality, 54* (4), 65-68.

Wagner, G. and Watkins, E. (1994). Pet peeves. *Lodging Hospitality, 50* (12), 117-119.

Walt Disney World Resorts. (1998, June). *Incentive,* 30-31.

Watkins, E. (1998). The guest is king. *Lodging Hospitality, 54* (1), 26-32.

Webster, C. and Hung, L. (1994). Measuring service quality and promoting decentring. *Tqm Magazine, 6* (5), 50-55.

Wolff, C. (1998). Making the guestroom "information central." *Lodging Hospitality, 54* (4), 35-36.

Wuest, B., Emenheiser, D., and Tas, R. (1996). What do mature travelers perceive as important hotel/motel customer services? *Hospitality Research Journal, 20* (2), 77-93.

Zeithaml, V., Berry, L., and Parasuraman, A. (1993). The nature and determinants of customer expectations of service. *Journal of the Academy of Marketing Sciences, 21* (1), 1-12.

## Chapter 4

# The Impact of People, Process, and Physical Evidence on Tourism, Hospitality, and Leisure Service Quality

### Karl Titz

### *INTRODUCTION*

The experience of great service vanishes in the blink of an eye. It is timeless, unobtrusive, and invisible. Great service is being seated for dinner at Charlie Trotter's in Chicago or Roger Verge's Le Moulin de Mougins in the south of France at 10:00 p.m. and looking at your watch at 1:30 a.m. not knowing where the time went. It is checking into your hotel room without effort. Some may argue that people remember only the extremes. However, while poor service is remembered, great service goes unnoticed. Creating a service environment where customers are given the gift of experience without interference from the service provider is the challenge in restaurants, hotels, transportation systems, and national parks.

Understanding the components of a quality service experience is critical to long-term business health in the hospitality, tourism, and leisure (HTL) organization. The lifeblood of HTL industries is the customer. Ensuring that the customer receives an appropriate level of service is critical to success. Establishing service at a level beyond what the customer expects or is willing to pay for is as problematic as establishing a level of service below what the customer expects. Customer perception of quality in an HTL context depends on his or her expectations. Some firms aim to delight the customer by exceeding expectations. However, is this a prudent business strategy for all firms? Businesses have the ability to manage customer expectations and, therefore, the experience of service.

The first challenge to anyone who sets out to discuss quality service is to establish a common meaning of what service is. Albrecht and Zemke

(1990) and others suggest that service is intangible. If service is intangible, how can one understand what quality service is? One aim of this chapter is to establish a foundation for defining service and quality for the HTL industries. One definition might be that service is useful labor that does not produce a tangible commodity. But is the act of being served somehow tangible? How do customers know they have been served and, if they have been served, how will they determine if the delivered service was of acceptable quality? Quality could be interpreted as the degree of excellence and superiority in kind. Both of these definitions together or separately do not capture the experience of quality service in an HTL context. The truth is, there is no single or simple definition of this complex phenomenon. And if we ask our customers what quality service is, they may ultimately tell us that quality service is not a "what" but a feeling. "I don't know what it looks like or what it takes to bring it together, but I know what I feel like when I have experienced it." It is difficult to evaluate a feeling, but the service encounter has tangible artifacts that we can evaluate.

"Service quality refers to customers' appraisals of the service core, the provider, or the entire service organization" (Duffy and Ketchand, 1998, p. 241). Langevin (1988) suggested that meeting expectations and needs of customers was the central issue in the perception of service quality. Parasuraman, Zeithaml, and Berry (1988) postulated that the difference between actual service provided and the customer's expectation was a true measure of customer service. SERVQUAL measures five dimensions of service space (Parasuraman, Zeithaml, and Berry, 1988):

1. *Tangibles:* Physical facilities, equipment, and appearance of employees
2. *Reliability:* Ability to perform the required service dependably and accurately
3. *Responsiveness:* Willingness to help customers and provide prompt service
4. *Assurance:* Knowledge and courtesy of employees and their ability to inspire trust and confidence
5. *Empathy:* Caring and individual attention provided by the staff

Perceived service quality measurement is based on gaps between the expected level of service in each of the domains and an evaluation of the actual service received. Three central components work in concert to produce a quality service experience in HTL: the people, the processes, and the physical evidence of the experience.

Service is not provided out of thin air but rather through interactions customers have with HTL organizations. Customers view their service experience through the lenses HTL creates. People, processes, and physical evidence are choreographed to focus the customer's experience of quality service. Traditionally, frontline service employees are the lowest paid but have the greatest impact on the HTL customer. Frontline employees are trained in the processes of providing guest service. The processes that support customer service may be standards and procedures, technology, communication flow, and organizational characteristics and culture. Because of the intangibility of service, the artifacts or physical evidence of service become critical to the service experience. This chapter discusses people, process, and physical evidence, laying a foundation for understanding quality service delivery in HTL.

## *PEOPLE*

Analysis reveals three distinct groups of people who participate in the customer's experience of quality service (Bateson, 1985; Schneider, 1980, 1990):

1. Customers
2. Employees
3. Management

A distinction must be drawn between different types of customers. Whether riding on an airline, checking into a hotel, or dining in a restaurant, homogeneity of the customer mix contributes to a positive customer experience. A heterogeneous customer mix may create problems. For instance, Disney has received significant attention in the press because of a boycott by one customer group intolerant of another customer group. Imagine a college fraternity being booked on the same floor of a hotel as a family reunion, or the last-minute business traveler seated next to a customer with a deeply discounted ticket. It is important to manage the customer mix with this reality in mind.

Before developing a service strategy in HTL, management and employees must understand customers' expectations. Failure to develop this basic understanding will result in organizational waste and dissatisfied customers (Lewis and Nightingale, 1991). Baker and Fesenmaier (1997) used a modified SERVQUAL instrument to measure responses from the three constituencies: employees, managers, and customers. The authors found that both employees and management significantly overestimated customers' service expectations at a Midwestern U.S. theme park. Interestingly, managers attributed significantly higher service expectations to customers than frontline employees did. This occurred in spite of the assumption that management was aware of marketing research and the nature of the relationship between product and customer. Balancing the level of service is requisite to successfully serve the customers' needs and maintain an economically viable presence in the marketplace.

J. W. Marriott had a simple philosophy about the treatment of employees. "Take care of your employees, and they will take care of your customers" (Marriott and Brown, 1997, p. 34). Diaz and Park (1992) found that employees who work in geographically isolated hotels and resorts experienced high levels of job satisfaction despite a significant dislike of isolation. The employees reported significant positive feedback from management. Pizam and Neumann (1988) noted two significant determinants in employee satisfaction: meaningful work, and feedback from peers and supervisors. Setting standards and communicating them to service employees is not enough to guarantee quality service in an environment devoid of other positive motivators and stimuli.

The service encounter and the customer's evaluation of the quality of the service encounter are critical to service business success. A common thread in creating a successful service climate is the employees who ultimately provide customer service. Not all employees have the temperament to work in a customer service capacity. It is important for the "health" of both the individual and the organization to select qualified candidates. However, management must cultivate a service environment, which is not accomplished by words alone but by observable actions that promote good service. Service must be part of the culture. Management's task is to identify viable and homogeneous markets, then create a service climate responsive to those markets. That service climate is neither overwhelming nor underwhelming, but a carefully orchestrated response to customer expectation. However, people are not the only component of a quality service experience. The processes that have been developed to aid employees in delivering a quality service experience are critical.

Quality service is a willful act. An intrinsic desire and willingness to serve distinguishes great service employees (Heskett, 1986). The challenge to managers in the service arena is to identify employees who demonstrate "flexibility, tolerance for ambiguity, the ability to monitor and change behavior during the service encounter, and empathy with the customer" (p. 123). Identifying quality service employees is difficult. However, there is a growing body of research on selection and retention of employees in the HTL industries.

## The Self-Monitoring Scale

The practice of preemployment screening was first introduced in the 1920s and 1930s (Anastasi, 1985) and has recently increased in the United States (Kiechel, 1985). Service settings have seen the use of a personality measure designed to evaluate an individual's service orientation and predict the qualities of the employee in the service encounter (Hogan, Hogan, and Busch, 1984). The self-monitoring scale, which measures the ability of an individual to monitor and change his or her behavior (Snyder, 1974), was used in a hospitality setting by Samenfink (1992). In addition to assisting in the identification of employees with a customer service orientation, Samenfink suggested that implementation of the self-monitoring scale might decrease employee turnover, increase the number of guest service employees likely to actively sell products, thereby increasing revenue, and aid in identifying employees with the ability to adjust their behavior to customer needs. Private companies often construct preemployment screening programs designed to identify qualified candidates. However, management actions play a crucial role.

## PROCESSES

Are a service delivery system and a quality service experience mutually exclusive? How do we build a service delivery system with the flexibility to adapt to individual needs? For example, try ordering a hamburger from McDonald's without pickles. The process collapses. Are we not shackling quality service with the nomenclature developed for a bygone industrial age? We need to examine the processes associated with quality service. Processes cover a spectrum of activities related to quality service delivery and deal with the procedures and policies a company establishes to deliver quality service. A discussion of operational-specific processes is beyond the scope of this work. However, the reader should gain a familiarity with the best practices that contribute to a quality service space. A service environment must be planned for the specific service activity that will take place. Significant processes related to quality service delivery discussed here are benchmarking, continuous quality improvement strategies, service evaluation, and application of technology.

Pye (1994) classified six approaches to service improvement:

1. *Task analysis:* Tasks were viewed as a series of trainable steps
2. *Models of behavior:* Makes a comparison of good and bad through video and pictures
3. *Influencing the environment:* Service training done with a whole group; little headway can be made if the manager fails to set a good example
4. *Recruitment approach:* Hiring people with a service orientation
5. *Objective setting approach:* Based on analysis of customer service ratings and setting appropriate objectives to meet future goals
6. *Structure approach:* Empowerment and moving the locus of control to the frontline employee

Pye suggests that these approaches are not universal in application. Management must consider three factors before implementing or changing a process:

1. Customer satisfaction level or expectations
2. Organizational culture
3. Nature of the transaction

Quality service improvement is not a prescriptive process but an analytical and dynamic process. Successful process implementation requires a systemic approach. The six change strategies Pye identified have appropriate applications. Applying them without consideration of the genesis of the problem may lead to unsatisfactory or less than optimum results. Increasingly, benchmarking has been used to examine internal practices as well as the practices of competitors to determine if a best practice exists.

## Benchmarking

Benchmarking measures performance in conjunction with improvement initiatives to measure comparative operating performance and identify best practices. Benchmarking, which is used by management to improve service quality and remain competitive, measures four domains:

1. Profitability
2. Service Quality
3. Marketing Effectiveness
4. Productivity

The National Association of Accountants (1998, p. 44) specified seven steps to implement a process called Multidimensional Balanced Benchmarking (MBB):

1. Define the service unit, which could be based on individual units, such as the front desk of a hotel or the entire hotel. It could be the central reservations center for a large travel agency or restaurants in a particular region of the country.
2. Identify the data needed to measure and rank the service unit on the four dimensions.
3. Compare the required measures with existing data and determine if additional measures must be made. Complete additional data collection as required.
4. Identify comparative service units and rank performance of the units in terms of strongest performer to weakest performer in each of the four domains. Verify with operation managers that no anomaly existed during the data collection period.
5. Compare the best practices with the weaker units to identify differences between operating practices. This comparison should be made in all four domains.
6. Implement best practices where applicable and consistent with company culture and philosophy.
7. Begin the analysis again, applying it to other service units and operating methods.

The Benchmarking Exchange (1998) ranked the top five business processes benchmarked in 1997:

1. Human Resources
2. Information Systems
3. Benchmarking
4. Purchasing/Accounting
5. Customer Service

The Benchmarking Exchange predicts that as companies become more externally focused, customer service issues will gain momentum in the years to come. Benchmarking will become critical as more companies explore opportunities over the Internet and develop processes to better serve customers through this medium.

### Blueprinting

Another method of evaluating process is blueprinting (Shostack, 1992). Blueprinting examines the flow of service. The question ultimately to be answered is, does this activity add value? If it does not add value, why do we do it (LeBoeuf, 1993)? For example, during the 1970s and early 1980s it was popular in many restaurants to serve a chilled salad fork. The forks were ceremoniously presented to each customer to ensure they were aware of the added "service." But, in the kitchen, we continued to hold the salad greens at room temperature and proceeded to put the greens on hot plates, fresh from the dishwasher! The amenity war of the late 1980s was another example of misplaced service. Hotels loaded guests up with toiletries but kept them waiting in line to check out. Examples of service gone awry in HTL are legion. Blueprinting is a way to systemically analyze the service process to ensure that customers are receiving the appropriate level of service.

Blueprinting requires two assumptions to be effective. First, the overall service design determines the quality of the service encounter. Second, the design and control of sensory input determines the nature of the service encounter (Shostack, 1984). Applied in a restaurant or other HTL setting, service blueprinting can be a useful tool in analyzing and providing an appropriate level of service (Smith, 1994). The three areas addressed in blueprinting are processes, means, and evidence (Shostack, 1992). Process relates to the procedures involved in service provision. An example would be scripting the reservation interaction in a hotel or airline reservation center. Means may include the frontline employee and increasingly technological interfaces over the Internet and in the facility. Evidence would include the ambiance, the physical facilities, the product, as in the case of a meal or a seat on an airplane, or the ease and speed of navigating a Web site. In spite of our best efforts to provide quality service, sometimes we fail. The way in which service breakdowns are handled is critical to the guest's perception of quality service.

### Handling Service Problems

There is an old saying, "It is not what you say but how you say it." Research in service breakdown and complaint resolution is receiving increased attention in the literature and is the subject of Chapter 11 in this book. Anyone who has managed or worked in operations knows the challenge of dealing with difficult situations and customers. HTL customers hope that everything will flow smoothly, but sometimes it does not happen that way. The way a service breakdown is dealt with will determine customer experience. Sparks and Callan (1996) measured the perceived level of effort in service recovery and the effect of effort on service evaluation. Effort was measured using explanations, offers, and communication style. Explanations were either internal, "This was our responsibility, and I assure you we will act to correct the situation," or external, "We are sorry, we have no control over the vending machines. You can call this number to get your money back." Customers measured the offer in terms of the service breakdown. The offer needed to be appropriate to the situation to mitigate the effects on service evaluation. Communication was evaluated on the basis of empathy. The more empathic the communication style, the greater the likelihood of a mitigating effect on service. Empathic communication was found to have mitigating effects even when the other two responses, explanation and offer, were rated lower by the customer. Keeping customers is more cost effective than finding new ones. Service industries need to recognize this reality and develop training programs to address weaknesses in their response to service breakdowns.

### Customer Comment Cards

Customer comment cards enjoy widespread use because they are economical and easy to administer. However, is the information provided by comment cards sufficient to facilitate analysis of the central issues of quality service? Prior work by Cadotte and Turgeon (1988), Herzberg, Mausner, and Snyderman (1959), Johnston (1995a), Johnston and Heineke (1998), and Silvestro et al. (1990) suggested that service evaluation consisted of four distinct factors:

1. Satisfiers
2. Dissatisfiers
3. Criticals
4. Neutrals

Satisfiers do not detract from a service evaluation if they are not present. But, when added to the service equation, satisfiers significantly improve the customer's perception of service. For example, fresh cut flowers and a heated towel rack would add significantly to a customer's quality service evaluation. In the absence of fresh flowers and heated towels, the service quality would not suffer.

Dissatisfiers can be classified as adequate or inadequate. HTL organizations will have service quality problems if the room is dirty or the food is cold. However, service providers will not be rewarded with higher evaluations for a clean room or hot food.

Criticals are the elements significantly impacting service evaluation positively and negatively. Timeliness would be a critical determinant of customer service, as would responsiveness to customer needs.

Neutrals have the smallest impact on customer service evaluation. New employee uniforms or an expensive change in china patterns may be examples of actions that have no impact on customer service evaluation. There is a debate as to whether customers' service antennae are as finely tuned as we give them credit for (Johnston and Heineke, 1998). Rather, there appears to be a zone of tolerance before a factor becomes significantly negative or positive in service evaluation (Berry and Parasuraman, 1991; Johnston, 1995b; Kennedy and Thirkell, 1988; Miller, 1977; Oliver, 1980; Woodruff, Cadotte, and Jenkins, 1985; Zeithaml, Berry, and Parasuraman, 1993). However, customer feedback will continue to be sought.

It is management's responsibility to ensure the information collection process is relevant to the operation and identifies satisfiers and criticals. Johnston and Heineke (1998) suggest that limited time and resources be spent on neutrals because of the relative lack of importance to customers. However, dissatisfying factors need to be brought up to an acceptable standard. By treating them as satisfiers, management can ensure they are executed at an appropriate level. Management must be economical and efficient in dealing with dissatisfiers.

Criticals are the facets of service that will significantly add or detract from a quality service experience. Criticals determine future purchase intention and are the issues to which management must pay closest attention. Travelers place a high value on safety. But how many customer comment cards in HTL inquire about safety? Timeliness and responsiveness to customer needs are also critical to customer satisfaction and quality service. Today, management has a variety of data collection alternatives in addition to the traditional customer comment card. A variety of technological innovations have made the process of quality service assessment and delivery easier.

### Technology

Technology is finding increasing application in HTL. Today technology allows customers to check into a hotel at an automated lobby kiosk and be issued a smart card for room access and charges. This scenario may not be appropriate for all settings but has dynamic application in HTL. Customers can click on Marriott Corporation's Web page and obtain a listing of available dates and rates for Marriott properties worldwide. A road map from either the local airport or places hundreds of miles away can be downloaded, airline tickets can be purchased, and seating for flights can be selected. Seamless technology is critical to quality service. As a matter of fact, travelers increasingly expect these technological enhancements, thus making them a competitive necessity (Sussmann and Baker, 1996). But successful technology implementation in hospitality has produced mixed results. Productivity improvement, one of the hoped-for and touted results of technology, is often not realized without a change in management approach and the preparation of the personnel affected (Haywood, 1990).

Three types of technology have been discussed in the business literature (Grosse, 1996):

1. Product technology
2. Process technology
3. Management technology

A systems approach to technology applications yields a somewhat different classification scheme:

1. Operating systems
2. Communication systems
3. Management systems

Specifically in hospitality, we have seen application of technology in four areas, according to Kirk (1996):

1. Building technology
2. Environmental management technology
3. Food production and service technology
4. Information technology

This discussion will focus on information technology. Grosse (1996) suggests that a firm's technology implementation may not distinguish it competitively. However, superior use of technology can create competitive advantage. For example, Harrah's Casinos recently patented a real-time table game tracking system. At present, the system contains over 12,000,000 customer records on Harrah's players worldwide (Harrah's Entertainment, 1998). Several questions must be answered prior to technology implementation (Ford, Ford, and LeBruto, 1995):

1. Why should the firm undertake technology implementation?
2. Who are the intended users?
3. What is the purpose of the system?
4. When is the information needed?
5. Where is the information stored?

The opportunity for technological application in HTL is only limited by imagination. Sumichrast and Olsen (1996) proposed a technological interface for the concierge. Presently concierge interfaces are a database of information, limited to "advertisers" who pay to be included in the database. The limitation of these systems is their inability to communicate with the customer. Sumichrast and Olsen recommend the use of an expert system designed to furnish recommendations, learn about the customer, and render services. Attempts to use information technology in destination management systems (DMS) have met with mixed results.

Although major hotel companies, airlines, and auto rental companies are quickly implementing technology applications, DMS that attempt to market a country or specific region have achieved fewer advances. Sussmann and Baker (1996) suggest that smaller HTL providers in defined destinations have the most to gain from technology. The Internet provides an economical vehicle for smaller locales and operators within those locales to gain widespread distribution of their product. Working together with regional tourism agencies, these products can be bundled and deliver a wide range of travel options for a broader segment of the market. A number of frameworks have been suggested for implementation of DMS (Cash, McFarlan, and McKenney, 1992; Griffiths and Willcocks, 1994; Keen, 1991). Griffiths and Willcocks (1994) identified six categories of risk associated with complex technology implementation:

1. *History:* Previous experience of success and failure
2. *Context or organizational characteristics:* This is complicated by the numerous stakeholders involved in a DMS
3. *External context:* Pressures from governmental agencies or competitive pressures
4. *Content:* The size and complexity of the project, the number and variety of participating entities
5. *Process:* The way the implementation is structured, project management
6. *Risk outcomes:* How closely the outcomes are tied to participant goals and objectives

Given the risks associated with technology implementation in DMS, Griffiths and Willcocks recommend four focal points for successful public/private technology initiatives:

1. *Governance:* The ability of major participants to reach consensus on objectives, resource allocation, and the decision-making process
2. *Project management:* There is a multidirectional flow of information involving localized input and clear direction
3. *Market need:* An identifiable need for the DMS exists, which may be predicated on economic survival of the participants

4. *Learning:* The development of a DMS is an incremental process and less likely to fail if some of the participants have prior experience with the technology

The challenge to management is the creation of competitive advantage through the use of technological processes. The impact of technology is further discussed in Chapter 16.

## *PHYSICAL EVIDENCE*

Physical evidence of a service experience may entail a number of variables. As has been discussed previously, the service encounter includes tangible and intangible attributes. Clearly, physical evidence of a service experience is easier for the customer to evaluate and understand because it is tangible. This poses problems for the HTL provider because physical evidence can be both controllable and uncontrollable. For example, the cleanliness of the service environment is under the operation's direct control. However, crime patterns impacting an inner-city hotel or rainy weather during a beach vacation are uncontrollable phenomena impacting the overall service evaluation. HTL businesses, including casino operators, McDonald's, and Disney, have a long tradition of cleanliness. The glass is free of fingerprints, the brass is polished, and the floors and walkways are free of debris. By maintaining this appearance of cleanliness and organization, management creates a sense of security for the customer. Casino management can mitigate the social stigma of gambling and create a sense of confidence that an operation is run honestly by maintaining an immaculate physical space. It has long been understood that the service environment has a significant impact on purchase behavior.

Atmosphere, design, and decoration are covered in marketing, retailing, management, and hospitality texts and periodicals. But physical changes to the service environment and the subsequent impact on purchase behavior remains little understood or investigated (Bitner, 1992). Unlike traditional industrial settings, service industries produce and distribute the product in the same space. The question becomes, what impact does physical space have on customers and employees? In and Out Burger, a successful Southern California hamburger chain, uses bright airy space with high ceilings. The production areas have large windows to provide an abundance of natural light. The space affords customers the opportunity to observe the sparkling cleanliness and employees at work in a large open space with natural light and an outside view. What impact does this sensitive and sensible design have on business health?

Bitner (1992) proposed a framework for examining the impact of physical space on employees and customers. Organizational behavior literature examined the impact of physical space on employees. Marketing literature examined its impact on customers. Employee motivational variables included pay, benefits, communication, promotions, and organizational relationships. Customer motivational variables included pricing, advertising, added features, and promotion. However, no prior attempt had been made to examine the simultaneous impact of design on customers and employees. Bitner suggested that employees and customers respond to physical stimuli on cognitive, emotional, and physiological levels. This epistemology mirrors the hedonic consumption paradigm as proposed by Hirschman and Holbrook (1982). Hirschman and Holbrook proposed that experiential activities such as gamesmanship, theater, and sporting events elicited hedonic responses. The constructs proposed were in the cognitive domain, the emotional domain, the physiological domain (excitement and arousal), and the absorption domain. The cognitive domain requires thinking, as in chess or mountain climbing. The emotional domain may be triggered through watching movies or spectator sports. The physiological domain may be triggered through eating or bicycle riding. Reading a great book or participating in a hobby may absorb the participant in the activity to the exclusion of outside stimulus.

Investigating these variables in a service context where tangible and intangible attributes are both so critical is the next logical step. Titz, Miller, and Andrus (1998) examined differences between casino gamblers using these constructs. Slot machine players were found to be escapist and tended to allow the experience to carry·them away from the problems and concerns of their everyday lives. Table game players were more adventurous and more willing to create their own experience. Bitner's typology and the hedonic consumption paradigm may increase our understanding of the impacts of physical space on business health. What experiences are elicited in restaurants, hotels, and entertainment complexes? The intention here is not to provide answers but instead to ask questions. As we understand more about service phenomena, we continue to develop new scales more·precisely able to measure the outcomes.

## CONCLUSION

This chapter reviewed current knowledge of the impact of people, process, and physical evidence on tourism, hospitality, and leisure service quality. Together these factors produce a synergistic relationship impacting on service quality expectation and perception. HTL management is responsible for charting the industry's future course. The successful executive will be prepared to think and act in a rapidly changing environment. The challenges are significant and dynamic.

# REFERENCES

Albrecht, K. and Zemke, R. (1990). *Service America*. New York: Warner.

Anastasi, A. (1985). The use of personality assessment in industry: Methodological and interpretive problems. In H.J. Bernardin and D.A. Bownas (Eds.), *Personality Assessment in Organizations* (pp. 1-20). New York: Praeger.

Baker, D.A. and Fesenmaier, D.R. (1997). Effects of service climate on managers' and employees' rating of visitors' service quality expectations. *Journal of Travel Research, 36(1)*, 15-22.

Bateson, J.E. (1985). Perceived control and the service encounter. In J.A. Czepiel, M.R. Solomon, and C.F. Suprenant (Eds.), *The Service Encounter* (pp. 67-82). London: Lexington Books.

Benchmarking Exchange (1998). *Benchmarking Past, Present, and Future* at <http://www.benchnet.com/bppf.htm>.

Berry, L.L. and Parasuraman, A. (1991). *Marketing Services: Competing Through Quality*. New York: The Free Press.

Bitner, M.J. (1992). Servicescapes: The impact of physical surroundings on customers and employees. *Journal of Marketing*, April, 57-71.

Brownell, J. and Jameson, D. (1996). Getting quality out on the street: A case of show and tell. *Cornell Hotel and Restaurant Administration Quarterly, 37(1)*, 28-33.

Cadotte, E.R. and Turgeon, N. (1988). Key factors in guest satisfaction. *The Cornell Hotel and Restaurant Administration Quarterly, 28(4)*, 45-51.

Cash, J., McFarlan, W., and McKenney, J. (1992). *Corporate Information Management*. Boston: Irwin.

Diaz, P.E. and Park, J. (1992). The impact of isolation on hospitality employees' job satisfaction and job performance. *Hospitality Research Journal, 15(3)*, 41-49.

Duffy, J.A. and Ketchand, A.A. (1998). Examining the role of service quality in overall service satisfaction. *Journal of Managerial Issues, 10(2)*, 240-255.

Earl, M.J. (1989). *Management Strategies for Information Technology*. Englewood Cliffs, NJ: Prentice Hall.

Ford, L., Ford, R.C., and LeBruto, S.M. (1995). Is your hotel MISsing technology? *F.I.U. Hospitality Review, 13(2)*, 53-65.

Griffiths, C. and Willcocks, L. (1994). *Are Major Information Technology Projects Worth the Risk?* Oxford Institute of Information Management/IC-Parc, Imperial College.

Grosse, R. (1996). International technology transfer in services. *Journal of International Business Studies, 27(4)*, 781-799.

Harrah's Entertainment (1998). Harrah's obtains patent for "Real Time" data on customer casino play technology. *Hotel Online,* <http.www.hotel-online.com/Neo/Ne...eases1998_4th/Nov98_HarrahsIT.html>.

Haywood, K.M. (1990). A strategic approach to managing technology. *Cornell Hotel and Restaurant Administration Quarterly, 31(1),* 39-45.

Herzberg, F., Mausner, B., and Snyderman, B. (1959). *The Motivation to Work.* New York: Wiley.

Heskett, J.L. (1986). *Managing in the Service Economy.* Boston: Harvard Business School.

Hirschman, E.C. and Holbrook, M.B. (1982). Hedonic consumption: Emerging concepts, methods and propositions. *Journal of Marketing, 47(Summer),* 92-101.

Hogan, J., Hogan, R., and Busch, C.M. (1984). How to measure service orientation. *Journal of Applied Psychology, 69(1),* 167-173.

Johnston, R. (1995a). The determinants of service quality: Satisfiers and dissatisfiers. *International Journal of Service Industry Management, 6(5),* 53-71.

Johnston, R. (1995b). Managing the zone of tolerance: Some propositions. *International Journal of Service Industry Management, 6(2),* 46-61.

Johnston, R. and Heineke, J. (1998). Exploring the relationship between perception and performance: Priorities for action. *Service Industries Journal, 18(1),* 101-112.

Keen, P. (1991). *Shaping the future: Business design through information technology.* Boston: Harvard Business School Press.

Kennedy, J.R. and Thirkell, P.C. (1988). An extended perspective on the antecedents of satisfaction. *Journal of Consumer Satisfaction, Dissatisfaction and Complaining Behavior, 1(1),* 2-9.

Kiechel, W. (1985, June 10). The managerial mind probe. *Fortune,* 113-116.

Kirk, D. (1996). Technology. In Haywood, M.K., Hobson, P., and Jones, P. (convenors). *Hospitality Management, The State of the Art,* <http://www.mcb.co.uk/services/conferen/apr96/hospitality/kirk/touch.htm>.

Kirk, D. and Pine, R. (1998). Research in hospitality systems and technology. *International Journal of Hospitality Management, 17(2),* 203-217.

Langevin, R.G. (1988). Service quality: Essential ingredients. *Review Business, 9(3),* 3-5.

LeBoeuf, M. (1993). *Fast Forward.* New York: G.P. Putnam's Sons.

Lewis, R.C. and Nightingale, M. (1991). Targeting service to your customer. *The Cornell Hotel and Restaurant Administration Quarterly, 32(2),* 18-27.

Marriott, J.W. and Brown, K.A. (1997). *The Spirit to Serve: Marriott's Way.* New York: Harper Business.

Miller, J.A. (1977). Exploring satisfaction, modifying models, eliciting expectations, posing problems and making meaningful measurements. In H.K. Hunt (Ed.), *Conceptualization and Measurement of Consumer Satisfaction and Dissatisfaction* (pp. 72-91). Cambridge, MA: Marketing Sciences Institute.

National Association of Accountants (1998). Implementing Multidimensional Balanced Benchmarking (MBB): A seven-step process. *Management Accounting, 79(7),* 44.

Oliver, R.L. (1980). A cognitive model of antecedents and consequences of satisfaction decisions. *Journal of Marketing Research, 17(4),* 460-469.

Parasuraman, A., Zeithaml, V., and Berry, L.L. (1988). SERVQUAL: A multiple-item scale for measuring customer perceptions of service quality. *Journal of Retailing, 64(1),* 12-40.

Pizam, A. and Neumann, Y. (1988). The effect of task characteristics on hospitality employees' job satisfaction, and burnout. *Hospitality Education and Research Journal, 12(2),* 99-106.

Pye, G. (1994). Customer service: A model for improvement. *International Journal of Hospitality Management, 13(1),* 1-5.

Samenfink, W.H. (1992). Identifying the service potential of an employee through the use of the Self-Monitoring Scale. *Hospitality Research Journal, 15(2),* 1-10.

Schneider, B. (1980). The service organization: Climate is crucial. *Organizational Dynamics,* Autumn, 52-65.

Schneider, B. (1990). Alternative strategies for creating service oriented organizations. In D.E. Bowen, R.B. Chase, T.G. Cummings, and Associates (Eds.), *Service Management Effectiveness* (pp. 126-151). San Francisco: Jossey-Bass.

Shostack, G.L. (1984). Designing services that deliver. *Harvard Business Review, 62(1),* 133-139.

Shostack, G.L. (1992). Understanding services through blueprinting. *Advances in Services Marketing and Management, 1(1),* 75-90.

Silvestro, R., Johnston, R., Fitzgerald, L., and Voss, C. (1990). Quality measurement in service industries. *International Journal of Service Industry Management, 1(1),* 54-66.

Smith, K. (1994). Blueprinting the restaurant for improved service quality. *Journal of Hospitality and Leisure Marketing, 2(4),* 21-35.

Snyder, M. (1974). Self-monitoring of expressive behavior. *Journal of Personality and Social Psychology, 30(4),* 526-537.

Sparks, B.A. and Callan, V.J. (1996). Service breakdowns and service evaluations: The role of customer attributions. *Journal of Hospitality and Leisure Marketing, 4(2),* 3-24.

Sumichrast, R.T. and Olsen, M.D. (1996). Expert-system technology for hotels: Concierge application. *Cornell Hotel and Restaurant Administration Quarterly, 37(1),* 54-60.

Sussmann, S. and Baker, M. (1996). Responding to the electronic marketplace: Lessons from destination management. *International Journal of Hospitality Management, 15(2),* 99-112.

Titz, K., Miller, J.L., and Andrus, D.M. (1998). Hedonic scales used in a logit model to explore casino game choice. *Journal of Hospitality and Tourism Research, 22(2),* 129-141.

Woodruff, R.B., Cadotte, E.R., and Jenkins, R.L. (1985). Modeling consumer satisfaction processes using experience-based norms. *Journal of Marketing Research, 20,* August, 296-304.

Zeithaml, V.A., Berry, L.L., and Parasuraman, A. (1993). The nature and determinants of customer expectations of service. *Journal of the Academy of Marketing Science, 21(1),* 1-12.

Chapter 5

# Understanding the Role of the Service Encounter in Tourism, Hospitality, and Leisure Services

Darren Lee-Ross

## INTRODUCTION

The nature of service, strategies for improving it, and understanding customers' perceptions of it have enjoyed tremendous popularity among researchers for the last two decades (for example, Leonard and Sasser, 1982; Johns, 1992; Lockwood, 1996; Johns and Lee-Ross, 1998). Moreover, the growing economic importance of service industries in many countries has seen increases in centrally driven quality-based initiatives including the European Foundation for Quality Management, the British Quality Foundation, the International Organization for Standardization ISO9000 Series, the Australian Quality Council, and the Quality Assurance Institute of America. In addition, according to Tenner and DeToro (1992), growth of international entrepreneurialism and an increased supply of more "sophisticated" customers has caused firms to seek competitive advantage by relying more upon their employees to satisfy and even exceed client expectations. Many hospitality, tourism, and leisure organizations have taken up this challenge by focusing upon employee performance at the customer interface, recognizing the crucial nature of the service encounter (MacVicar and Brown, 1994; Dodwell and Simmons, 1994; Breen and Liddy, 1998; Bouldner, Baker, and Fesenmaier, 1997).

In addition, the term "service encounter" may have negative connotations, for example:

Encounter: Meet in conflict. *Collins English Dictionary and Thesaurus.* (1992, p. 161)

According to this definition, customer/employee encounters have the potential for conflict. In a service context this meaning cannot be taken literally, but it provides a cautionary note for service managers because customer perceptions of composite product quality often depend upon the interaction between customers and frontline employees.

Management of the service encounter is notoriously problematic because direct provision relies solely on the employee. This is where managers have the least direct control over what their workers say and do (Jones and Lockwood, 1989). The ubiquitous manager is also both impractical and not particularly desirable in busy organizations. However, managers may influence service encounters by focusing on broader issues such as organizational culture, system design, selection, and training. In other words, frontline employees can perform adequately at the customer interface so long as there is a culture of support, an appropriate service delivery system, and adequate training. Clearly, this is a complex mix of variables and interactions which managers of hospitality, tourism, and leisure organizations must understand if they are to influence the process and outcome of service encounters.

This chapter focuses on the role of the service encounter in service organizations. The nature and main features of social interactions are first explored, followed by an outline of service encounters and how to manage them. The chapter continues by considering other issues of encounter management including service delivery and system design, "scripting," and organizational culture. Personal interaction and relationships between customers and frontline employees are key elements in service provision, so selection and training strategies are also discussed.

## SOCIAL INTERACTIONS

Service encounters are complex affairs, not least because the social contact between actors carries a variety of expectations. For example, employees who provide the service need to feel satisfied with their performance almost as a justification for their career choice. They also need to satisfy the immediate demands of the client. Similarly, customers desire satisfaction in terms of their immediate purpose for the interaction, such as hiring particular facilities in a leisure center, exchanging currency, or ordering a drink at the hotel bar. They also desire to be treated in a polite and "appropriate" manner. Horney (1996) simplifies these expectations into procedural and convivial aspects of service delivery.

Understanding these two dimensions of service is obviously necessary for managing the encounter; however, it is a mistake to believe that each situation is similar. The role played by customers in the interaction has a significant bearing on the subsequent turn of events. A normal exchange pattern contains a number of stimuli and responses communicated verbally and nonverbally. Actors provide cues for each other to react in specific ways. Usually these cues are determined by the actual situation and stereotyping from experience of previous exchanges. Perceptions of social status, economic and personal characteristics, appearance, and so on also impact upon the relationship between participants. In addition, expectations and behavior are particular to specific occasions, which may cause changes in the service encounter dynamic (Farber-Canziani, 1996). For example, an individual using the clubhouse facilities of St. Andrew's Golf Club will have significantly different service encounter expectations than one using those of a nine-hole municipal course.

Despite the impact of these dynamics upon the service encounter, psychological research (for a summary see Eysenck and Eysenck, 1985) has shown that people possess a more or less stable set of characteristics that predispose them to react in certain ways in a variety of encounters. These include culture, introversion and extroversion, stability and neuroticism, aggression and passivity, self-esteem, and desire for approval. Clearly managers would be well advised to account for these innate predispositions prior to hiring and training their employees. For example, an introverted employee would probably not be suited immediately to the job of cocktail bartender. Similarly, a hotel employee displaying extrovert behavior would possibly feel unfulfilled as a night porter or internal auditor.

## SERVICE ENCOUNTERS

According to Czepiel, Solomon, and Surprenant (1985), a number of key features distinguish service encounters from other social interactions:

- They have a narrow focus
- They are purposeful
- Roles are defined
- Providers are performing a job
- There is often no prior acquaintance
- Task-related information predominates
- There may be temporary status differences

These features modify the properties of social interactions to a greater or lesser extent depending upon situational specifics, and all occur within the workplace. Usually, the narrow and purposeful focus of the encounter is understood by participants and all will have expectations modified by the tasks and functions of the job. For example, fine dining customers will expect the experience to be somewhat formal and "silver-served" by competent, unobtrusive, and polite waiting staff. In addition, perceptions of status may be altered or suspended because of the possibility of temporary status shift. Outside the workplace the service provider may have a higher status than the customer but will nonetheless be expected to defer during the encounter. Task-related information also characterizes the exchange because it focuses on encounter-based goals of which actors are aware. For example, the activities involved when booking a holiday with a travel agent are restricted by the nature and content of the service.

Service encounters have a significant impact on participants. The interaction is an essential ingredient in the total quality perception of the customer and the employee. Successful encounters are positively correlated with employee motivation, performance, and job satisfaction. Hospitality, tourism, and leisure organizations must manage the service encounter effectively for the benefit of customers and employees and for long-term organizational success.

## ENCOUNTER MANAGEMENT

There is no doubt that service organizations are characterized by high levels of service encounters. It is also the case that employees act as ambassadors for their organizations and play a crucial role influencing overall customer perceptions of quality. Consequently, researchers and some service organizations have sought to provide a context for managing the encounter indirectly using service-related techniques of "blueprinting" and other quality assurance systems (Comen, 1989). For example, once a service delivery system has been blueprinted it may be appreciated as a series of interconnected stages. Areas may then be identified in which the service could be modified or customized. This technique allows managers to see the amount and nature of the stages involved in the service and also the range of options at each point in the process. The more complex the system in terms of stages and extent, the more sophisticated the service encounter is likely to be. This has a direct impact on the expectations of the service provider and customer. For example, the Belfry Hotel in the United Kingdom offers a package that includes extensive leisure facilities and a championship golf course, whereas a TraveLodge offers a limited range of accommodation and catering services. Belfry employees need greater knowledge of facilities and how to interact with clients whose purpose of visit and social status may be different than those of Trave-Lodge clients. Alternatively, consider the potential for differences in the service encounter between a McDonald's fast-food restaurant and a full silver-service fine dining restaurant. In the former organization, the encounter is fleeting, noncustomized, and product oriented (interestingly, without the server wishing you well as you leave the building!). However, in a fine dining restaurant, the service is highly customized, with the server having a more integral role in the complex service delivery process.

Some other general control measures include minimizing risk by limiting employee contact with customers. For example, it is fairly common practice for hotels to incorporate buffet style self-service food systems (particularly for breakfast). In addition, hotels are increasingly using beverage vending in corridors and public rooms and "minibars" in bedrooms. In this way customers are forced to play a more active role, the interface is eliminated, and thus risk reduced.

Another approach considers that if employees are trained or "scripted" to respond in a preprogrammed way at the service interface, then service quality will be enhanced. Simply, the roles of bartender, tour guide, and receptionist, for example, can be conceptualized as the typical series of tasks and behavior of someone in that position. Part of this role is interaction with customers in a particular manner. Typically, a script includes routines for greeting, probing, empathy, and positivity. Notwithstanding problems of role conflict, role overload, role incompatibility, and multiple-role conflict (see Jones and Lockwood, 1989, for an explanation) some managers are fairly prescriptive about the script content and how it is presented to the customer.

However, care must be taken when scripting if the subsequent encounter is to be successful. Managers need to be flexible when designing scripts because each encounter is unique (although some commonality usually exists). In addition, if the procedure is not carefully planned and employees are not encouraged to share in the developmental process, scripted responses will not truly be their own. Simple repetition of learned "lines" at predetermined points of the service encounter may give a shallow, unoriginal, and uncaring impression to customers. In addition, employees may become bored and lose their self-esteem.

Farber-Canziani (1996, p. 143) summarizes the major limitations associated with scripting as follows:

- Minimal employee involvement in service operation diagnostics
- Minimal development of employee observation and attention skills
- Overemphasis on rote memorization of limited categories of service problems and standard solutions

- Minimal employee ownership of management-designed service scripts and standards
- Little empowerment of employees to manage the unavoidable contingencies in the service encounter

An alternative approach for managers is to rely more on methods that improve employee observation, diagnostic, and improvisation skills. In other words, managers should consider empowering employees to deal with each individual situation as it arises. However, a full training support system should be in position for this approach to be useful. Otherwise there is a danger that employee incompetence and inexperience will lead to poorer levels of service and increased worker stress.

## SELECTION

Perhaps one of the most controllable issues in managing the service encounter is selecting the right person for the right job. Managers can attempt to influence employee behavior at the customer interface in a variety of ways, such as job design, scripting, empowerment, and so on. However, it is equally important (and makes the manager's job easier) that people with a predisposition toward providing organization-determined quality service are selected in the first place. This idea is based on the notion that there are differences in people's skills and personality characteristics which can be matched to specific jobs. Detailed explanation of techniques and procedures involved in employee selection are beyond the scope of this chapter, but further information is provided by Goldthorpe and colleagues (1968), Shamir (1975), and Dickinson and Ineson (1993).

Developments in selection techniques for service encounter staff include situational interviews based on identified critical incidents occurring during performance of the job. The incidents are then explained in terms of behavior and provide benchmarks for a range of activities at the customer interface. These descriptions are then turned into interview questions asking how applicants would deal with the situations. Answers are transposed by interviewers into Likert-type responses on a behaviorally anchored rating scale.

Other approaches for measuring the "fit" of candidates for service encounter jobs include those which focus on personality traits. Overall, these procedures suggest that personality dimensions such as sociability and conscientiousness, for example, influence job performance and therefore reflect innate competencies related to service encounters. According to Lewis and Entwhistle (1990) the resulting service orientation index constructed from such dimensions has successfully discriminated between suitable and unsuitable candidates.

These techniques have been subjected to much criticism because of their apparent inability to predict behavior at work. However, the key issue is that they should not be used in isolation but as part of a composite approach to employee selection. In this way, any bias or weakness specific to a technique may be counteracted by strengths of another.

## TRAINING

Augmenting results of the selection process is an obvious objective of the training procedure. On the basis of organizational goals and priorities, the best training procedures are usually effective if they consider fundamental issues of total commitment at all levels, involvement of everyone, opinions of staff at all levels, and chief executives willing to participate in the program.

According to Jones and Lockwood (1989), staff training has several dimensions including the following:

- *Traditional:* Staff are shown the correct way of dealing with customers based on previously identified standards. Staff are then encouraged to adopt this approach through role play, video, and so on. This is effective but may engender inflexibility which may be unsuitable for all situations.
- *Quality circles:* Staff are encouraged to consider how they can improve the service given to the customer. This approach (like others) needs everyone's support and the provision of resources by which ideas generated can be tried and tested.
- *Encouragement:* Staff develop their customer service skills by using incentives where they are judged against previously identified standards of performance.

Lewis and Entwhistle (1990) advocate a two-pronged approach for effective staff training:

- *Evangelical:* This usually involves large numbers of employees coming together for a sophisticated and polished performance designed to generate a high degree of excitement, enthusiasm, and "togetherness." The leader is someone who inspires and is viewed as representing something to identify with and belong to. Unfortunately the fervor is not usually maintained in the workplace.

- *Exploratory:* Raises enthusiasm more subtly than evangelism and over a longer period. Individualism and resistance to change is acknowledged. This approach aims to "overcome" by creating a climate in which people can grow and learn based on a premise that staff involvement and participation in the decision process brings commitment.

This type of training is a key element in "customer care programs" being developed by forward-looking hospitality, tourism, and leisure organizations. Often the starting point for these programs is a policy or vision statement. Training needs analysis may then be undertaken by internal trainers or external consultants. Staff work attitudes are usually investigated in interviews. Information elicited includes feelings toward their jobs and customers and how they feel about their employing organization generally. Subsequent training programs are then designed, typically containing information and guidance about the composite service product and how to deal with the service encounter. It is also important for service organizations to have some form of feedback mechanism so employee performance can be monitored.

## ORGANIZATIONAL CULTURE

Customer care and the provision of excellent service at the customer interface needs more than a simple shift of organizational focus. The transition requires a repositioning of the total organizational culture, and managers would do well to remember the adage that one can rewrite a constitution without changing people's attitudes. For the purposes of this chapter, culture refers to underlying attitudes and beliefs held by everyone and how they impact on the service encounter.

Expressions of organizational culture range from complex and convoluted definitions to simply "the way things get done here." In smaller hospitality, tourism, and leisure organizations, culture may be quite "fuzzy," a function of owners and managers who may be equally unclear about their attitudes and beliefs. Larger organizations, however, should have clearer aims, objectives, and procedures to achieve and thus satisfy their cultural aspirations. To develop an appropriate service culture, managers need to understand the concept itself and the key change triggers. The main elements cited by Jones and Lockwood (1989, p. 123) include the following:

- *Values:* Sense of direction and identity guiding day-to-day behavior
- *Heroes:* Individuals who are successful because of their adherence to organizational values

- *Rites and rituals:* Communicate what is expected of employees
- *Cultural network:* Informal organization through which communication of the culture takes place

Understanding these elements should assist managers to establish the "right" organizational culture. Lewis and Entwhistle (1990) suggest that the correct climate creates responses in customers as well as employees. That is, the organization establishes a climate that affects the way in which employees behave during the service encounter and, therefore, the customers' perceptions of the organization and its service.

## SUMMARY

The service encounter is a complex affair and difficult to manage; therefore, it has been illustrated in a number of ways. Initially, it was presented as a meeting between individuals, focusing upon their differences and how this transforms the actual exchange. The nature of the service encounter was then shown to affect ensuing attitudes and behavior between the employee and customer because of its specific purpose.

Dialogue, attitudes, and behavior during service encounters are effectively beyond the control of management. However, if no attempt is made to at least influence events, the outcome could be potentially disastrous. There are a number of ways to manage service encounters, and those in authority would be well advised to adopt strategies featuring all approaches. Encounters may be controlled directly and indirectly with approaches focusing on service delivery and system redesign, a knowledge of organizational culture, and appropriate selection and training procedures.

Service quality stands or falls by the outcome of the service encounter. Excellence can only be achieved by commitment starting at the top of the organization and being translated by managers providing leadership by example. Clearly, this is only workable with appropriate support systems that focus on service quality.

## REFERENCES

Bouldner, A., Baker, D.A., and Fesenmaier, D.R. (1997). Effects of Service Climate on Managers' and Employees' Rating of Visitors' Service Quality Expectations. *Journal of Travel Research,* 36 (1): 15-22.

Breen, P. and Liddy, J. (1998). The Ramada Revolution: The Birth of a Service Culture in a Franchise Organization. *National Productivity Review,* 17 (3): 45-52.

Comen, T. (1989). Making Quality Assurance Work for You. *Cornell Hotel and Restaurant Administration Quarterly,* November, 22-29.

Czepiel, J.A., Solomon, M.R., and Surprenant, C.F. (1985). *The Service Encounter: Managing Employee/Customer Interactions in Service Businesses.* Lexington, MA: Lexington Books.

Dickinson, A. and Ineson, E. (1993). The Selection of Quality Operative Staff in the Hotel Sector. *International Journal of Contemporary Hospitality Management,* 5 (1): 16-21.

Dodwell, S. and Simmons, P. (1994). Trials and Tribulations in the Pursuit of Quality Improvement. *International Journal of Contemporary Hospitality Management,* 6 (2-3): 14-18.

Eysenck, H.J. and Eysenck, M.W. (1985). *Personality and Individual Differences.* New York: Plenum Press.

Farber-Canziani, B. (1996). Integrating Quality Management and Customer Service: The Service Diagnostics Training System. In M.D. Olsen, R. Teare, and E. Gummesson, *Service Quality in Hospitality Organizations* (pp. 140-163). London: Cassell.

Goldthorpe, J.H., Lockwood, D., Bechhofer, F., and Platt, J. (1968). *The Affluent Worker: Industrial Attitudes and Behaviour.* Cambridge, UK: Cambridge University Press.

Horney, N. (1996). Quality and the Role of Human Resources. In M.D. Olsen, R. Teare, and E. Gummesson, *Service Quality in Hospitality Organizations* (pp. 69-115). London: Cassell.

Johns, N. (1992). Quality Management in the Hospitality Industry: Definition and Specification. *International Journal of Contemporary Hospitality Management,* 4 (3): 14-20.

Johns, N. and Lee-Ross, D. (1998). A Study of Service Quality in Small Hotels and Guesthouses. *Progress in Tourism and Hospitality Research,* 3(4): 351-363.

Jones, P. and Lockwood, A. (1989). *The Management of Hotel Operations: An Innovative Approach to the Study of Hotel Management.* London: Cassell.

Leonard, F.S. and Sasser, W.E. (1982). The Incline of Quality. *Harvard Business Review,* 60,September/October: 163-171.

Lewis, B.R. and Entwhistle, T.W. (1990). Managing the Service Encounter: A Focus on the Employee. *The International Journal of Service Industry Management,* 1 (3): 41-51.

Lockwood, A. (1996). A Systematic Approach to Quality. In A. Lockwood, M. Baker, and A. Ghillyer (Eds.), *Quality Management in Hospitality* (pp. 14-32). London: Cassell.

MacVicar, A. and Brown, G. (1994). Investors in People at the Moat House International, Glasgow. *International Journal of Contemporary Hospitality Management,* 6 (2-3): 53-60.

Shamir, B. (1975). *A Study of Working Environments and Attitudes to Work of Employees in a Number of British Hotels*. Doctoral thesis, London School of Economics.

Tenner, A.R. and DeToro, I.J. (1992). *Total Quality Management: Three Steps to Continuous Improvement*. Cambridge, MA: Addison-Wesley.

# Chapter 6

# Service Quality, Customer Satisfaction, and Value: An Examination of Their Relationships

Geoffrey N. Soutar

## *INTRODUCTION*

A great deal of discussion has occurred in the fields of marketing and strategy in recent years about consumer satisfaction and how it can be created and maintained. Most organizations now recognize the central role that their customers' satisfaction plays in their long-term success; hospitality, leisure, and tourism organizations are no exception. Marketers have argued for the centrality of customer satisfaction for at least forty years, giving the approach a variety of names, including the marketing concept, having a customer orientation or, more recently, having a market orientation. However, all of these approaches argue that good marketing is much more than merely being concerned about customers' needs. All agree that managers must understand the marketplace in which they operate, which includes not only customers, but also competitors, governments, and regulatory agencies and the overall market environment (e.g., Narver and Slater, 1990; Kohli and Jaworski, 1990). Further, all recognize that an organization's interest in satisfaction is not for its own sake but because of a recognition that satisfied customers give an organization its best chance of achieving its objectives, whatever they happen to be, as satisfied customers are much more likely to come back, remain loyal, and provide positive word of mouth. However, it is fair to say that customer satisfaction has taken pride of place in many discussions about marketing (e.g., Kotler, 1988). Consequently, a great deal of research has been undertaken to understand what creates and maintains customer satisfaction and to determine how it should be measured, as it is clearly a key marketing variable.

Peters (1987) and many others have pointed out that today's customers are searching for quality, which in service industries, such as hospitality, tourism, and leisure, equates with service quality. Not surprisingly, therefore, service quality has become a major issue for managers in these areas, with many people arguing that service quality has a central role in the success or failure of such organizations (e.g., Lee and Hing, 1995; Ford and Bach, 1997; Hudson and Shephard, 1998) and that successful organizations will have to compete on the basis of the quality of the customer service they provide. If an organization succeeds in such a competitive strategy, it has been argued, it will be well rewarded, as it is likely to obtain the following:

- A competitive differentiation that favors the organization
- Favorable word-of-mouth advertising
- Greater productivity
- Better employee morale

However, perhaps most important, as Buzzell and Gale's (1987) examination of the Profit Impact of Marketing Strategy (PIMS) database suggested, private sector organizations at least may achieve:

- Better profits and rates of return

Managers must, therefore, understand how quality and satisfaction are determined in their marketplace and how the two constructs are related, as without such an understanding, the development of appropriate marketing strategies and service quality programs will be impossible. Further, as should be obvious, such understanding cannot come from internal information alone. Quality and satisfaction must be investigated in the marketplace with customers, which means that organizations must undertake appropriate marketing research and have well-developed and long-term quality and satisfaction measurement and monitoring programs that provide management with the information they need. As a starting point for suggesting a model of this relationship, the next section briefly discusses some key aspects of service quality, while subsequent sections discuss customer satisfaction and their relationship.

## SERVICE QUALITY

The central link in most service strategies is quality, which has been a major issue for many years, dating back at least to Deming's work in Japan in the 1950s. Ideas about total quality management (TQM) and quality assurance (QA) have been well developed over the last thirty years (e.g., Crosby, 1979, 1984) and are a central part of many organizations' operations. However, most of the early work on quality concentrated on products. Thus, Gummesson (1989) found only three of the 145 papers presented at the 1988 American Society for Quality Control included "services" in their titles, while none of the 102 papers at the 1987 European Organization for Quality Control did so. Despite this, many service organizations have also realized that quality is essential (e.g., Albrecht and Zemke, 1985; Peters, 1987; Carlzon, 1987; Gronroos, 1990; Albrecht, 1990; Berry and Parasuraman, 1991). While service organizations have recognized a need to improve quality, and many have introduced service quality programs, service quality is still a major problem that needs to be addressed, for a number of reasons:

1. Many managers have a short-run view of the world, especially when organizational systems are designed to reward short-, rather than long-term achievements. Quality programs have financial and human resource costs, especially when first developed, which is a major problem if such resources are in short supply, as is often the case in leisure and hospitality organizations. However, as Gronroos (1990, p. 51) has pointed out, "quality does not cost—a lack of quality does," at least in the long term.
2. Many organizations offer too many services. With limited budgets this often means that nothing within the organization can be done excellently. However, pruning activities can be an extremely difficult issue as it requires considerable change in the things people do and may require substantial organizational restructuring, all of which are costly, both financially and in human resources terms.
3. Existing operating systems may not be efficient or effective. As a consequence, staff find it difficult to deal effectively with customers, especially when problems arise. Often, systems are also expensive to repair or replace, making choices in this area difficult.
4. Reasonable status may not be given to the "frontline troops," whether they are desk clerks, pool attendants, or housekeepers. Consequently, these people have little job satisfaction or organizational loyalty and are not inclined to exert themselves for their organization when it might be required.
5. An "it's not my job" syndrome exists in many organizations, which means people try to avoid helping instead of providing support to customers or to other staff who are dealing with customers. Removing this syndrome requires a major culture change, which can be

difficult and which must come from an organization's most senior managers.

6. Staff think "customers are a nuisance," making it difficult to develop strong customer service programs, as they have other agendas.

Despite these problems, organizations must be concerned with the level of service quality being provided. If service quality is to be assessed, however, it must be operationally defined. People find it difficult to articulate what they mean by service quality, although they know when they have not received it. As Buzzell and Gale (1987, p. 111) have noted, "quality is whatever the customer says it is and the quality of a particular good or service is whatever the customer perceives it to be." There is even more ambiguity about service quality as it

1. is multidimensional;
2. has underlying quality dimensions, some of which change over time;
3. is intangible, although it is often assessed through tangible clues (e.g., a hotel's appearance or a tour bus's design or seats);
4. is the result of both service processes and service outcomes (i.e., it arises from how customers are treated and whether their problems are solved); and
5. depends on the difference (or gap) between customers' expectations and perceptions.

Clearly, organizations must have a good understanding of their customers if they are to understand their quality perceptions or have a chance of successfully implementing service quality programs. They also need knowledge about how and when customers interact with their organization and its various operations. Such interactions are critical as it is at these times that service quality is assessed and the organization judged. Carlzon (1987) is generally given credit for this insight, terming these interactions "moments of truth" and arguing that the first phase in understanding service quality is to define these moments of truth and determine how they can go wrong.

Shostack (1984) provided an excellent approach to developing such an understanding with her "blueprinting" concept, which examines interactions from a customer's viewpoint. Carlzon (1987) also stressed that moments of truth are more likely to go wrong if staff do not have the capacity to deal with customers. Consequently, he argued for "empowering" customer interaction staff and giving them the authority to solve problems, rather than forcing them to respond bureaucratically, something that hospitality managers need to understand more than most.

Process and outcome are both vital to service quality, and these two aspects are integral parts of Gronroos's (1990) service quality model, which emphasizes the "what" and "how" of services but also points out that service quality results from gaps between expectations and perceptions of service received. This "gap" idea is also a critical part of the "disconfirmation" approach to measuring both quality and satisfaction (e.g., Oliver, 1981; Parasuraman, Zeithaml, and Berry, 1988). If performance is less than customers expected, quality is perceived to be low and dissatisfaction results. If performance meets or exceeds customers' expectations, quality is perceived to be high and satisfaction results. Gronroos (1990) also noted the importance of image in the generation of quality perceptions. If an organization (service provider) has a good image then small service gaps are more likely to be accepted. However, if there is already a poor image, even small gaps are likely to create negative quality perceptions.

Of course, if gaps continue, previously good images are likely to be overturned, with negative long-term consequences. Even great service providers cannot live on their reputation forever. However, institutions with relatively poor images will find it harder to overcome the past and will need to be extremely vigilant about service quality. The gap model provides a useful guide to understanding quality problems. Brown and Swartz (1989, p. 97) found that the "gap analysis is a straightforward and appropriate way to identify inconsistencies between provider and client perceptions of service performance. Addressing these gaps seems to be a logical basis for formulating strategies and tactics to ensure consistent expectations and experiences, thus increasing the likelihood of satisfaction and a positive quality evaluation."

As has already been noted, service quality cannot be determined from within an organization, for quality is about meeting consumers' needs (Wyckoff, 1984). If an organization does not know much about its customer needs, it will find it extremely difficult to meet them. Consequently, most service researchers recommend customer surveys as the starting point in the development of quality programs.

There is no better general comment about service quality than that suggested by Berry (1988), who stated:

1. Customers define quality.
2. Quality is a journey.
3. Quality is everyone's job.
4. Quality, leadership, and communication are inseparable.
5. Quality and integrity are inseparable.

6. Quality is a design issue.
7. Quality is keeping the service promise.

As these points emphasize and, as with all other areas of service management, the success of service quality programs will depend on an organization's people and the capacity of the organization's systems to support them effectively. As Lee Iaccoca (1988, p. 249) noted, "the only job security anybody has . . . comes from quality, productivity and satisfied customers" but if you "start with good people, lay out the rules, communicate with your employees, motivate them, and reward them if they perform . . . you can't miss." Clearly, management, human resource management, operations management, and marketing must all come together in the service quality area, suggesting that we need to look as much within as outside the organization if we are to really understand service quality.

### Inside the Organization

What is sometimes forgotten in the necessary external evaluation of service quality is that any strategies that are developed will have to be implemented by an organization's people and that managers need to understand as much about their staff, especially their customer contact staff, as they do about their customers. Indeed, Gronroos (1990) argued that excellent service quality cannot be provided without committed, dedicated, and capable staff. Such arguments suggest that internal marketing and employee satisfaction are as vital to organizational success as is effective external marketing and, further, that internal marketing comes before external marketing.

This suggestion has led to a new model that puts the frontline workers first and designs the service systems around frontline interactions with customers, as can be seen in Shostack's blueprinting procedures. This approach also led to the development of the upside down organization chart, which is often associated with Carlzon's (1987) management view.

It also led to Albrecht's (1990) suggestion of a quality service triangle, which notes the relationship between organizational success and customer contact staff and the need to ensure that operating systems support all staff who deal with customers. The new approach to staff is well outlined by Schlesinger and Heskett (1991), who suggested managers should:

1. Value investments in people at least as much as investments in machines (customers and staff are assets while machines are a liability)
2. Use technology to support the front line, not to monitor or replace them

3. Remember that recruitment is at least as important when hiring front desk clerks or housekeepers as it is when hiring managers and senior executives
4. Link compensation to performance at all levels, not just at the top

Such a model requires organizations to measure their internal as well as external quality. Internal quality is related to an organization's ability to attract, develop, motivate, and retain quality employees, not for its own sake but because the model recognizes that internal quality leads to external quality, which leads to customer satisfaction, long-term loyalty, and profitability. Effective internal quality programs must, therefore:

1. Compete aggressively for service talent
2. Offer a real vision that brings purpose to those at the front line
3. Provide training to equip staff to perform their service roles
4. Understand that good and committed teams perform better
5. Provide real freedom for staff to solve customers' problems
6. Acknowledge achievement publicly
7. Base job design on research with employees (viewing them as "customers")

Nevertheless, at some point, an organization must understand how it is viewed in the marketplace and so must measure its service quality. While a number of suggestions have been made, the SERVQUAL model remains the most commonly used approach. It is discussed briefly in the next section.

### The SERVQUAL Model

Parasuraman, Zeithaml, and Berry's (1988) service quality model (SERVQUAL) has been outlined in many papers in recent years. Despite criticism from a number of detractors, SERVQUAL remains the most commonly used diagnostic model for evaluating service quality and the development of service quality strategies. As mentioned previously, the SERVQUAL model assumes quality is the result of gaps between people's expectations and their perceptions of service performance. The model does not examine actual performance and so cannot be evaluated from within the organization; it can only be evaluated from outside. Nel and Pitt (1993), Saleh and Ryan (1991), and Samson and Parker (1994), among many others, have used SERVQUAL in a variety of settings and found that, although there are some problems with the instrument, it has good descriptive power and can generate useful managerial insight and understanding.

## SATISFACTION

As has already been noted, satisfaction has been a concern for a number of years (Cardozo, 1965) and is generally recognized as a postpurchase construct that is related to how much a person likes or dislikes a product or service after experiencing it (Woodside, Frey, and Daly, 1989). It can be defined as an evaluation that an "experience was at least as good as it was supposed to be" (Hunt, 1977, p. 459). Satisfaction is a response to a perceived discrepancy between prior expectations and perceived performance after consumption (Oliver, 1981; Tse and Wilton, 1988). Consequently, managers need to understand how expectations are created and how these expectations are influenced by people's consumption experiences. Satisfaction is often described as a confirmation of expectations (Cadotte, Woodruff, and Jenkins, 1987) and, while there has been some discussion as to whether satisfaction and dissatisfaction are opposite poles on the same dimension (Churchill and Surprenant, 1982), most researchers seem to have accepted that dissatisfaction and satisfaction reflect the same continuum (e.g., Westbrook and Oliver, 1991). Customers are assumed to have developed expectations prior to use, and perceived performance is compared to these expectations on a "better than" or "worse than" model. This comparison is "labelled negative disconfirmation if . . . worse than expected, positive disconfirmation if better than expected, and simple confirmation if as expected" (Oliver and DeSarbo, 1988). However, at least in some circumstances, satisfaction also seems to be related directly to perceived performance, which customers evaluate on a "good" to "bad" dimension (Churchill and Surprenant, 1982; Tse and Wilton, 1988; Bolton and Drew, 1991). Thus, performance impacts on satisfaction directly and indirectly (through disconfirmation).

## THE SERVICE QUALITY–SATISFACTION RELATIONSHIP

At the heart of the discussion is the assumption that, for service marketers, such as those in hospitality, tourism, and leisure, service quality impacts on satisfaction directly and, so, is the crucial variable marketers need to control strategically if they are to be successful in the long term. This has led to suggestions that customer service is the key operational variable and that, if service quality is improved, customer satisfaction and, hopefully, profitability will be improved, a result supported by research undertaken by Getty and Thompson (1994) and Woodside, Frey, and Daly (1989). The simplest suggested relationship is shown in Figure 6.1.

FIGURE 6.1. A Simple Relationship Between Service Quality and Satisfaction

It should be kept in mind that service quality is a global measure of a number of quality dimensions (e.g., the tangibles, reliability, responsiveness, assurance, and empathy dimensions suggested in Parasuraman, Zeithaml, and Berry's [1988] SERVQUAL model). It has also been suggested that satisfied customers are also more likely to repurchase and/or recommend the product or service to others, and the prior research cited suggested that this may also be true. Consequently, there are antecedents to and consequences of this simple relationship.

However, the relationship may not be as simple as Figure 6.1 depicts, as recent research has suggested that service quality may be only one of a number of factors that influence "value" and that it is value, rather than service quality alone, that determines people's willingness to buy and subsequent satisfaction. Given this suggestion, the present chapter concludes by outlining some of the research undertaken into the value construct and discusses its implications for hospitality, tourism, and leisure organizations.

## THE VALUE CONSTRUCT

Zeithaml (1988, p. 14) suggested that value is a "consumer's overall assessment of the utility of a product (or service) based on perceptions of what is received and what is given," which she termed a product or service's "get" and "give" dimensions. The most common such definition of value is product quality and price tradeoff (e.g., Monroe, 1990; Cravens et al., 1988), although some have suggested that a two-factor model may not be a sufficient explanation (Schechter, 1984; Bolton and Drew, 1991) and that other variables that might impact on value are service quality, perceived risk, and image.

Sheth, Newman, and Gross (1991) have also suggested that value is a complex construct with multiple dimensions (social, emotional, functional, epistemic, and conditional) that may impact differently in various situations. While functional value has generally been presumed to be the key influence, Sheth, Newman, and Gross found that the other value dimensions were influential in some situations. For example, while functional and social values dominated a decision to use filtered or unfiltered cigarettes, emotional value was paramount in the overall decision to smoke. Whatever dimensions are in the value construct, it is a mediating variable between service quality and satisfaction, as shown in Figure 6.2.

The implications of this small change to the model are significant as, if value plays a central mediating role, a reliance on service quality to generate satisfaction may be misplaced. If customers are more concerned about what they get, then service quality may play a major role in generating satisfaction and, more important, such customers are more likely to be willing to pay a premium for higher quality. On the other hand, if customers are more concerned about what they give, then better quality is unlikely to compensate for a higher price, organizations are unlikely to be able to charge higher prices and, thus, will be unable to cover the additional costs inherent in many customer service programs. It is clearly vital that organizations understand the nature of the market and the value derived from quality before embarking on expensive customer service programs.

Research by Bolton and Drew (1991), Dodds, Monroe, and Grewal (1991), Baker, Levy, and Grewal (1992), and Sweeney, Soutar, and Johnson (1997, 1999) suggests that such a model is plausible and that managers need to understand the much more complex relationships than that implied by the simple service quality-satisfaction nexus. Service quality still plays an important role but it has indirect, as well as direct, effects on people's intentions and satisfaction. Managers need to understand both types of effects if they are to develop effective customer service strategies.

Indeed, it seems that value is a complex construct with multiple dimensions that are influenced by price, perceived risk, and "brand" (hotel, tour company, or whatever) image, as well as service quality. Sweeney, Soutar, and Johnson's (1999) later research, undertaken in a retail environment, suggests that service quality's most important contribution may be indirect, as good quality service reduces the risk people feel and, so, increases value indirectly rather than directly. If this is true in the hospitality, tour-

FIGURE 6.2. Value As a Mediating Variable

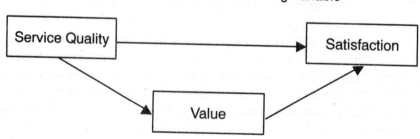

ism, and leisure area, then service quality is no less important. However, its role may be different, suggesting managers may need to alter the way they approach customer service programs that have traditionally focused on the direct role service quality plays in increasing satisfaction. If the indirect role through risk is more important, staff will need to be trained to provide "risk reducing" service and ensure that they are seen as appropriately qualified to do so.

## *CONCLUSION*

The present chapter examined the two constructs that are at the heart of the debate about the nexus between service quality and customer satisfaction and outlined some of the issues relevant to understanding and measuring both constructs. It also discussed a simple service quality–satisfaction model and suggested that this model was not a sufficient explanation of the way service quality impacted on consumer decision making. Some very recent research into value was outlined which suggests that service quality is only one of a number of factors that influence value and that managers need to understand the interactions of all of these factors and the mediating role that value plays before designing customer service programs.

Further, little research has been undertaken to understand the role that different value dimensions (such as functional value, emotional value, social value, and epistemic or novelty value) play in different situations. Given the nature of the hospitality, tourism, and leisure market, it may be that social and emotional aspects play more important roles, and these roles need to be examined carefully as they could have significant implications, not only for customer service programs but also for the very nature of the hospitality, tourism, and leisure experience. Managers in these areas clearly need to look beyond the simple service quality–satisfaction relationship to the more complex value relationships that make this area exciting but often frustrating. An understanding of the service quality–value–satisfaction path would not reduce the excitement, but it would reduce managers' frustration and make it possible for them to better plan the experiences their customers receive and the way their organizations interact with them.

## REFERENCES

Albrecht, K. (1990). *Service Within: Solving the Middle Management Crisis.* Homewood, IL: Irwin.

Albrecht, K. and Zemke, R. (1985). *Service America!* Homewood, IL: Dow Jones-Irwin.

Baker, J.A., Levy, M., and Grewal, D. (1992). An Experimental Approach to Making Retail Store Environmental Decisions. *Journal of Retailing,* 68(Winter): 445-460.

Berry, L.L. (1988). Delivering Excellent Service in Retailing. *Retailing Issues Letter,* 1(4).

Berry, L.L. and Parasuraman, A. (1991). *Marketing Services: Competing Through Quality.* New York: The Free Press.

Bolton, R.N. and Drew, J.H. (1991). A Multistage Model of Customers' Assessments of Service Quality and Value. *Journal of Consumer Research,* 17(4): 375-384.

Brown, S.W. and Swartz, T.A. (1989). A Gap Analysis of Professional Service Quality. *Journal of Marketing,* 53(2): 92-98.

Buzzell, R.D. and Gale, P.T. (1987). *The PIMS Principles: Linking Strategy to Performance.* New York: The Free Press.

Cadotte, E.R., Woodruff, R.B., and Jenkins, R.L. (1987). Expectations and Norms in Models of Consumer Satisfaction. *Journal of Marketing Research,* 24(3): 305-314.

Cardozo, R.N. (1965). An Experimental Study of Customer Effort, Expectation and Norms in Models of Consumer Satisfaction. *Journal of Marketing Research,* 2(3): 244-249.

Carlzon, J. (1987). *Moments of Truth.* Cambridge, MA: Ballinger.

Churchill, G.A. Jr. and Surprenant, C. (1982). An Investigation into the Determinants of Customer Satisfaction. *Journal of Marketing Research,* 19(4): 491-504.

Cravens, D.W., Holland, C.W., Lamb, C.W. Jr., and Moncrief, W.C. (1988). Marketing's Role in Product and Service Quality. *Industrial Marketing Management,* 17(4): 285-304.

Crosby, P.B. (1979). *Quality Is Free.* New York: McGraw Hill.

Crosby, P.B. (1984). *Quality Without Tears.* New York: The American Library.

Dodds, W.B., Monroe, K.B., and Grewal, D. (1991). Effects of Price, Brand and Store Information on Buyers' Product Evaluations. *Journal of Marketing Research,* 28(3): 307-319.

Ford, R.C. and Bach, S.A. (1997). Measuring Hotel Service Quality: Tools for Gaining the Competitive Edge. *FIU Hospitality Review,* 83-95.

Getty, J.M. and Thompson, K.N. (1994). The Relationship Between Quality, Satisfaction and Recommending Behavior in Lodging Decisions. *Journal of Hospitality and Leisure Marketing,* 2(3): 3-22.

Gronroos, C. (1990). *Service Management and Marketing.* Lexington, MA: Lexington Books.

Gummesson, E. (1989). Nine Lessons on Service Quality. *Total Quality Management,* 1(2): 83-87.

Hudson, S. and Shephard, G.W.H. (1998). Measuring Service Quality at Tourist Destinations: An Application of Importance-Performance Analysis to an Alpine Ski Resort. *Journal of Travel and Tourism Marketing,* 7(3): 61-77.

Hunt, H.K. (1977). CS/D: Overview and Future Research Directions. In H.K. Hunt (ed.), *Conceptualization and Measurement of Consumer Satisfaction and Complaining Behavior* (pp. 455-488). Cambridge, MA: Marketing Science Institute.

Iacocca, L. (1988). *Talking Straight*. New York: Bantam Books.

Kohli, A.K. and Jaworski, B.J. (1990). Market Orientation: The Construct, Research Propositions, and Managerial Implications. *Journal of Marketing,* 54(2): 1-18.

Kotler, P. (1988). *Marketing Management: Analysis, Planning, Implementation and Control,* Sixth Edition. Englewood Cliffs, NJ: Prentice Hall Inc.

Lee, Y.L. and Hing, N. (1995). Measuring Quality in Restaurant Operations: An Application of the SERVQUAL Instrument. *International Journal of Hospitality Management,* 14(3/4): 293-310.

Monroe, K.B. (1990). *Pricing: Making Profitable Decisions,* Second Edition. New York: McGraw-Hill Book Company.

Narver, J.C. and Slater, S.F. (1990). The Effect of a Market Orientation on Business Profitability. *Journal of Marketing,* 54(4): 20-35.

Nel, D. and Pitt, L. (1993). Service Quality in a Retail Environment: Closing the Gaps. *Journal of General Management,* 18(3): 37-56.

Oliver, R.L. (1981). Measurement and Evaluation of Satisfaction Processes in Retail Settings. *Journal of Retailing,* 57(Fall): 25-48.

Oliver, R.L. and DeSarbo, W.S. (1988). Response Determinants in Satisfaction Judgments. *Journal of Consumer Research,* 16(3): 372-383.

Parasuraman, A., Zeithaml, V.A., and Berry, L.L. (1988). SERVQUAL: A Multiple-Item Scale for Measuring Consumer Perceptions of Service Quality. *Journal of Retailing,* 64(Spring): 12-37.

Peters, T. (1987). *Thriving on Chaos*. New York: Harper Perennial.

Saleh, F. and Ryan, C. (1991). Analysing Service Quality in the Hospitality Industry Using the SERVQUAL Model. *Journal of Service Industries,* 11(July): 324-345.

Samson, D. and Parker, R. (1994). Service Quality: The Gap in the Australian Consulting Engineering Industry. *Journal of Quality Management,* 3(1): 43-59.

Schechter, L. (1984). A Normative Conception of Value. *Progressive Grocer, Executive Report,* 12-14.

Schlesinger, L.A. and Heskett, J.L (1991). The Service-Driven Service Company. *Harvard Business Review,* 69(5): 71-81.

Sheth, J.N., Newman, B.I., and Gross, B.L. (1991). *Consumption Values and Market Choice*. Cincinnati, OH: SouthWestern Publishing Company.

Shostack, G.L. (1977). Breaking Free from Product Marketing. *Journal of Marketing,* 41(2): 73-80.

Shostack, G.L. (1984). Designing Services That Deliver. *Harvard Business Review,* 62(1): 133-139.

Sweeney, J.C., Soutar, G.N., and Johnson, L.W. (1997). Retail Service Quality and Perceived Value: A Comparison of Two Models. *Journal of Retailing and Consumer Services,* 4(1): 39-48.

Sweeney, J.C., Soutar, G.N., and Johnson, L.W. (1999). The Role of Perceived Risk in the Quality-Value Relationship: A Study in a Retail Environment. *Journal of Retailing,* 75(1): 77-105.

Tse, D.K. and Wilton, P.C. (1988). Models of Consumer Satisfaction Formation: An Extension. *Journal of Marketing Research,* 25(2): 204-212.

Westbrook, R.A. and Oliver, R.L. (1991). The Dimensionality of Consumption Emotion Patterns and Consumer Satisfaction. *Journal of Consumer Research,* 18(2): 84-91.

Woodside, A.G., Frey, L.L., and Daly, R.T. (1989). Linking Service Quality, Customer Satisfaction, and Behavioral Intention. *Journal of Health Care Marketing,* 9(4): 5-17.

Wyckoff, D.D. (1984). New Tools for Achieving Service Quality. *Cornell Hotel and Restaurant Administration Quarterly,* 25(3): 78-91.

Zeithaml, V.A. (1988). Consumer Perceptions of Price, Quality, and Value: A Means-End Model and Synthesis of Evidence. *Journal of Marketing,* 52(3): 2-22.

# Chapter 7

# Competitive Advantages of Service Quality in Hospitality, Tourism, and Leisure Services

Chris Roberts

## *INTRODUCTION*

Virtually every competitive organization seeks some sort of advantage over its rivals; that is, it seeks some way to distinguish itself in the eyes of its customers. The challenge for a business is to find an advantage that is long lasting and not easily imitated. Of what use is an advantage if competitors can quickly copy it? Any gain from such actions is short lived, and may not be worth the cost.

What does it take for a firm to create a competitive advantage? It is not as simple as lowering prices or adding a new feature to a product. Both of these actions may be rapidly copied. In response, competitors can also lower prices quickly. But price discounting usually comes at a cost if a compensating gain in production or delivery is not found. Without such a change, it is unlikely firms could sustain deep price cuts for very long.

Similarly, product improvements add costs to production. The value added of the new feature in the eyes of the customer must be equal to or more than any increase in price. It is frequently very easy for a competitor to become aware of a product enhancement, analyze it, and then imitate it. Some firms adopt a "follower" approach, waiting for leading firms to introduce new ideas. When these actions prove successful, the followers quickly move to duplicate them to share in any market gains.

Benefits from such competitive actions may be enjoyed for only months, weeks, or less. For example, in the airline industry, gains from price changes are limited to hours. Knowledge of lower ticket prices on selected routes is quickly learned by rivals, and reservation computer systems are rapidly reprogrammed to match. From this example it is easy to see that both time and uniqueness play vital roles in the creation of an advantage.

This chapter explores the concept of competitive advantage and how firms may use service quality as a competitive tactic. The role of strategic management and the competitive environment are explained as important factors in the development of a competitive advantage. Next, core competencies, the foundation of any firm's competitive strength, are explored. The chapter ends with a discussion of how service quality can be used as a key competitive advantage.

## *COMPETITIVE ADVANTAGE*

The various processes that a firm develops to create and deliver its product may become competitive advantages. Many firms use secret ingredients as part of a unique production operation. Coca-Cola has never revealed its syrup formula, and continues to use it as a basis for creating an advantage over rival soft drink producers. It no longer matters whether the syrup formula has special qualities; customers and competitors perceive that it does, and so it acts as a sustainable advantage. Other firms develop a service delivery process to set themselves apart from competitors. For example, the sorting, routing, and package processing routines that Federal Express developed revolutionized the small parcel delivery industry. Although eventually rivals were able to duplicate FedEx processes, it was a matter of years before they could do it effectively. In that time, FedEx accumulated a significant lead in market share and has since dominated the small parcel delivery industry (Lovelock, 1996).

Skills may also develop into a competitive advantage. Hyatt Hotels has developed what they call "the Hyatt touch." It is a level of service delivery that consistently aims to surpass customer expectations. To achieve it, they have carefully identified customer needs and the levels of service customers expect to fulfill those needs. Hyatt then takes the next step and determines what additional actions can deliver the expected service with higher quality. Techniques include simple actions such as training bell staff to notice names on luggage tags in order to personally address guests, or more complex actions, such as conducting ongoing training programs for all employees through its Hyatt University that explore what customer satisfaction and service are about. Hyatt uses "the Hyatt touch" as a key element in its advertising and in its routine delivery mechanisms. Customers and employees are educated about it, and taught to believe in it and to expect it. While rival hotel firms may seek to deliver a similar level of service, Hyatt has created a competitive advantage in the full service market segment.

Sometimes a competitive advantage is an asset such as real estate. In the hospitality industry, only one hotel or restaurant at a time can occupy a highly desired location. The Plaza Hotel is the only hotel that can be located at the corner of Fifth Avenue and Central Park South in New York City. Its location alone gives the Plaza a prestigious advantage. Only one hotel can be at the end of the bluff overlooking Niagara Falls. A restaurant that is located at a freeway access point has a clear advantage over a competitor who is located blocks away. However, there are few situations in the hospitality industry in which real estate can be a true competitive advantage. In most cases, customers are willing to be served short distances from where they ideally want to be. Although location may be a factor in the purchasing decision price, product and service may be more important.

Architectural design can be a competitive advantage (Roberts and Shea, 1996). The first large interior atrium hotel was constructed in Atlanta, Georgia, in the late 1960s. For the times, its unique design was dramatic, and initially the building owners had some difficulty finding a hotel chain that would operate the new project. Hyatt Hotels finally agreed after several other companies turned away the project, and Hyatt has continued to use unique architectural designs to distinguish itself. Competitors could not easily modify existing buildings, so the distinctive designs used by Hyatt endured for many years as a competitive advantage. Thirty years later the concept of interior atriums is no longer unique, but Hyatt continues this approach by seeking other dramatic architectural compositions. The tubular, oblong-shaped Hyatt Hotel near the Charles De Gaulle Airport in Paris and the three-story, open air lobby of the Hyatt Regency Maui are but two examples.

## Strategic Management

A sustainable competitive advantage is the combination of firm processes, skills, and/or assets that together create an edge in the eyes of the customer (Prahalad and Hamel, 1990). These unique strengths are called *core competencies,* and usage of them is considered *strategic intent.* That is, firms select various sets of activities in planning efforts that they feel will help them reach specific goals. This act of planning is very deliberate, with choices made about specific tactics that are expected to achieve desired results (Olsen, West, and Tse, 1998).

However, the concept of *strategy* is about more than just planning. It is about allocating organizational resources and crafting actions that are in concert with the mission or primary purpose of the firm (Olsen, West, and Tse, 1998; Schulze, 1992). The field of strategic management is the study of an organization's ability to align itself with forces driving change in its competitive environment (Ansoff, 1988). It is a decision-making approach to managing that integrates a firm's mission, goals, and organizational resources to create the most value over time (Porter, 1980).

## *Environment*

The environment in which firms currently operate has changed dramatically. It is no longer steady and predictable, as it was in prior decades. Rather, it is turbulent, and the rate of change is highly unpredictable. These changes occur in both the general environment (in which we all live) as well as within the highly competitive hospitality industry environment.

In the general environment, a number of social, technological, political, economic, and environmental forces continually alter our world. For instance, the aging of the baby boomers is having a significant impact on consumer buying patterns. Advances in electronic and computer technology have revolutionized the computer and telecommunications industries. These advances have had an impact on our homes, schools, and businesses through the new products we use. All of these environmental forces have an effect to one degree or another. As managers, then, we must be aware of these environmental forces, assess their impact, and craft appropriate organizational responses (Wright, Pringle, and Kroll, 1992).

Forces are at work in the competitive environment, too. The competitive environment is called the task environment, as it represents the subset of the environment in which the firm operates. Customers, suppliers, rivals, and the government all act in ways that influence the task environment. Customers change their preferences, often influenced by competitors who offer new products or services. Legislatures increase taxes or regulate business actions.

Consider companies that made typewriters. They are virtually out of business today unless they learned to produce something radically different, such as word processing software or personal computers. To keep ahead of these forces of change, firms must seek out news of such changes. They must carefully analyze these changes and take appropriate actions in order to maintain a strategic alignment between their mission, goals, strategies, and the environment.

Strategies are not built with a view only to the firm's goals, resources, and capabilities. The alignment of a firm's strategy with the forces at work in the environment is an absolute necessity to succeed. It is this "fit" that managers seek when they build strategic plans. And since the environment rarely remains perfectly stable and unchanging, strategies must be designed to be flexible to allow the firm to adapt to change. Most of the time such adapting requires only small adjustments to existing plans, some minor variation or shift. This is referred to as incremental change. Other times the environmental impact is so strong as to require frame-breaking adjustments. This is referred to as radical change. Regardless of which type of change action is needed, the firm must be cognizant of these environmental forces. It must be prepared to adapt in order to maintain a proper alignment between the firm's goals, strategies, resources, capabilities, and the environment.

## CORE COMPETENCIES

Although all organizations may desire a core competency to create a competitive advantage, not all firms possess the essential mix of resources. Many firms may think they have one but really do not, while other firms may be unaware of their core competencies. A core competency has four critical elements (Prahalad and Hamel, 1990). First, as described previously, it must be a unique asset, process, or skill. Second, it must be useful over a wide range of markets. The 3M Company's expertise with adhesives gives it the ability to create products that range from office supplies such as Post-it notes and Scotch tape to industrial glue used in aircraft construction. Third, there must be an increase in benefits in the eyes of the consumer. For example, the Intel Corporation is widely known for the microprocessors it makes for personal computers. Customers perceive a greater value if a PC has an Intel chip rather than some other brand because of their reputation for performance reliability and quality. Finally, a core competency should be difficult to imitate. Competitors may acquire some of the resources that make up a competency, but often they will lack the human resources and production skills that are used to create the product or service, and so are unable to exactly duplicate it.

These core competencies may be either internal or external to the firm. For instance, Sony Electronics has a core competency in its ability to miniaturize. They have nearly perfected the process of shrinking electronic products. As consumers, what we see is an array of well-crafted, useful, and smaller versions of popular products such as radios and televisions. What we do not see is the carefully integrated array of research and development techniques they employ to miniaturize products.

On the other hand, firms such as Disney have built external competencies. As with the majority of service firms, the customer is very involved in the delivery of the Disney entertainment experience at their amusement parks. They have developed a wealth of people management skills. From quickly and smoothly orchestrating the parking of tens of thousands of automobiles daily to the movement of people around the parks, Disney demonstrates moment after moment its expertise in entertainment. Where else are customers willing to wait in such long lines—many times more than an hour—just to experience a product?

Disney has even made the waiting entertaining, a skill that is the envy of many other companies. Disney has also mastered the concept of merchandising, tying product sales to the many images in the Disney portfolio. All of these competencies work together to create the perception of a quality entertainment experience, and all of these activities are performed externally, in full view of the customer. Disney has indeed developed a competitive advantage from this strong set of core competencies.

## SERVICE QUALITY AS A COMPETITIVE ADVANTAGE

The Disney experience is a good example of how service may be used to create a competitive advantage. However, service products are often much more difficult to produce than physical products. Services are delivered much differently than products. Grönroos (1990) suggests that there is an important distinction between the process of service delivery and the actual output of a service. He believes customers will compare their expectations against the combination of both the service process and the actual service output. In the hospitality industry, the customer is involved to some degree in virtually all that we do. What we strive for is the ability to design service systems that are customer friendly, and that allow positive interaction between staff (service providers) and guests (service receivers).

Service quality can be used as a competitive advantage (Hamel and Prahalad, 1989). Firms have learned to create superior service levels that are not easily duplicated. The Ritz-Carlton Hotel Company is a good example. A basis for their service quality approach is their motto: "We Are Ladies and Gentlemen Serving Ladies and Gentlemen." This statement sets a tone for service delivery that is easily understood by all employees, and is a clear benchmark of high expectations in service quality. However, to build a competitive advantage using service quality is not easy. Services are quite different from products. A customer does not see a product until a firm believes it is ready for the marketplace. In contrast, services cannot be held until ready for delivery.

Because this topic is of great interest to managers, much research has been conducted to learn about these differences in great detail. Based upon this research effort to date, we conclude that services are different from products in four primary ways. First, service is a performance, not a physical item. It cannot be stored and inventoried. It cannot be quality checked before delivery. Its creation cannot be automated or computer controlled. Second, the customer is always involved in the service process. Services performed in the absence of the customer are not seen or valued. Third, service delivery must be managed. Customers want services when and where they perceive they need them. Therefore, service firms must adapt to customer needs and deliver services under conditions that satisfy the customer.

Finally, quality control of services is very difficult. Manufactured products can be checked in the production area before any customer is aware of a defect (Juran, 1992). Automation can be used to standardize production processes to ensure consistency. This is simply less possible with services. Since the customer is involved in the service delivery process, there is no opportunity to check for quality in advance. Customers are instantly aware of a breakdown in service. Further, since humans deliver services to other humans, automation can rarely be used. Therefore, staff training in service delivery becomes a high priority for service firms. Management also needs to maintain a high level of awareness of service failures (Bateson, 1995). An unhappy customer does not easily forget a service failure. To keep a customer, management knows it must swiftly act to correct a service failure plus offer additional services to appease the unhappy customers.

Given these differences between services and products, how can we control quality? In manufacturing concerns, conformance to an established standard or set of specifications is emphasized (Juran, 1982). We can do this in service firms, too. Standards for employee behavior in service delivery can be identified and taught. For example, staff can be trained to greet customers with standard phrases. A specification is developed and learned, and management can perform a quality control check by listening to employees greet guests.

However, this alone is not enough to control quality. Service delivery is performed in response to a customer need. It is important that the service delivered *match* the customer need. While greeting phrases can be developed that appropriately vary with the time of day or the weather outside, they can hardly be prepared to respond to the wide range of human emotions. Further, because customer expectations and perceptions are constantly shifting, customer concepts of quality shift as well. Therefore, quality must be viewed as having two important dimensions: responsiveness and consistency.

Responsiveness is the process of reacting easily or readily. Many firms attempt to be responsive to market trends and changing customer demands. Hyatt Hotels demonstrates a very high level of individual responsiveness with their "Hyatt touch" program, which prepares employees to respond to specific guest needs as they occur. It is not a program of prepared (or canned) responses. Rather, it permits the employee to identify a unique guest need and to respond accordingly. Not all firms have empowered their staff in this manner. This approach permits Hyatt to maintain a high level of responsiveness—on an individual guest basis—in order to deliver their goal of a high-quality lodging experience.

Consistency is the process of repeatedly producing a good or service in the same manner. The concept is not centered on the level of quality, which can be low or high. Rather, the item (or service) is delivered in exactly the same fashion, with the same level of quality, each time it is produced or performed. For example, McDonald's is well known for its consistency in the production of hamburgers. Each of us expects every McDonald's sandwich to be similar to the last one. We expect consistency without regard to geography or time of day. McDonald's meets this expectation by maintaining rigorous standards in their production process.

## MATCHING SERVICE QUALITY WITH STRATEGY

Service quality can be used as a competitive strategy. However, a competitive strategy based upon service quality does not necessarily mean adopting a premium level of service. The restaurant meal, the hotel room,. and the package tour are the primary products in the hospitality and leisure industries. How they are delivered to customers is where service quality can make the difference.

What is of utmost importance is that the firm should carefully match the level of service quality with the product design. If a firm offers an economy-level product, it can be delivered in both a responsive and consistent manner, yet still maintain desired cost efficiencies. For example, McDonald's offers products in the fast-food segment of the food service industry. Although their product positioning and price are at the lower end of the competitive spectrum, McDonald's has built a very strong reputation for offering quality products that people want, when they want them. Uniformity in production is a major goal. They use fine quality ingredients, but not necessarily the absolutely highest premium meats, condiments, or breads.

Their product design concentrates on maintaining consistency in how products are prepared as well as what raw food components are used.

McDonald's also concentrates on efficient service delivery that meets the time demands of customers. They ensure this through careful employee training efforts. Quickly and cheerfully greeting customers and then swiftly filling their orders is a key focus of staff training programs. What they do *not* do is offer an obsequious level of service, which is both time consuming for customers and costly in terms of increased labor expenses for the firm. Customers do not desire such service because it would not meet their need for fast service. Further, given the large numbers of people they serve every day, McDonald's would see excessive increases in labor costs. It would require more workers to provide higher levels of individualized attention. Therefore, given McDonald's strategic intent of competing in the fast-food business, they have accurately matched the quality of their product with the quality of their service delivery. Both are consistent and responsive to customer desires.

The same attention is needed at higher levels of product positioning. Firms that operate in full-service segments should be just as keenly aware of the service expectations of customers. A full-service hotel should carefully consider whether they should include self-service activities in their operations. For example, providing luggage trolleys at the reception desk for guest use when the bell staff is busy would likely not be perceived as an acceptable level of service. Customers select full-service operations because of the higher level of service they perceive they will *consistently* receive. Although self-service trolleys would be useful in moving luggage, customer expectations would not be met. Hotel guests at full-service properties expect the bell staff to always be available for baggage handling.

However, too much service can also be inappropriate. A hotel in San Francisco attempted a service strategy combining five-star Asian service with five-star American lodging. Employees were to be personal valets, catering to every guest's need and whim. While many guests in this international business city were from Pacific Rim countries, a larger percentage were from North America. Therefore, the majority of guests were not familiar with the extremely high level of personalized service provided in five-star Asian hotels. Even Asian guests did not expect such service in the United States. Most customers were uncomfortable with the level of service offered because it was viewed by American cultural standards as too personal. Guests were often confused by what services these personal valets would provide.

The staff spent most of their time cleaning rooms rather than servicing. Thus, they were not always available when needed to provide certain services in a timely manner. Furthermore, the personal valets were hired with the expectation that they would earn a large portion of their income from tipping in exchange for the high level of personalized service. The combination of guests not desiring the personalized service as expected and personal valets spending much of their time cleaning resulted in very low tips. Therefore, the strategy did not succeed. Guests were confused and workers were unhappy. A good match was not achieved between service quality and product.

These examples show that firms can use service quality to create a competitive advantage, but the issues of responsiveness and consistency play key roles. The service quality provided must be built upon core competencies. Firms must offer what is desired and offer it in the same way each time to meet customer perceptions of service quality.

### Service Quality and Process Competencies

Service quality strategies can be built using many different process competencies. Most apparent are those transactions that directly involve the customer. As shown in the examples previously cited, the level of service quality applied in the service delivery function can be intentionally targeted and finely tuned. However, service quality in processes can be applied widely across the organization. The issue is not limited to interactions with customers. It can be embedded not only in operational issues, but also in financial management, organizational design, and the corporate culture. For example, how a firm manages its relationships with lenders, suppliers, and investors can easily impact its ability to negotiate favorable financial terms and conditions. Further, how employees of organizations choose to interrelate with one another can be impacted by service quality. Every enterprise can inculcate its own culture with the same focus on consistent and responsive staff interaction that is often created for customer interaction. In the hospitality business, where so many employees perform their tasks in front of the guest, the consistency and responsiveness in how they treat one another is very visible to customers.

## SUSTAINABLE COMPETITIVE ADVANTAGE

The turbulent general and competitive environment is a force driving radical change in hospitality and leisure services. Globalization, the increasing sophistication of consumers, and dramatic changes in information technology are forcing hospitality and leisure firms to create distinctive competitive advantages. Firms seek to successfully align their mission, goals, and resources with their environments in order to maximize performance. They draw upon inner strengths to build enduring strategies. In these ever-changing times, merely imitating rivals does not create a lasting competitive edge.

The pattern of adding amenities to continue to attract customers (amenity creep) is reducing the distinction between firms. Similar to the airline industry, where air travel is viewed as a commodity and there are only minor differences in service perceptions, within product segments hospitality and leisure products are becoming more homogenized. As products move toward each other in terms of features and quality (within product segments) it becomes more difficult to effectively compete. To create a sustainable competitive advantage, firms seek to develop core competencies: unique combinations of processes, skills, and/or assets. As competitors move closer together in terms of product quality, it is the service quality developed by these core competencies that will be used more often to create a competitive distinctiveness.

Service quality can be utilized in how a business produces and delivers its products and services; in how it manages its employees; and in how it builds a strong brand identity and reputation. It is a process that includes both the responsiveness of the service and the consistency of the service delivery. Firms that learn how to match service quality as an operational approach with their competitive methods can create a formidable and sustainable competitive advantage.

## REFERENCES

Ansoff, H.I. (1988). *The New Corporate Strategy.* New York: John Wiley and Sons.

Bateson, J.E.G. (1995). *Managing Services Marketing.* Fort Worth, TX: Dryden Press.

Grönroos, C. (1990). *Service Management and Marketing.* Lexington, MA: Lexington Books.

Hamel, C. and Prahalad, C.K. (1989). Strategic Intent. *Harvard Business Review,* May-June: 63-76.

Juran, J.M. (1992). *Juran on Quality by Design: The New Steps for Planning Quality into Goods and Services.* New York: The Free Press.

Lovelock, C.H. (1996). *Services Marketing* (Third Edition). Upper Saddle River, NJ: Prentice Hall.

Olsen, M.D., West, J.J., and Tse, E.C. (1998). *Strategic Management in the Hospitality Industry* (Second Edition). New York: John Wiley.

Porter, M.E. (1980). *Competitive Strategy: Techniques for Analyzing Industries and Competitors.* New York: The Free Press.

Prahalad, C.K. and Hamel, G. (1990). The Core Competence of the Corporation. *Harvard Business Review,* May-June: 79-91.

Roberts, C. and Shea, L.J. (1996). Core Capabilities in the Hotel Industry. *Hospitality Research Journal,* 19(4): 141-153.

Schulze, W.S. (1992). The Two Resource-Based Models of the Firm: Definitions and Implications for Research. *Best Papers Proceedings, Academy of Management,* 52, 37-41.

Wright, P., Pringle, C.D., and Kroll, M.J. (1992). *Strategic Management.* Boston: Allyn and Bacon.

# Chapter 8

# Approaches to Enhance Service Quality Orientation in the United Kingdom: The Role of the Public Sector

Gillian Maxwell
Susan Ogden
Victoria Russell

## INTRODUCTION

The origins of the U.K. "quality movement" arguably lie in the British Standards Institution's (BSI) definition of quality as the "totality of features and characteristics of a product or service that bear on its ability to satisfy a need" (British Standards Institution, 1983) and the publication of the British national standard, BS 5750, in 1979. The international equivalent, ISO9000, was launched in 1987 by the International Organization for Standardization (ISO). ISO9000 was subsequently adopted as the European standard (EN9000) to promote industry competitiveness throughout the world and to assist development of the European internal market. Nationally and internationally, this approach has therefore provided the key guiding principles for quality management (DETR, 1998). Quality by the original BSI and ISO definitions is explicitly derived from a manufacturing approach which adopts a process control perspective to prevent errors. However, this approach to quality orientation is limited in relation to the complex task of managing tourism services (Maxwell, 1994), because tourism experiences are delivered by a range of suppliers from the public, private, and voluntary sectors and are then purchased, experienced, and evaluated by consumers over time and distance (Augustyn, 1998).

Since the early 1980s, though, a number of approaches to service quality management have evolved to stress the importance of satisfying the needs of increasingly sophisticated customers by delivering intangibles such as flexibility and friendliness (Becker, 1996). Again, there are limitations in this emphasis in the context of tourism as intangible offerings are, to some extent, predicated on tangible, finished standards such as cleanliness—although the delivery of the tangible services is often intangible (Murdick, Reuder, and Russell, 1990). Instead, wider approaches, effective in meeting customer expectations regarding both the softer (intangible) and hard (tangible) elements of quality, are required (Maxwell, 1994). One result has been a continuing emphasis on training to enhance service delivery skills. Acknowledgment of the importance of training to achieve service quality is evident in the 1990 introduction of a national training standard, Investors in People (IiP). The widespread and successful implementation of this standard since 1990 and the impact of other quality assurance schemes has increased the United Kingdom's international competitiveness in tourism provision.

U.K. public sector policy for promoting quality awareness and improvement is now gradually becoming more sophisticated, reflecting development in the understanding of service quality across both hard and soft constituents. This can be seen particularly in relation to the U.K. tourism sector where the framework for promoting quality is multifaceted. Here, a wide array of national and regional initiatives has been aimed at both public and private sector organizations responsible for contributing to the tourist experience; some of these are discussed in this chapter. As will be seen, the range of initiatives is a direct reflection of the complexity and variety of stakeholders involved in the U.K. tourism industry.

## THE U.K. TOURISM INDUSTRY:
## THE QUALITY CONTEXT

The domestic and international tourism markets of the United Kingdom of Great Britain and Northern Ireland (U.K.), worth over £17 billion per annum (Ernst and Young, 1998), are characterized by a high degree of volatility and seasonality. U.K. tourism attracts a wide range of visitors and is usually classified by type: urban and rural; industrial; conference and business; retail; historical, arts, and cultural tourism; and sports, leisure, and events tourism, for example. The effects of market volatility and seasonality, set in an increasingly mature and competitive marketplace, are diverse and sometimes differentiated in product and service offerings (Maxwell and Connell, 1994).

U.K. tourism provision is characterized, above all, by its fragmentation and diversity. This can be seen in geographical dispersion, organizational size and characteristics, and public sector involvement, each of which is outlined in the following sections.

## Geographical Dispersion

Tourism sites span the length and breadth of the mainland island of Britain, with the geographical and cultural diversity of the United Kingdom providing attractions for both domestic and international visitors. On the north/south axis, popular tourist destinations are found at John O'Groats at the northernmost tip of Scotland and Land's End at the southernmost tip of England. On the west/east axis, County Kerry in Northern Ireland, across the Irish Sea from mainland United Kingdom, is a scenic tourist destination, as are the Norfolk Broads, at the easternmost North Sea coastline in England, which also are renowned as a nature reserve and boating area. With communication and transport links ever improving, the range of islands, most notably the Outer Hebrides, Orkney, and Shetland off Scotland, beyond mainland Britain are increasingly accessible to tourists. That the United Kingdom is an island destination is particularly significant for international tourism, in that overseas tourists have to be dedicated to making the specific journey to the United Kingdom. The recent opening of the Channel Tunnel train service linking the United Kingdom and France is, however, increasingly making exit from and entry to continental Europe more accessible.

## Organizational Size and Employment Characteristics

Companies with interests in tourism range in size from international, public limited company operators such as British Airways, British Airports Authority, and Hilton hotels to a legion of small bed-and-breakfast operators and independently owned visitor attractions. In between are national organizations such as The National Trust, one of the most well-known and largest voluntary organizations in the United Kingdom, which maintains a wide range of historic properties, parks, and woodlands; the public sector National Tourist Boards (NTBs) of Scotland, England, Wales, and Northern Ireland; and regional, public sector organizations such as Area Tourist Boards (ATBs).

Employment in the tourism sector is typically characterized by labor intensity and intensification, and part-time and seasonal work undertaken in particular by female and young employees. In the hotel sector especially, employment practices can be conspicuously poor (Wood, 1992; Price, 1994), as manifest in, for example, low pay, long working hours, and casual employment contracts. Employment management is conspicuously marginalized (Goldsmith et al., 1997). In the face of such employment circumstances and conditions, employees may be generally disinclined to offer quality service (Barron and Maxwell, 1998).

## Public Sector Involvement

At a national level in the United Kingdom, several government departments have responsibility for tourism, with Secretaries of State for the Departments of National Heritage, Sport, Environment, and Transport, for example. Also, the Departments of the Chancellor of the Exchequer and Trade and Industry encompass tourism-related issues within their portfolio. Tourism interests even extend to the Ministry of Defense, which grants access to walkers and ramblers as a major landowner. Central government also provides subsidies to various organizations or QUANGOS (quasi-autonomous nongovernmental organizations), e.g., the Arts Council, the Sports Council, and the Countryside Commission, in order to assist in the development of the tourism industry. An important current political development in the United Kingdom is the formation of national assemblies in Scotland, Wales, and Northern Ireland.

Public sector influence extends to a local government level. Local authorities are an important provider of a wide range of tourist and leisure facilities, such as museums and art galleries, libraries, parks, golf courses, swimming pools, and leisure centers, which are either provided for free or with heavily subsidized entry fees. Local government management of these facilities is becoming more commercialized in response partly to private sector competition and pressures on public funding, but also due to the need to appeal to more sophisticated domestic and international visitors. For example, local authority museums and galleries, which have historically had free admission for all visitors, are increasingly relying on the full exploitation of ancillary services, such as retailing and catering, to maximize revenue from visitors while simultaneously improving the total visitor experience (McPherson, 1997). Within a public sector leisure or museum facility, as a result of compulsory competitive tendering, visitor catering may be provided by a private sector contractor. Also increasingly common is the use of joint ventures, termed public-private partnerships, where the local authority and a private developer unite to develop a new leisure complex with management of all or part of the facility transferred to the private sector. This approach has encouraged the shift from municipal swimming baths to themed leisure centers, for example. Often, joint ventures have the effect of merging local resident and tourist markets. The use of Charitable Trust Status is similarly gaining importance due to the inherent regulatory benefits in tax, employment, and operational conditions.

Thus the very nature of the U.K. tourism industry, in its individual and interrelated characteristics, makes for a challenging context in which to embrace theories of service quality. The following sections focus on the role of the U.K. public sector in the drive for service quality.

## DRIVING QUALITY FORWARD IN U. K. PUBLIC SERVICES

### Compulsory Competitive Tendering

Despite the evolution of customer-focused approaches to service quality, the manufacturing approach to quality largely dominated quality enhancement of public services in the United Kingdom up until the mid-1990s. This can be demonstrated by examining the implementation at the local government level of the compulsory competitive tendering (CCT) system, first in 1988 for "hard" (tangible) services such as catering, cleaning, and grounds maintenance in museums and galleries, leisure centers, and parks, and then in 1989 to "soft" (more intangible) services such as sport and leisure management. The belief of the (then) conservative government in introducing CCT was that competition is the best guarantee of quality and value for money. The overriding principle was that the public sector should only continue to provide services if they could demonstrate value for money in their management of them in comparison with the private sector. Value for money was usually defined by three criteria:

- Economy (cost of services)
- Efficiency (comparing the amount/quality of outputs for any given level of inputs)
- Effectiveness (a judgment on whether the right outcomes are being achieved)

However, it is now widely accepted that given the strict mechanisms imposed for the management of CCT, the main incentive for local government managers has been to concentrate on using economy as the basis for service provision (ILAM, 1997, p. 2).

Central to the implementation of CCT was the introduction of a client/contractor division in the management of services whereby the client had the responsibility for the developing the service specification, inviting tenders from both the in-house contractor and private sector contractors, awarding the contract to the tender offering the most value for money, and subsequently monitoring contract performance. The winning contractor had the responsibility for delivering the service to the contract specification at the agreed contract price. In awarding contracts, the quality of processes and systems contained in the tender documentation could also be taken into account. Thus, the incentive to gain an external quality award such as ISO9000 as a badge of respectability increased under CCT. Indeed, many authorities sought ISO-9000 accreditation from potential contractors (both internal and external) as assurance that the contractor had quality systems in place. This became a justification for awarding the contract internally even where the tender price was slightly higher. Consequently, the implementation of CCT, at its simplest, encouraged a quality control approach to service management, and, at best, a quality assurance approach (see Table 8.1).

As quality management theory predicted, relying on such a products-based approach to service quality caused problems when dealing with complex services, which contain a large degree of intangible and experiential elements. As Figure 8.1 illustrates, quality gaps can arise if the specification is not designed to meet customer expectations and needs (Gap 1 and 2), or if the service delivery does not meet the contract specification (Gap 3). CCT was, therefore, criticized for achieving the goals of efficiency and economy to the detriment of effectiveness; that is, delivering the service to the specification at the prespecified price taking precedence over the specification design and service innovation and development. Contract specifications concentrated on numerically measurable outputs due to the difficulty of specifying and monitoring intangibles such as the "enjoyability" of the visitor experience or the needs of the local community. Furthermore, the client/contractor division, where it has been rigidly applied, has hindered the development of services. Of course, the extent to which CCT has had any impact at all on the quality of service delivery has depended on the perceived level of competitive threat within each locality. Thus it has been alleged that "under CCT service quality has often been neglected and efficiency gains have been uneven and uncertain, and it has proved inflexible in practice" (DETR, 1998).

The approach to quality embedded in the CCT example, therefore, constitutes a defining stage in the development of service quality orientation in the United Kingdom on two counts. First, it provides valuable and extensive experience of the implementation of a national, product-based quality system. Second and consequently, it provides an example of how planning for quality has to be continuously reviewed; CCT itself is currently subject to a moratorium.

FIGURE 8.1. Quality Gap Model

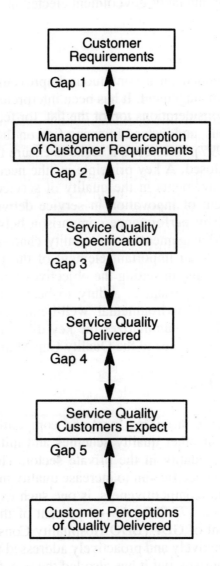

Source: Adapted from Brogowicz, Delene, and Lyth, 1990.

The focus on service quality within the United Kingdom is now matur-ing from the initial products-based initiatives, such as CCT, imported from the manufacturing sector, to an approach based more on process orienta-tion. This more recent and revised approach is reflected, for example, in the recent policy shift away from CCT to the introduction of the Best Value (BV) policy by the labor government elected in 1997.

## Best Value

Best Value is founded on a continuous improvement, process-based approach to quality management. It has been interpreted as a "move away from putting price considerations top of the list, for fear of falling foul of Government sanctions, and instead focusing first on the question of effectiveness" (ILAM, 1997). In essence it seeks to ensure that all quality gaps are monitored and closed. A key principle is "the need to establish plans and targets for improvements in the quality of services" (ILAM, 1997). Thus the development of innovation in service delivery is encouraged. This is underpinned by performance comparison between organizations via benchmarking. Management of the quality chain—both internal and external customers—is an important element of the policy: "greater involvement of local people in setting the objectives for service provision" (ILAM, 1997). Also important is a duty to be taken into account the "social, economic and environmental well-being of the community" (ADLO, 1997). Table 8.1 summarizes the key differences between CCT and Best Value, with reference to the Quality Gap Model.

## The Scottish Tourist Board

The developments in providing local and competitive public services have been reflected in other quality schemes and initiatives, which can extend to facilitating quality in the private sector. The Scottish Tourist Board (STB), with its specific aim to increase quality in tourism provision to enable international competitiveness, is one such example. Tourism in Scotland now supports 177,000 jobs—8 percent of the workforce—and accounts for 5 percent of GDP (BDO Hospitality Consulting, 1998). Not only has the STB effectively and proactively addressed the issue of quality service in Scottish tourism, but it has also led the way for its counterparts in the rest of the United Kingdom and Europe.

One of the four National Tourist Boards in the United Kingdom, the STB launched the first NTB quality assurance scheme for accommodation provision in the mid-1980s and was followed by the English Tourist Board (ETB) and Welsh Tourist Board (WTB). This scheme was introduced initially as a classification of accommodation facilities symbolized by crowns, and an optional assessment of quality grading which included a range of service measures and facilities (see Table 8.2).

TABLE 8.1. The Shift from CCT to Best Value—A Quality Perspective

| | CCT | BEST VALUE |
|---|---|---|
| Policy Imperatives | Economy and efficiency:<br>- cost control<br>- revenue generation | Economy, efficiency, and effectiveness:<br>- customer focus |
| Gap 1 (External customer focus) | Distancing of external customer and supplier via the client/contractor split. | Full involvement of all parties in setting service levels (internal and external customers and suppliers). |
| Gap 2 (Service design) | Set service specifications over length of contract—client role. | Continuous review and service improvement—provider role. |
| Gap 3 (Service delivery) | Measurement of outputs against service specifications and contract price. Contract penalties for failure. | Measurement of outcomes against performance of similar authorities via benchmarking. |
| Gap 4 and 5 (Service review) | Competition every 4/5 years. | A duty to regularly:<br>- publicize targets and service standards<br>- monitor customer satisfaction<br>External auditing with public reporting |
| | **Quality Control (product orientation)** | **Total Quality Management (process orientation)** |

*Note:* Another illustration of a quality assurance initiative in the public sector is included in Best Practice Example 1: The QUEST for Quality in Sport and Leisure.

TABLE 8.2. NTB's Quality Assurance Scheme

| | |
|---|---|
| **Classification Scheme** (determining the range and type of facilities offered) | Listed<br>One Crown<br>Two Crowns<br>Three Crowns<br>Four Crowns<br>Five Crowns |
| **Grading Scheme** (determining the quality of facilities offered) | Approved<br>Commended<br>Highly Commended<br>Deluxe |

Two motoring organizations, the Automobile Association (AA) and Royal Automobile Association (RAC), had long provided examples of quality grading for accommodation providers. However, it was the introduction of the NTB schemes that provided for the first time both large-scale coverage and increased consumer recognition of the accommodation facilities and services available. The STB provides an example of facilitating and addressing quality by constantly developing its scheme in response to consumer demand, including the following:

- Making the optional grading assessment mandatory (in 1991), resulting in raising standards in hotel provision
- Introducing a new quality grade, "Deluxe," to encourage quality provision at the highest end
- Introducing "specifications" that ensure accommodation providers only achieve a grade through a minimum, as opposed to average, grading percentage
- From 1996, basing ATB membership on quality assurance membership

The NTB scheme, though a significant milestone, proved a source of customer dissatisfaction as it was perceived as difficult to understand. Hotels with five-crown facilities, for example, did not necessarily provide an equivalent quality of service. As a result, all four NTBs and the two motoring organizations embarked on discussions in 1994 with a view to providing a uniform scheme that would help promote an increase in the number of overseas visitors. However, these organizations were unable to agree on a harmonized scheme. Consequently, the STB introduced its own "STAR" classification and grading scheme, based on awarding an appropriate level of STARs to each accommodation provider, which began to operate on August 1, 1997. (Best Practice Example 2, at the end of the chapter, outlines the STAR scheme.)

Important for the STB is the high membership it enjoys in relation to overall accommodation provision in Scotland (see Figure 8.2) and in comparison to that of the ETB. Following the introduction of the STAR scheme, a significant number of STB members have increased their grading assessment, and it has been argued that they have been encouraged to invest in property improvements (Segal Quince Wickstead Ltd., 1998). In 1998, versions of the STAR scheme were introduced elsewhere in the United Kingdom. The ETB, with the support of AA and RAC, planned that its own STAR scheme—for hotels only—would be fully operational by the year 2000.

FIGURE 8.2. Accommodation Breakdown in Scotland

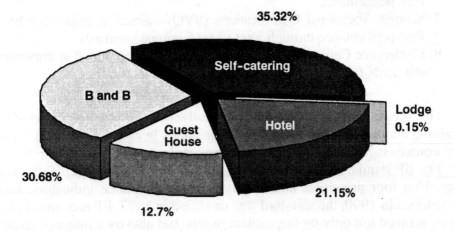

*Source:* Campbell, 1997.

## *Training in Scotland*

The STB also has a firm commitment to providing support for training initiatives across Scotland, which are delivered through the Local Enterprise Company (LEC) network. Tourism Training Scotland (TTS) is a national initiative set up to promote effective training and staff development across Scotland. Its mission is "to transform Scotland's competitive position in tourism, through promoting quality training and career development for all who work in the industry, to ensure that a world-class quality of service is enjoyed by all visitors to Scotland" (Scottish Tourist Board, 1997b). Typical programs delivered or supported under this initiative include the following:

1. Investors in People (IiP) national standard—a long-term process that ties training to business objectives
2. Welcome Host—a one-day awareness seminar aimed at improving the standard of service and hospitality offered to visitors to Scotland
3. Scotland's Best—a one-day course for frontline staff and a two-day course for managers and supervisors, aimed at developing a service strategy
4. Natural Cook—a one-day awareness workshop aimed at raising the profile of cooking using Scottish produce
5. Tourism Business Success—a tailor-made package to improve business management skills

6. Scottish Quality Retailing (SQR)—aiming to improve retailers' business performance
7. Scottish Vocational Qualifications (SVQ)—aimed at improving business performance through a set of professional standards
8. Conference Care—a one-day awareness workshop aimed at improving standards for the conference and business traveler

The local enterprise network also delivers a number of customized training courses depending on market demands in each LEC region. Typical courses include marketing and housekeeping.

The IiP standard has been particularly successful (Alberga, 1997). It is based on four principles and twenty-three performance indicators. First developed in 1990, the standard was modified in 1997. IiP recognition has been secured not only by large chain hotels, but also by a range of leisure and tourism attractions such as visitor attractions, tea rooms, and coach companies. (Examples of this are included in Best Practice Examples 3 and 4 at the end of the chapter.) Government policy is to continue to actively support the IiP standard with targets set for increasing the number of establishments with IiP recognition. Businesses initially commit to the principles of IiP, then are formally assessed and, if appropriate, officially recognized as Investors in People. With reassessment mandatory every three years, the full IiP cycle from commitment to reassessment ensures continuous review (see Figure 8.3).

FIGURE 8.3. IiP Cycle

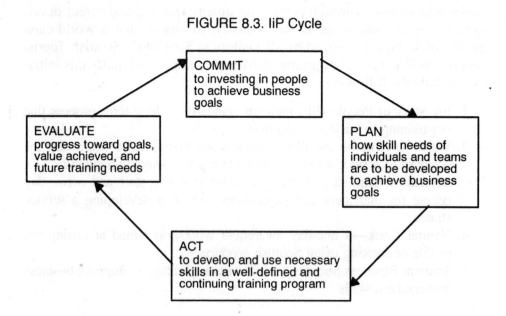

## CONCLUSION: EMERGENT ISSUES
## IN SERVICE QUALITY
## IN THE UNITED KINGDOM

U.K. public sector policy impacts on visitor experiences in both a direct (Tourist Board accommodation classification schemes) and indirect (CCT, Best Value) fashion. The variety of publicly supported national and regional quality initiatives (QUEST, IiP, STARS) is indicative of the diffusion of public sector bodies that influence the development and support of tourism. Public policy can therefore be seen as an important catalyst for the development of tourism in a diverse, but fragmented, way.

In overview, however, it can be seen that the initiatives impacting on quality are generally shifting from a product to a process and, more recently, a user-based approach to quality assurance (Becker, 1996), which is founded upon the premise that quality is a subjective perception which is best evaluated from the perspective of the consumer. The user-based approach is particularly pertinent in the management of services, where the total quality package is skewed away from the objective, physical attributes toward the intangible, experiential elements. As Baum, Amoah, and Spivack (1997) acknowledge, delivering quality products and services in tourism focuses increasingly on intangibles and the human factor in service. The wide range of training initiatives supported by public funding is evidence that the importance of enhancing the soft elements of services is recognized. Furthermore, attempts are increasingly being made to measure these intangibles in order to develop better control systems to monitor service quality. This is particularly well illustrated with respect to the QUEST accreditation system for sport and leisure facilities (see Best Practice Example 1) and in examples of successful IiP implementation (see Best Practice Examples 3 and 4). The challenge of developing a holistic approach to service quality management is ongoing, but within the U.K. context, the recent design and redesign of initiatives aimed specifically at the hospitality, tourism, and leisure sectors serve as examples of how this challenge can be met. Monitoring the success of these schemes in terms of enhancing the customer experience will be necessary to evaluate the prospects for increasing service quality in the United Kingdom.

A danger of many of these schemes is that some service providers may continue to see them in terms of gaining an emblem of respectability primarily for promotional and marketing advantages, rather than for genuinely improving customer satisfaction and the competitiveness of U.K. tourism. Finally, it is asserted that the success of any quality initiative is to varying degrees predicated on training.

**Best Practice Example 1:**
**The QUEST for Quality in Sport and Leisure**

A further development in quality assurance has been the development of QUEST, the only U.K. quality assurance scheme specifically designed for sport and leisure facilities. Launched in 1996, the quality management initiative was developed by a joint committee of various professional and public sector sport and leisure associations in the United Kingdom chaired by the Sports Council—"developed by the industry, for the industry" (AQS, 1996b:2). It is targeted primarily at publicly owned sport and leisure facilities, whether operated by the local authority, private sector contractors, or voluntary sector organizations, with the aim of "setting clear industry standards and providing a focus for raising standards and encouraging continuous improvement" (AQS 1996a:1). However, it is hoped that QUEST has the potential to develop appropriate standards for other sectors such as health and fitness centers operated in the private sector.

The main principles of QUEST are quality improvement, shared knowledge, and best practice. The scheme encourages managers to consider their operation from the customer's point of view. Service improvement is achieved through a process of ten steps starting with self-assessment against recognized industry standards through to mystery customer visits and on-site assessment visits by trained assessors and endorsement via a rating system with three categories: registered, highly commended, and excellent. The assessment criteria cover twenty-four management issues listed under four categories: facility operations, customer relations, staffing, and service development and review.

1. Facility Operation
   - Service Planning, Delivery, and Control
   - Cleanliness
   - Housekeeping
   - Maintenance of Buildings, Plant, and Equipment
   - Equipment
   - Environmental Control
   - Changing Rooms
   - Health and Safety Management
   - Inspection of Service Quality

2. Customer Relations
   - Customer Care
   - Research
   - Customer Feedback
   - Advertising and Promotion
   - Reception
   - One-off Bookings

3. Staffing
   - Supervision and Staff Planning
   - People Management
   - Management Style

4. Service Development and Review
   - Programming and Sports Development
   - Objectives
   - Measurement and Review
   - Usage
   - Awards Achievement
   - Service Development (AQS, 1996b:8)

**Best Practice Example 2:**
**Scottish Tourist Board "STARS" Classification and Grading Scheme**

Within the "STARS" scheme introduced in August 1997, a number of classifications exist to inform customers of the type of business they wish to book:

* *Hotel:* a minimum of six letting bedrooms, of which at least 50 percent will have en suite or private facilities (this will increase to 75 percent by the year 2001). A hotel will normally be licensed (may be a restricted license) and serve breakfast and dinner.
* *Guest House:* a minimum of four letting bedrooms, of which at least 20 percent (minimum of one) will have en suite or private facilities. Breakfast to be available and evening meals may be provided.
* *Bed-and-Breakfast:* accommodation offering bed and breakfast, normally, but not always in a private house. B and B's will usually have no more than six bed spaces, and may or may not serve an evening meal (STB, 1997b).

The visit is classified into many areas. For a hotel, this can include up to nine categories:

1. *Exterior:* includes the appearance of the building, grounds and garden, environment, and parking
2. *Bedrooms:* includes decoration, furnishings, furniture, flooring, beds, linen, bedding, lighting, heating, accessories, and spaciousness/overall impression
3. *Bathrooms and WC:* includes decoration, flooring, fixtures, furniture, linen, lighting, heating, accessories, and spaciousness
4. *Public areas:* includes decoration, furnishings, fixtures, flooring, lighting, heating, atmosphere, and ambience
5. *Restaurants:* includes decoration, furnishings, furniture, flooring, lighting, heating, menu presentation, table appointment, atmosphere, and ambience
6. *Food:* includes dinner and breakfast (presentation and quality)
7. *Hospitality and service:* includes reception (welcome, friendliness, attitude), reception efficiency, reception porterage, housekeeping (bedrooms, guest bathrooms, public areas), bedrooms, room service, public area service, restaurant (wine service, breakfast service), and checkout efficiency
8. *Other:* appearance of staff, tourist information, and public toilets
9. *Leisure facilities:* cleanliness, maintenance/decor (STB, 1997a)

A hotel will only be graded on existing facilities and service and will therefore not be downgraded if, for example, it does not have a leisure center.

This assessment is based on the grading element of the previous scheme employed with some notable changes; the total grading percentage is no longer based on an average percentage, which introduces a minimum standard for each category, and grading assessment sheets are automatically forwarded to establishments after their visit (previously this was done only on request).

**Best Practice Example 3:**
**Knockhill Racing Circuit—The Business Benefits**
**of Investors in People Recognition**

*Profile*

Knockhill, established over twenty years ago near Dunfermline, is Scotland's national motor sport center. Skilled instructors provide expert coaching and guidance in many activities including: race and rally training, clay pigeon shooting, four by four vehicles, go-carting, and thunder buggies. The company has grown in the last five years from a family business to an organization which employs thirty-six full-time and 100 part-time employees. Commitment to IiP was made in 1993, championed by the owner of the business, and recognition achieved in 1996. People are recognized as the source of all business activities, as the circuit manager explains: "It is a philosophy of this business that it's people first—the staff and the customers. Without them there is no business, so the training aspect is vital."

*Benefits of Investors in People*

The personnel and circuit managers indicate that positive customer effects of Investors in People achievement include:

• customer satisfaction;
• high levels of repeat business;
• positive image in the community and with customers;
• word-of-mouth recommendation; and
• staff responsiveness to customers.

Above all, customers emphasize that staff responsiveness ensures that they have a unique and enjoyable experience and that good customer care will always bring them back.

Thus the business strategy is focused on both customers and employees through the Investors in People award, and there is a strong organizational commitment to quality service.

*Source:* Maxwell et al., 1998.

**Best Practice Example 4:
The Freedom of the Glens Family of Hotels—
Business Focus and Development Through Investors in People**

*Profile*

The Freedom of the Glens Hotels is a privately owned group of hotels and a visitor attraction that has been in the hands of the Young family for four generations. The hotels are situated in the beautiful scenery of the Fort William area, on the west coast of Scotland, and number three distinctive, small, and personal establishments. The visitor attraction is Mysteryworld, a recently developed attraction which explores the myths and legends of Scotland's history. Each of the hotels has its own particular identity and is no more than a two-hour drive from the Scottish central belt which extends from Glasgow in the west to Edinburgh in the east.

The group is a major employer in the village area, with some ninety staff on the payroll. The staff have a dedication to the provision of good service and a desire for a team approach. Having secured Investors in People in 1994, the Youngs are ardent advocates of the IiP process, which has brought them clarity of business focus and allowed them to increase the scope of their organization. Lawrence Young, managing director, expresses the value of IiP: "The culture and ethos of a 'family business' is central to our success, but as we grew in size, how was this to be maintained? Investors in People became the brilliant solution."

*Business Approach*

The commitment of the Freedom of the Glens Hotels to customer satisfaction through staff development is highlighted, especially in 1997 when the annual business planning session was devoted entirely to staff matters. Staff development was the business's key priority for 1998. The focus is on improving customer and staff relationships as well as enhancing internal customer communications. Further examples of good practice include the managing director attending all staff induction sessions to explain the business philosophy and the role of Investors in People in the company. Thus investment in internal and external customers, to secure long-term goals, is at the core of the business. Expansion is very much part of the group's aspirations, with plans to develop leisure facilities at two of the hotels. In addition, given the right property, acquisition may be considered. The Freedom of the Glens Hotels asserts that to secure a successful future, the key lies in the interactions between its management, staff, and customers.

*Source:* Maxwell et al., 1998.

# REFERENCES

ADLO (1997). *A Duty of Best Value,* Association of Direct Labor Organizations. London, UK: Sports Council.

Alberga, T. (1997). Time for a Check-up, *People Management,* 3(3), pp. 30-32.

AQS (1996a). *QUEST—The Quest for Quality in Sport and Leisure,* Sports Council, Ref. No. 0618. London, UK: Sports Council.

AQS (1996b). *QUEST—Manager's Guidance Pack* October 1996. Ref. No. 0619. London, UK: Sports Council.

Augustyn, M. (1998). The Road to Quality Enhancement in Tourism, *International Journal of Hospitality Management,* 10(4):145-158.

Bailey, S. and Reid, G. (1994). Contracting Municipal Sports Management, *Local Government Policy Making,* 21(2), pp. 55-65.

Barron, P. and Maxwell, G. (1998). Employee Job Perceptions: A Comparison of Scottish and Australian Fast Food Outlets, *Australian Journal of Hospitality Management,* 5(1):33-40.

Baum, T., Amoah, V., and Spivack, S. (1997). Policy Dimensions of Human Resource Management in the Tourism and Hospitality Industries, *International Journal of Contemporary Hospitality Management,* 9(5/6): 221-229.

BDO Hospitality Consulting (1998). *The UK Hotel Industry.*

Becker, C. (1996). Implementing the Intangibles: A Total Quality Approach for Hospitality Service Providers. In Olsen, M.D., Teare, R., and Gummeson, E. (Eds.), *Service Quality in Hospitality Organizations*, (pp. 278-295). London: Cassell.

British Standards Institution (1983). *BS 5750 Part 8 "Quality Systems,"* London: HMSO.

Brogowicz, A.A., Delene, L.M., and Lyth, D.M. (1990). A Synthesised Service Quality Model, *International Journal of Service Industry Management,* 1(1).

Campbell, P. (1997). *Grading and Classification Statistics for 1997 Scheme Year,* Scottish Tourist Board internal report, September 12.

Department for Enterprise (1992). *S5750/ISO9000/EN29000: 1987 A Positive Contribution to Better Business,* DETR.

DETR (1998). *Modernising Local Government: Improving Local Service Through Best Value,* Department for the Environment, Transport and the Regions [also available at <http://www.local.doe.gov.uk/cct/improvbv/preface.htm>]. March 1998, Green Paper. London, UK: DETR.

Ernst and Young (1998). *British Hospitality: Trends and Statistics, 1998,* British Hospitality Association Report. London, UK: British Hospitality Association.

Goldsmith, A., Nickson, D., Sloan, D., and Wood, R.C. (1997). *Human Resource Management for Hospitality Services,* London: International Thomson Business Press.

ILAM (1997). *Best Value—An Alternative to CCT,* Discussion Paper, Factsheet, No. 7, Institute of Leisure and Amenities Management. London, UK: Institute of Leisure and Amenity Management.

Maxwell, G.A. (1994). Human Resource Management and Quality in the UK Hospitality Industry—Where Is the Strategy? *Total Quality Management,* 5(3):45-52.

Maxwell, G., Adam, M., Farquharson, L., MacRae, M., and MacVicar, A. (1998). *Customer Perceptions of Investors in People: Market Research in Scottish Hotels and Visitor Attractions—Summary Findings,* Glasgow: Glasgow Caledonian University.

Maxwell, G. and Connell, J. (1994). Retailing and the Foreign Tourist—The Retailer Perspective, *Marketing Intelligence,* English Tourist Board 6:1-6.

McPherson, G. (1997). The Changing Role of Marketing in Local Authority Museums. In Foley, M., Lennon, J.J., and Maxwell, G. (Eds.), *Hospitality, Tourism and Leisure Management: Issues in Strategy and Culture* (pp. 131-142), London: Cassell.

Murdick, R.G., Reuder, B., and Russell, R.S. (1990). *Service Operations Management,* Needham Heights, MA: Allyn and Bacon.

Price, L. (1994). Poor Personnel Practice in the Hotel and Catering Industry, *Human Resource Management Journal,* 4(4):44-63.

Scottish Tourist Board (1997a). Annual Report.

Scottish Tourist Board (1997b). *Tourism Training Scotland,* information leaflet.

Segal Quince Wickstead Ltd. (1998). *Impact of the Scottish Tourist Board's Accommodation Quality Assurance Scheme,* May. Edinburgh, Scotland: Scottish Tourist Board.

Wood, R. (1992). *Working in Hotels and Catering,* London: Routledge.

## Chapter 9

# Service Quality Monitoring and Feedback Systems

Bonnie J. Knutson

### *BACKGROUND*

As the time approached for the coffee break, someone in the group asked, "What factors are important in a good coffee break?"

The server, the food and beverage manager, and the hotel manager all agreed that the coffee should be of the highest quality, well brewed, and served in attractive china. It would be served from a polished, elegant coffee urn on a clean, attractively arranged table.

None of the people in the workshop mentioned any of these factors. They wanted to get through the line quickly. They also wanted the coffee service area to be located close to the rest rooms and telephones. They thought of a total break that would take care of a variety of needs. None of them even mentioned the quality or flavor of the coffee. (Albrecht and Zemke, 1985, p. 59)

An old axiom says, *You can't manage what you can't measure.* Grades are used in school so teachers can monitor and manage the education of children. Highways have speed limits to monitor and manage traffic safety. Organizations have incorporated concepts such as Zero Defects and Total Quality Management standards to monitor and manage production, distribution, and service throughout the value chain.

Ever since Peters and Waterman (1982) admonished us to listen to our customers, managers have looked for ways to accurately measure and monitor the delivery of service quality in their organizations. Both the popular and academic press have noted the link between high service quality and business success. Measures of customer satisfaction and service quality are widely used as a barometer of business performance.

AT&T reported that changes in customer-perceived quality caused changes in market share (Gale, 1994). Also consider this: Businesses having low service quality average only a 1 percent return on sales and lose market share at the rate of 2 percent per year. On the other hand, businesses with high service quality average a 12 percent return on sales, gain market share at the rate of 6 percent per year, and charge significantly higher prices (LeBoeuf, 1987). If service quality is critical to the financial well-being of an organization, then knowing what constitutes service quality is essential to accurately measure and manage its delivery.

## CONCEPTUALIZING SERVICE QUALITY

What is service quality? Unfortunately, there is no universal interpretation. It means different things to different people at different times and on different occasions. To parents with small children, it may mean a swimming pool and extra towels in a hotel. For a businessperson, it may mean a prompt wake-up call and accurate billing. For a couple celebrating their twenty-fifth wedding anniversary, service quality may take on the guise of a romantic view from the room or unobtrusive room service. However each person may define it, service quality is generally thought to be the aggregate of his or her perceptions of the service experience.

While some studies view service quality as the sum of anywhere from twenty-four to ninety-nine individual activities, others see it as having one or more dimensions (Bennington and Cummane, 1998). Regardless of how the construct is conceptualized, service quality is always a combination of two major factors—procedure and conviviality (Martin, 1986a). The procedural factor deals with the technical systems involved in getting products and services to customers. It includes such elements as the flow of service, the timing of service, anticipation, supervision, and customer feedback. The conviviality factor reflects an employee's ability to relate to customers as people. It includes attitude, body language, attentiveness, suggestive selling, and problem solving.

Gronroos (1984) reasons that service quality is composed of three dimensions. The first he calls technical quality. It represents what the consumer actually receives as a result of interaction with the organization and lends itself to an objective measurement by the customer. Examples include a restaurant meal, a hotel room, or the roller coaster ride at an amusement park. The second dimension, functional quality, represents the actual performance of the service. Attitude, tact, skills, knowledge, and friendliness are examples. They are seen subjectively by customers. Together, technical quality and functional quality represent a bundle of goods and services that create an image, which Gronroos sees as a third dimension of service quality. Although they use different labels—materials, facilities, and personnel, or physical quality, corporate quality (image), and interactive quality—other researchers support Gronroos' notion of three service quality dimensions (Lewis and Klein, 1986).

Perhaps the most widely cited measurement tool of service quality is SERVQUAL (Parasuraman, Zeithaml, and Berry, 1985). SERVQUAL is a generic instrument for measuring the gap between what consumers expect (*should* be provided) and what customers perceive (thought organizations *did* provide) vis-à-vis service quality. The researchers hypothesized that service quality has five dimensions: reliability, assurance, responsiveness, tangibles, and empathy. Their work used expectations to define service quality and identify consumer expectation levels. In 1993, Boulding and colleagues conducted a two-part study that supported earlier findings about perceptions, clarified issues regarding expectations, and established the relationship between perceptions and behavioral intentions. Genestre and Herbig (1996) extended the SERVQUAL concept by adding product attributes, then examining the combined results. They conclude that the product dimensions are uppermost in the customer's mind, and by excluding it, SERVQUAL only tells a part of the service quality story.

### A Note About Expectations

Expectations are an integral part of how researchers conceptualize service quality. In fact, they form the foundation against which perceptions are measured, and thus service quality gaps are identified. It is important, therefore, to have a clear understanding of what expectations are and how they are formed.

> But there is a price to pay for the experience of substantial progress and the expectation of further progress. When expected progress is not achieved, we feel disappointed or even frustration. What we have today, even if it is much more than that which we had and which gave us full satisfaction yesterday, is no longer enough tomorrow. (Katona, 1964, p. 120)

Expectations are personal intervening variables. In its most elementary form, the theory of expectations may be graphically represented as follows:

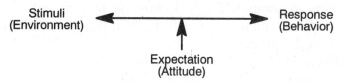

Personal intervening variables mediate between changes in the environment (stimuli) and people's responses to these changes (overt behavior or action). They influence both the perceptions of the stimuli and the responses to them. Katona points out that expectations are of particular importance when people have substantial discretion of action and when a problem arises about how to respond to the stimuli.

*(continued)*

---

*(continued)*

Expectations are considered to be a class of attitudes that point to the future and reflect the degree of probability of an occurrence. Attitudes constitute important intervening variables; they are generalized perspectives with affective connotations, indicating what is good or bad. Attitudinal variables are learned; that is, acquired and modified by past experiences with the environment. People's time perspective extends both backward and forward. Expectations, then, constitute a forward-looking class of attitudes of particular importance for purchase behaviors.

Expectations also tend to be stable as well as directionally consistent; that is, they tend to remain favorable or unfavorable over time. Katona argues that people do not generally change their expectations without valid reasons but concludes that the formation of new expectations is not always based on a careful consideration of all facets of a situation.

---

Boulding et al. (1993) distinguish between two types of expectations. One type is a prediction of future events, an expectation of what *will* happen; the second is normative, an expectation of what *should* happen. The second type is characteristic of earlier service quality literature (Parasuraman et al., 1988).

The Boulding group concluded that service quality should be measured via a perceptions-statements instrument. Further, they believe that perceptions result from a combination of a priori expectations of both what will and should happen with the reality of the actual service encounter. Given the same service encounter, the lower the *should* expectation, the higher the perception; the higher the *will* expectation, the higher the perception. Finally, the researchers found that the higher the perception of service quality, the greater the intention to return and the greater the intentions to recommend the establishment to others.

## MEASURING SERVICE QUALITY

A hospitality manager needs to understand computers, managerial accounting, how to compute ROIs (Return on Investment), establish cost control procedures, and manage staff. Each of these functions is an essential support to the purpose of the business—guests. While many people may be influenced to try a hotel, restaurant, or attraction through the mass media, loyal guests are made one at a time through top service quality. This appears to be a mind-boggling task. Think about a hotel that checks in a thousand guests a day, or a restaurant that serves two thousand people daily, or the hundreds of thousands who walk through the gates at Disney World every day. Hospitality managers in these operations, and thousands more like them, must have knowledge, understanding, and managerial skills to establish a standard operating performance (notice I did not say procedure) for hospitality or caring. The customer who first walks through the door can be turned into a loyal guest only through high service quality. Thus, in reality, it is impossible to separate marketing from operations; they are two sides of the same coin. Every employee is both a salesperson and a goodwill ambassador for the hospitality business. In fact, to your guest, the employee *is* the business. Therefore, identifying opportunities to increase sales and/or guest counts, through measuring customer feedback about service quality, is a primary function of any hospitality enterprise.

Hospitality professionals know that customer feedback is the basis for effective management decisions. If you talk with successful managers in major hospitality chains—McDonald's, Walt Disney, Hyatt International, Hilton, or any other first-tier enterprise—you will get the same response: Customer feedback works. They all believe in it, do it, and use it. It stands to reason that if they develop new products, services, or concepts, the market had better want them and be willing to pay what is needed to cover costs.

Occasionally, an entrepreneur who manages a small hotel or restaurant may say, "That stuff! Who needs it?" That response cannot be taken at face value because, chances are, the entrepreneur *is* gathering customer feedback without knowing it, such as the following:

- Recording and monitoring customer counts, sales information, and costs
- Being personally on the floor at meal times or at peak check-in times observing guests' behavior
- Using comment cards
- Talking with bussers and dishwashers to find out what is being left on plates, or watching how a guest moves furniture in the hotel room to make it more convenient
- Reading the complaint log
- Following up on the comments in the suggestion box
- Visiting competitors, attending seminars, and reading trade magazines

Managers who do any of these things are using customer feedback to make better management decisions. They understand guests' wants and needs by being close to those being served. It is simply not a formalized process. But the growth of multiunit operations brought with it a need to formalize the guest information system. First, because the final decision makers (corporate management) become removed from the end user (guest). Second, the impact of a management decision on hundreds or thousands of units is far greater than on one. Therefore, trial and error can cause financial disaster.

For example, the owner/operator of a 200-seat restaurant finds it relatively easy to obtain feedback from guests and employees. She can be in the dining room almost every meal period, observing guests and probing for perceptions, preferences, and habits. Her method of adapting to changing guest needs can be trial and error. Before listing an item on a menu as a regular offering, it can be carefully tested for taste (by sampling), appearance (again, by sampling), portion size, and price (usually first as a special). Single unit owner/operators continually obtain feedback from guests and employees to aid in predicting what the customers will like and buy, and what they will not. On the other hand, the president of a 500-unit restaurant chain finds it impossible to have the same personalized and direct feedback to guests. The bigger the distance between decision makers and customers, the greater the need for accurate, thorough, and continual customer information—thus, the need for a formalized customer feedback system. The bottom line is this: Customer feedback about an operation's service quality is necessary whether it is a ten-room bed-and-breakfast or a 1,000-unit chain. The question is how to best get it. Several methods are commonly used to accomplish this task.

### Service Audit

Martin (1986b) claims that the service audit is a form of "management by walking around" (MBWA), which Peters and Waterman (1982) found was one technique used by successful organizations. The service audit goes beyond MBWA because it gives a structured process for walking around. Through the service audit, management can examine service quality and get a feeling for how the operation is functioning. The auditing process requires careful scrutiny of each service step and function. As a result, it provides a sense of direction and identifies any areas that require remedial attention.

Martin's audit form is a series of forty service quality indicators that have been identified as important to customers and to the success of an organization. Half of the items are procedural, while the other half are convivial. This audit form utilizes a four-point rating scale on which the frequency and quality of each behavior item are recorded. The scale (Customer-Service Assessment Scale, CSCA) is used to determine how adequately the firm is meeting customers' needs. The scale can be used to assess service quality in an individual property, a group of properties, or competitors. Regardless of how it is used, the CSCA's usefulness lies in its ability to expose service strengths and weaknesses. Its weakness, of course, lies in the fact that the evaluation (perceptions) is not done by customers.

## Shoppers' Studies

This type of feedback tool is akin to a service audit. In a shopper's study,* a field worker poses as a customer and, following a list of predefined steps and criteria, makes mental notes (and later written notes) about the service quality he or she receives from the organization. "This technique was first used over a half-century ago . . . [when] an investigator posed as a customer and observed relationships with company employees in areas such as quality of service and personality" (Blankenship and Breen, 1993, p. 465). To be useful to hospitality managers, these studies have to concentrate on what the guest thinks is important. A colleague often tells the story about the district manager for a major fast food company. The manager went to visit his mother, who lived in a distant city. On the way to her home from the airport, he decided to visit one of the company-owned stores as a mystery shopper. After they finished eating, he walked out of the store and headed around back. When his mother asked what he was doing, he said that he wanted to check the garbage bins. "Oh," his mother replied, "I didn't know I was supposed to be concerned about the garbage."

Shoppers' studies are best done by an outside research company. Although it may cost more, an outside firm is generally more skilled in gathering this type of customer feedback, and they can evaluate the service quality from an unbiased perspective. They would have no reason to slant the findings either positively or negatively. In addition, it is unlikely that any employee would know that the shopper is indeed evaluating the quality of service being given.

## Critical Incident

A second alternative for assessing service quality is critical incident analysis (Johns and Tyas, 1997). First used to identify critical requirements in job performance, the technique has been developed to study satisfactory and unsatisfactory service quality in industries such as airlines, hotels, and restaurants (Bitner, Booms, and Tetreault, 1990; Lockwood, 1994). This technique involves collecting a large number of service incidents by interviewing customers and/or staff. These incidents are then

---

*Shoppers' studies are also called shopping surveys or mystery shoppers.

inventoried, analyzed, and prioritized to identify those that are truly critical. These incidents are then traced back to their origins and action taken
on the most significant satisfiers and dissatisfiers. A case in point: Airlines
have discovered that one of the biggest irritants for passengers is not being
informed about changes in scheduled or normal flight operations—and
why a change occurred. They not only want to know that a flight will be
delayed; they want to know why, for how long, and what the airline will do
about connecting flights. In the air, knowing that the flight will experience
turbulence for ten minutes is far better than starting the bumpy ride with
no warning. To get the information to the passengers that they want (high
service quality) the airline must first conduct a critical incident analysis
(pert chart) to identify all the elements involved in delivering each step of
the process. Only then can the airline implement policies and procedures
to make sure that customers get the information they want, when they
want it.

### Comment Cards

The hospitality industry is notorious for using comment cards to get
customer feedback about their service quality. Despite their widespread
use, there are two major problems with using comment cards (Stevens,
1988, pp. 41-42). First, most customers do not fill them out. Those that do
are far from being a representative sample of customers. They are usually
either very happy or very unhappy with the service quality; rarely are they
in the middle. While some may argue that comment cards can help management spot a small service failure before it becomes a big problem, you
could also argue that the negative (or positive) incident is simply a fluke—
a one-time occurrence. The second problem with comment cards is that,
even when they are filled out and turned in, it is often impossible to tell
what they mean. "Some people rate almost everything as 'fair'; some think
mediocre is 'good.' If yours is a coffee shop restaurant and someone says
that the food was 'fair,' do they mean 'fair' relative to a chain fast-food
outlet, another family sit-down place, or to Le Francais?" (Stevens, 1988,
p. 42).

### Complaint Logs and Special Request Logs

Hospitality managers should love to hear complaints and receive suggestions or special requests. They are a valuable form of customer feedback.
Because employees are often the first to hear them, all personnel should
enter customer comments in a daily log. *The line is too long. I couldn't find*

*the place. Can I have applesauce instead of a salad? Beautiful room. Great coffee.* Personnel at one luxury hotel chain even carry a small notebook in which they write any comments, requests, or suggestions they hear. In one case, a bellman heard a guest comment on how he loved Snickers candy bars and wished they were in the VIP fruit basket. That information was entered into the gentleman's guest profile and, from that time on, whenever he checked into any of the hotel's properties, there were some bite-size Snickers bars in his room. These comments provide valuable customer' feedback. In each case, they give valuable information on how you can "tweak" your operations to better provide what the customer wants.

The key, of course, in making these logs successful is twofold. First, the manager can never "shoot the messenger," especially if the employee is relaying a complaint or a service failure. There is a management principle that states: We get the behavior we reward (LeBoeuf, 1987). Employees soon learn whether their managers want to hear this valuable customer feedback. The second key is follow-up. Just as with comment cards, the organization must use this feedback as an opportunity to add value to the guest's experience.

### Focus Group

There are three primary uses of the focus group technique. One is to identify a comprehensive list of service quality attributes that are important to customers. Often, focus groups are used to narrow concepts and issues so that the "right" questions are asked in a subsequent survey. They can also be used as a follow-up to surveys and other data gathering techniques to help clarify the findings. For example, feedback from a hotel survey might indicate that security is a major concern for guests. To better understand what customers mean by "security," focus groups can be used to probe the term. How does security relate to items such as key locks, lighting in the parking lot, or front desk personnel not saying your room number out loud? In one focus group with older travelers, security took on the aspect of name tags being printed large enough for aging eyes to read easily. Who would have thought that type size is part of hotel security?

Finally, focus groups are an excellent tool to pretest aspects such as menu design, media messages, or proposed new names or logos. Several years ago, there was a restaurant company named Mr. Steak. As American consumers became more health conscious and started eating less beef, the company was concerned that their name would begin to drive customers away—even though they offered a good selection of chicken, fish, and pasta on the menu. Following a comprehensive telephone survey, several possible new names were identified. In focus groups, each name was "tested" relative to image, and how well it represented the menu design, interior and exterior design of the buildings, and price structure of the restaurant. From this research, Findley's American Restaurant was selected as the new name; it was successfully launched six months later.

Focus groups are popular with hospitality organizations because they are relatively low cost and can be implemented rather quickly. Management can view the discussion process so that they get a real feel for not only what consumers say, but also how they say it—i.e., the intensity of their feelings. Focus groups can also help generate new product ideas. *Wouldn't it be nice if I could get soup to go at a drive through? I sure wish the phone in my hotel room were portable. Gee, if I had known you have a store in that city, we would have stopped there for lunch.*

### Customer Value Workshop

Although akin to the traditional focus group, the customer value workshop (CVW) overcomes many of the problems inherent in the focus group technique. Bennington and Cummane (1998) summarize the workshop technique as follows: The CVW is more structured than a focus group and generally involves more customers, about twelve to fifteen. The workshop begins with customers completing a brief questionnaire that focuses on identifying irritating elements in the service process as well as the level of that irritation—disappointed, annoyed, angered. Participants then move on to "imagineering," which involves a visioning process designed to build a picture of the ideal product and service—i.e., service quality—in the relevant area. All the ideas generated by customers are organized into categories based on the natural relationship among the items. This process, known as affinity diagramming, is more creative than logical (Brassard, 1989).

Affinity diagramming is both efficient and inclusive. Groups can organize more than 100 separate ideas or issues in less than an hour. Ideas are not lost in the process because all are recorded and incorporated into the diagramming. The customer group then names each attribute of the "ideal" product and service. It is important that each attribute category is independent from the other categories and that participants can easily differentiate among them.

The final step in the CVW involves the use of computer technology. Participating customers are asked to rate the firm's current service quality against each of the "ideal" attributes by pressing a number from 1 (poor) to 9 (excellent) on wireless, hand-held keypads that are linked to a computer. Real-time processing allows both customers and management to see the results of the group and/or segments within the group. A follow-up discussion helps clarify any points of confusion or differentiation.

This collaborative process addresses the service quality issues that customers want to address and allows them to provide direction for improving quality and customer loyalty. It likewise allows customers to help organizations to design innovative products and services to meet their present and future needs (Flores, 1993).

## *Survey*

Even with its inherent methodological flaws, the survey is still the most commonly used tool for measuring service quality. Consumer surveys have become a widely used barometer of business performance over the past decade (Hurley and Hooman, 1998). For instance, Parasuraman and colleagues (1985) used surveys to develop SERVQUAL. Today, it is the dominant service quality survey instrument, although it has been widely criticized in recent years (Bennington and Cummane, 1998).

While a full discussion of the pros and cons of survey research is beyond the scope of this chapter, it is helpful to list a few of its characteristics as they relate to our ability to measure service quality. First, survey data are often reported in the aggregate. Yet averaging consumers' preferences and perceived performance do not necessarily represent the views of anyone. Thus, their value is limited. Several researchers conclude that the survey does not represent the customer viewpoint in a useful manner because it cannot adequately probe the consumers' mind-set. They conclude that it should be replaced by methods that better identify the perspectives of individual customers (Hiam, 1992, p. 113; Lytle, 1993). This becomes increasingly important as people demand more customization of products and services.

## *RELATING SERVICE QUALITY*
## *TO CUSTOMER SATISFACTION, VALUE,*
## *INTENTION TO RETURN, AND LOYALTY*

The primary reason organizations measure service quality and customer satisfaction is to better understand how they may enhance customer value and loyalty, and thus the overall financial performance of the firm. Consequently, it is necessary to establish links among these measures. Research has established a relationship among customer perceptions of service quality, customer satisfaction, and customer defection and retention rates.

There has been less success, however, in clearly defining and distinguishing service quality from customer satisfaction, and determining the best tools to measure each. In fact, the two terms are often used interchangeably because both are evaluation variables relating to consumers' perceptions about a given product or service. The dominant view in the literature is that satisfaction is the more global of the two constructs, and that perceptions of service quality affect feelings of satisfaction, which will then affect loyalty and future buying decisions (Hurley and Hooman, 1998).

## RISING COST OF OBTAINING CUSTOMER FEEDBACK

Many of us have placed a catalog order over the telephone. We have also made hotel, restaurant, or airline reservations on the Internet. Most have completed a survey or customer warranty card and returned it. And how many of us are now using the new money cards and smart cards? One swipe of their magnetic strip through the store's scanner and the store is paid in full. Companies are making it more convenient for us to spend money. But they are also doing something else. They are making it much easier to collect information (feedback) about us—about what we buy, what we want, and what we do.

Consumer information is today's business currency. Knowing more about who comes to a hotel, resort, or other tourist destination, and why, helps managers focus their marketing and operational strategies. They can better target high-potential prospects, tailor their services to meet individual needs, improve customer satisfaction and loyalty, and even find opportunities to develop additional products or services. With new technologies and databases, it is easier than ever for managers to capture information from their guests and about their guests.

But a funny thing is happening on the way to the "information well." Consumers are in revolt. Until now, people have divulged information about their lifestyles rather freely. They have completed surveys, participated in focus groups, typed in their e-mail address and preferences, and applied for the money card. This will not be the case in the future.

Some consumers see this as a privacy issue. Others look at it from a security standpoint. Still others rebel at the thought that Big Brother is alive and well and living in a computer chip. In reality, the growing reluctance of customers to disclose personal data is really an issue of value. People are realizing that they get very little in exchange for the information they give so freely through their commercial transactions and survey responses. There is a growing body of managers who believe that consumers are going to take ownership of information about themselves and demand something in exchange for it. In a recent article in the *Harvard Business Review*, management experts John Hagel III and Jeffrey Rayport (1997) point out that businesses are seeing the rise of a privacy backlash among consumers. They believe that this backlash has less to do with privacy, however, than with value. People are coming to realize that they are "selling" information about themselves to corporations too cheaply.

Of course, for some, privacy is an abstract concept that is an absolute right. Most consumers, however, are willing to give their opinion or release personal facts if they can get something tangible in return—make a "profit" from it. Think about the next time you take a vacation or go on a business trip. Are you a member of a frequent flyer program? Passengers will give airlines detailed data about their flying history in exchange for items of value to them—e.g., upgrades, discounts on future flights, or the ability to buy tickets, hotel rooms, and other products at a discount. The same is true of hotel and car rental companies. Their application forms often request credit card information, business and home addresses, phone and fax numbers, e-mail, driver's license, Social Security number, and myriad other information.

The same trend is evident in the market research industry. Once, people would complete a survey or participate in a focus group for little more than a thank-you or some coffee. Those days are gone forever. Today, consumers want something for their time and information. In the United States, the going rates for focus group participants can range from $50 and up. Restaurants offer certificates for complimentary appetizers, desserts, or meals to encourage patrons to complete surveys. Even private clubs are entering the fray. They will often "purchase" a new member referral from a current member by offering a month's dues free, a gym bag, or a logo jacket if the prospective member joins. Telecommunications giant MCI used a similar strategy with its Friends and Family program in which customers were given discounts in return for listing the names of people they called most often—e.g., prospective MCI customers.

A few years ago, there was a movie in which someone leans out of a window and yells: "I'm madder than hell and I'm not going to take it anymore!" When it comes to data about themselves, a similar scenario can be applied to today's consumers. So what does this mean to hospitality and tourism industries? It means that people are increasingly taking ownership of their personal information, forcing researchers to rethink their approach to gathering consumer feedback. Historically, consumer data has been something that hospitality businesses have obtained for free as a by-product of their transactions with their customers. According to Hagel and Rayport (1997, p. 60), this means that academe and business "have every incentive to overinvest in collecting information about . . . customers and to underinvest in using it." But the days of the "free lunch" are over. When companies have to pay for information, the incentives change. As hospitality companies pay more, they will become more selective about the feedback data they collect, focusing on what is needed to increase value and better satisfy consumers. They will also have to establish a stronger partnership with customers so that they can continue to collect this vital information. Finally, companies will have to establish a schedule of payments for the data they want to collect.

Futurist Faith Popcorn (Popcorn and Marigold, 1997) talks about the rise of the vigilante consumer. Nowhere is this more evident than in the arena of consumer feedback. While we still are not sure how this whole trend will play out for the hospitality and tourism industry, the direction is clear. As consumers take tighter control of their own personal data, access to it will become more costly, much like the old supply and demand curves that we all learned in Economics 101. Those hotels, resorts, restaurants, and other travel destinations that develop innovative strategies to collect this data will have a competitive head start in the new century.

## TOWARD THE FUTURE

In the twenty-first century, organizations will find themselves in a more competitive landscape greatly altered by new technologies, business practices, and consumer demands. Through its Hospitality 2000 study, consulting firm Arthur Andersen (Cline, 1996) concluded that businesses need to shift their primary focus from physical assets (property) to virtual assets (customers). This view is one held by hospitality industry executives around the world by a margin of five to one.

It is clear that service quality is a complex, confusing concept. If this shift does indeed take place, it will require organizations to pay closer attention to consumers' expectations and perceptions about service quality, then respond to them. McKenna (1997) says technology will enable organizations to collapse this feedback loop in real time. Real time ". . . applies not to any device but to the technologically transformed context of everything we do. Real time is characterized by the shortest possible lapse between idea and action; between initiation and result. . . . It is instant response" (p. 6). He believes that the application of the powerful real-time concept— using an information feedback loop from customers and market infrastructure to design and service, and back out again—has just begun. Successful organizations in the future will use information and telecommunications technology to respond to changing customer expectations within the shortest possible span of time. They will understand that customers' expectations are being reset for hyperaccelerated, if not immediate, company response. The competitive environment will no longer tolerate slow responses or delayed decision making, McKenna declares.

The task of developing more effective and efficient ways to measure and monitor service quality will fall to all stakeholder groups involved in its delivery: customers, staff, and management. Real time will make it easier; it will also make it more imperative. Each group will have to see what the other groups see relative to the delivery of service quality, and they will have to see it simultaneously. It will be an exciting challenge—especially in light of a growing global economy. Only then will the coffee break described at the beginning of this chapter reflect true service quality.

## REFERENCES

Albrecht, K. and Zemke, R. (1985). *Service America.* Dow Jones-Irwin, Homewood, IL.

Bennington, L. and Cummane, J. (1998). Measuring Service Quality: A Hybrid Methodology. *Total Quality Management.* 9 (6) 395-406.

Bitner, M.J., Booms, B.H., and Tetreault, M.S. (1990). The Service Encounter, Diagnosing Favorable and Unfavorable Incidents. *Journal of Marketing.* 54 (1) 71-84.

Blankenship, A. and Breen, E. (1993). *State of the Art Marketing Research.* PTC Business Books, Chicago.

Boulding, W., Kalra, A., Staelin, R., and Zeithaml, V.A. (1993). A Dynamic Process of Service Quality: From Expectations to Behavioral Intention. *Journal of Marketing Research.* 3 (February) 7-17.

Brassard, M. (1989). *The Memory Jogger Plus.* Metheun, Goal/QPC, London.

Cline, R.S. (1996). Hospitality 2000: A View to the Millennium. *Lodging Hospitality.* 52 (8) 20.

Flores, F. (1993). Innovation by Listening Carefully to Customers. *Long Range Planning.* 26 (3) 95-102.

Gale, B.T. (1994). *Managing Customer Value: Creating Quality and Service That Customers Can See.* Free Press, New York.

Genestre, A. and Herbig, P. (1996). Service Expectations and Perceptions Revisited: Adding Product Quality to SERVQUAL. *Journal of Marketing Theory and Practice.* 4 (4) 72-82.

Gronroos, C. (1984). A Service Quality Model and its Marketing Implications. *European Journal of Marketing.* 18 (4) 36-44.

Hagel III, J. and Rayport, J.F. (1997). The Coming Battle for Customer Information. *Harvard Business Review.* 75 (1) 53-61.

Hiam, A. (1992). *Closing the Quality Gap.* Prentice Hall, Englewood, NJ.

Hurley, R.F. and Hooman, E. (1998). Alternative Indexes for Monitoring Customer Perceptions of Service Quality: A Comparative Evaluation in a Retail Context. *Academy of Marketing Science Journal.* 26 (3) 209-221.

Johns, N. and Tyas, P. (1997). Customer Perceptions of Service Operations: Gestalt, Incident or Mythology? *The Service Industries Journal.* 17 (3) 474-488.

Katona, G. (1964). *The Mass Consumption Society.* McGraw-Hill, New York.

LeBoeuf, M. (1987). *How to Win Customers and Keep Them for Life.* G.P. Putnam, New York.

Lewis, R.C. and Klein, D.M. (1986). The Measurement of Gaps in Service Quality. Paper presented to the American Marketing Association's Services Marketing Conference. September 7-10, Boston, MA.

Lockwood, A. (1994). Using Service Incidents to Identify Quality Improvement Points. *International Journal of Contemporary Hospitality Management.* 6 (1/2) 75-80.

Lytle, J.F. (1993). *What Do Your Customers Really Want?* Probus, Chicago.

Martin, W.B. (1986a). Defining What Quality Service Is for You. *The Cornell Hotel and Restaurant Administration Quarterly.* 26 (February) 32-38.

Martin, W.B. (1986b). Measuring and Improving Your Service Quality. *The Cornell Hotel and Restaurant Administration Quarterly.* 26 (May) 80-87.

McKenna, R. (1997). *Real Time: Preparing for the Age of the Never Satisfied Customer.* Harvard Business School Press, Boston, MA.

Parasuraman, A., Zeithaml, V.A., and Berry, L.L. (1985). A Conceptual Model of Service Quality and Its Implications for Future Research. *Journal of Marketing.* 49 (Fall) 41-50.

Peters, T.J. and Waterman, R. Jr. (1982). *In Search of Excellence.* Harper and Row, New York.

Popcorn, F. and Marigold, L. (1997). *Clicking.* HarperCollins Publishers, Inc., New York.

Stevens, P. (1988). *Winning!!!* Hospitality Resource Inc., East Lansing, MI.

# Chapter 10

# Measuring Service Quality and Customer Satisfaction

## Martin O'Neill

## *INTRODUCTION*

The increased significance of the services sector to the global economy has led to a heightened concern by practitioners as well as consumers regarding the quality of services being offered (Sung et al., 1997). Not surprisingly, the concept of quality and its relationship with the service industries has become a major preoccupation of many within this sector, not least the hospitality industry. Hospitality operations now have to serve an increasingly discerning public, who are now more eager than ever to complain and transfer their allegiances to perceived providers of quality services. This, coupled with the increasingly hostile nature of the hospitality environment, has forced many within the industry to invest in the delivery of higher levels of service quality as a means to achieving competitive differentiation. An integral part of any organization's attempt to deliver on this front is a commitment to a process of continuous quality improvement. In turn, this requires the support of a systematic approach to quality measurement.

Interest in the measurement of service quality is thus understandably high, and measuring the quality of the service experience is now an integral part of most managers' responsibilities. The challenge, however, is to identify and implement the most appropriate measurement tools for their operation. In stressing the importance of service quality to the hospitality sector, this chapter seeks to investigate the conceptualization and measurement of service quality and the relationships between service quality, customer satisfaction, and customer retention. In so doing, it shall identify and critically examine a number of the more popular techniques commonly employed within the hospitality industry.

## DEFINING QUALITY
## IN THE CONTEXT OF SERVICE

Numerous attempts have been made to define service quality and the closely related concept of customer satisfaction (Oliver, 1980; Tse and Wilton, 1988). Unlike product quality, which in itself is particularly hard to define, the search for a working definition of service quality is further complicated by the highly transitory and intangible nature of most services. At its most basic, quality has been defined as "conforming to requirements" (Crosby, 1984). This implies that organizations must establish requirements and specifications. Once established, the quality goal of the various functions of an organization is to comply strictly with these specifications. However, the questions remain, whose requirements and whose specifications (Palmer, O'Neill, and Beggs, 1998)? Thus a second series of definitions state that quality is all about fitness for use, a definition based primarily on satisfying customers' needs (Juran, 1982). These two definitions can be united in the concept of customer-perceived quality, where quality can be defined only by customers and occurs where an organization supplies goods or services to a specification that satisfies their needs.

There have been numerous attempts to encapsulate the essential nature of the service quality construct in the form of theoretical models. One of the earliest models is that described by Gronroos (1983), which relates the level of experienced quality to both technical and functional dimensions of service provision (see Figure 10.1):

- *Technical quality* refers to the result of the service and/or the question, what has been provided?
- *Functional quality,* on the other hand, refers to the way the service has been delivered and relates to the question, how has the service been provided?

Technical quality refers to the relatively quantifiable aspects of the service that consumers experience during their interactions with a service firm. Because it can be easily measured by both consumer and supplier, it becomes an important basis for judging service quality (Palmer, 1998). According to Gronroos (1988, 1990), however, these more technical aspects of a service are easily copied, and competitive positioning may be easily lost. Functional quality, in contrast, can be used to create a competitive edge by focusing on the more personal aspects of the service encounter. Gronroos (1984) argues that technical quality is a necessary but not sufficient condition for higher levels of service quality and that functional quality is likely to be more important than technical quality if the latter is at least of a sufficient standard. Saleh and Ryan (1991) concur with this

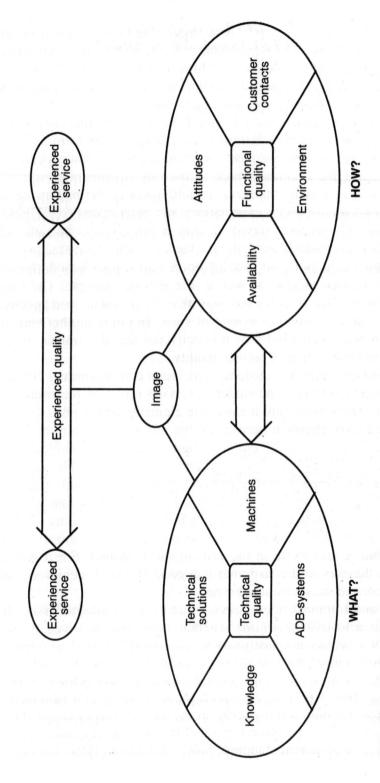

FIGURE 10.1. Service Quality Model

*Source:* Gronroos, 1983.

viewpoint and take it a step further, suggesting that the quality of functional service may even offset problems with the technical component experienced by consumers. While a technical problem should not occur, the reaction of the service provider to it, if it does, may contribute to positive customer perceptions of the service provided.

Berry, Parasuraman, and Zeithaml (1988) support this concept by arguing that Crosby's (1984) definition of quality as "conforming to requirements" should be rephrased as "conformance to customer specifications." In addressing the evaluation process used by customers to assess service quality, they conclude that service quality may be defined as the discrepancy between customers' expectations and perceptions (see Figure 10.2). If expectations are met, service quality is perceived to be satisfactory; if unmet, less than satisfactory; if exceeded, more than satisfactory.

Quality evaluations are both process and output based. They derive from the service process as well as the service outcome. The manner in which the service is delivered may thus be a crucial component of the service from the customer's point of view. To put it another way, it is not just what is delivered but how it is delivered that determines the customer's overall perception of service quality.

In most instances, the customer receives a combination of both material and personal service. The material service refers to the more tangible, technical, and objectively measurable elements of the product or service being supplied. Personal service, on the other hand, refers to what might be better described as the more intangible, functional, subjective, and/or relational elements of the service encounter. To provide good service, therefore, a balance is needed between both personal and material needs. More often than not it is the more relational factors that will create a lasting impression in the customer's mind. By concentrating on the development and provision of these relational elements, organizations are now better able to add value in the eyes of the customer. For it is in adding value in the eyes of the customer that good service is achieved, quality is perceived, and satisfaction achieved.

First and foremost, then, service quality is a customer issue. It is the customer who will determine whether they have received it. To put it another way, customer perception is everything. As harsh as it may sound, it does not matter what the service provider thinks; if the customer is not satisfied then the service has failed. Customers' perceptions are their reality (Cook, 1997). In turn, their perception of the service provided will be determined by their expectations. If the service experienced lives up to their expectations, customers will be satisfied. If the treatment they receive is less than expected, this constitutes bad service. In short, customers want

FIGURE 10.2. Service Quality: The Fit Between Customer Expectations and Perceptions

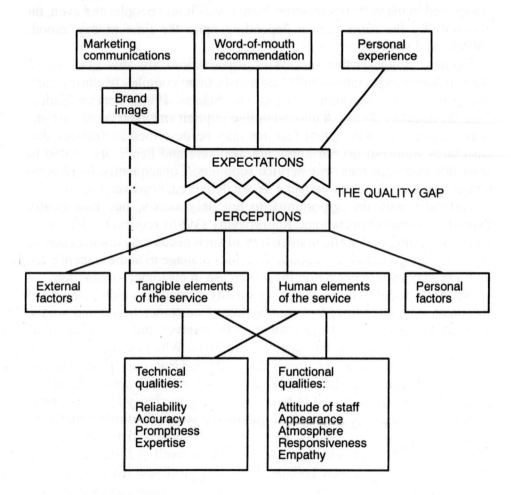

*Source:* Morgan, 1996.

their expectations to be met completely and consistently. One critical question remains, however: What do customers want and how do they define quality?

## DETERMINANTS OF SERVICE QUALITY

This is the difficulty from a provision and measurement point of view. The factors affecting customer satisfaction and service quality are as many and as varied as the number of potential customers themselves. Different things are important to different people for different reasons and as such are perceived in different ways. For example, the same factor can be interpreted in many different ways, by many different people, and even, on occasion, by the same person depending upon the time of day, mood, attitude, and so on.

Evidence suggests that successful organizations are able to diagnose their customer expectations fully and satisfy them completely, during each and every service encounter (Zemke and Schaaf, 1990). Service leaders have the uncanny ability of understanding implicit and even latent customer requirements. These latent features may be described as features that customers want but do not know are available and hence are unable to articulate in discussions with service suppliers. Consequently, there is no way of guaranteeing their delivery. When delivered, however, they present the provider with the opportunity to not only satisfy, but also greatly exceed customer expectations. Ramaswamy (1996) reinforces this viewpoint by arguing that while nondelivery of such needs may not necessarily dissatisfy the customer, a company that does manage to address them even partially may experience a nonlinear increase in customer satisfaction.

Naturally, identification of service quality dimensions aids in the measurement, understanding, and satisfaction of customer needs and wants. This information comes from customers themselves and also from frontline staff who daily come into contact with them. While extensive research has been carried out in the area (Berry, 1983; Gronroos, 1984; Garvin, 1987; Fitsimmons and Maurer, 1991), the work of Parasuraman, Zeithaml, and Berry (1988) stands out in terms of helping to clarify how customers define service quality. Their initial qualitative study identified underlying dimensions of service quality, each of which relates to the customers' confidence in those providing the service. As a result of further extensive research these criteria were collapsed into five more specific components: tangibles, reliability, responsiveness, empathy, and assurance, which have formed the basis of many measurement techniques. Although widely referred to as SERVQUAL, the five elements can more easily be remembered through the acronym "RATER" (Tenner and DeTorro, 1992):

1. *Reliability:* Ability to perform the promised service dependably and accurately
2. *Assurance:* Knowledge and courtesy of employees and their ability to inspire trust and confidence
3. *Tangibles:* Physical facilities, equipment, and appearance of personnel
4. *Empathy:* Caring, individualized attention, and appearance of personnel
5. *Responsiveness:* Willingness to help customers and provide prompt service

According to Zeithaml, Parasuraman, and Berry (1990), the various statistical analyses conducted in constructing SERVQUAL revealed considerable correlation among items representing several of the original ten dimensions for evaluating service quality. The authors believe that these five dimensions are a concise representation of the "core criteria that customers employ in evaluating service quality" (p. 20).

## SERVICE QUALITY AND CUSTOMER SATISFACTION

Previous reference has been made to the concept of customer satisfaction in the context of customer-perceived service quality. Indeed, a review of the literature will reveal that both terms are quite often used interchangeably, which has caused confusion. While both concepts are related and appear to be merging, there are still gaps in the understanding of the two constructs, their relationship to each other, and their antecedents and consequences (Gwynne, Devlin, and Ennew, 1998). A distinction needs to be made between both. According to Cronin and Taylor (1992, p. 56), "this distinction is important to both managers and researchers alike, because service providers need to know whether their objective should be to have consumers who are satisfied with their performance or to deliver the maximum level of perceived service quality."

Oliver (1981, p. 27) takes the view that satisfaction is "the emotional reaction following a disconfirmation experience." Getty and Thompson (1994, p. 9) define it as a "summary psychological state experienced by the consumer when confirmed or disconfirmed expectations exist with respect to a specific service transaction or experience." In fact, the most commonly used representation of customer satisfaction is the disconfirmation approach (Ramaswamy, 1996), in which satisfaction is related to the variation between a customer's prepurchase expectations and their postpurchase perceptions of the actual service performance. According to disconfirmation theory, the extent of satisfaction or dissatisfaction that a customer has with a particular service encounter is determined by the difference between the customer's expectations of performance and the actual perceived performance of the service (Oliver, 1996). Any difference between them is referred to as disconfirmation.

If the service experienced is better than expected, then positive disconfirmation or high levels of satisfaction will result. If, however, the service performance falls short of what was expected, then negative disconfirmation or dissatisfaction will result. Confirmation or zero disconfirmation results when perceived performance just meets the customer's expectations or when the service experience is much as expected in the customer's eyes. Satisfaction may thus be viewed as being situation, encounter, or transaction specific.

Perceived quality, on the other hand, may be viewed as a global attitudinal judgment associated with the superiority of the service experience over time (Getty and Thompson, 1994). As such, it is dynamic and less transaction specific (Parasuraman, Zeithaml, and Berry, 1988). In other words, it has attitudinal properties and acts as a global value judgment. According to Lovelock, Patterson, and Walker (1998), the important distinction is that " . . . satisfaction is experience-dependent—you must experience the service to feel a degree of satisfaction/dissatisfaction. Perceived service quality on the other hand is not experience-dependent . . . perceived service quality is formed over multiple service encounters."

Both constructs are distinct but related concepts, which can be used to evaluate a specific service incident or overall attitudes toward a service encounter. Service quality does differ from satisfaction, however, in that it is a cognitive evaluation and objective attributes are used to assess quality. While satisfaction can result from any aspect of an organization, whether quality related or not, service quality perceptions are specifically related to quality attributes or dimensions (Oliver, 1993).

Not surprisingly, there has been considerable debate concerning the nature of the relationship between these constructs. Although the majority of research suggests that service quality is a vital antecedent to customer satisfaction (Parasuraman, Zeithaml, and Berry, 1985; Cronin and Taylor, 1992) there is now strong evidence to suggest that satisfaction may be a vital antecedent of service quality (Oliver, 1981; Bitner, 1990). Regardless of which view is taken, the relationship between satisfaction and service quality is strong when examined from either direction. Satisfaction affects assessments of service quality, and assessments of service quality affect satisfaction (McAlexander, Kaldenberg, and Koenig, 1994). In turn, both are vital in helping today's customers frame their future purchase intentions. The importance of both to today's hospitality professional is thus paramount.

## SERVICE QUALITY AND THE HOSPITALITY INDUSTRY

In today's hospitality environment, the true measure of company success lies in an organization's ability to continually satisfy customers. Increasingly, customers are demanding value for money in terms of both the price/quality ratio and the actual quality of the product or service being offered. To ensure market success, hospitality organizations of all types are now being forced to stand back and take a long hard look at the way they are currently doing business.

Given the increasingly competitive nature of the hospitality environment, industry professionals must now concern themselves with not only increasing market share, but also satisfying and maintaining the existing customer base. Consequently, a large proportion of organizational effort is now being directed at "both getting and keeping customers" (Christopher, Payne, and Ballantyne, 1991). Evidence suggests that an organization's ability to deliver consistently on the service quality front will without doubt go a long way toward achieving this central business objective. Indeed, the importance of service quality and its relationship with customer satisfaction, brand loyalty, and market share has long been lauded by those in the hospitality field (Knutson, 1988). Both are now viewed as fundamental to the well-being of individual customers, which will have a significant effect on postpurchase perceptions and, in turn, future purchase decisions.

In an attempt to achieve sustained competitive advantage, hospitality organizations are now investing quite heavily in a host of service quality improvement initiatives. By and large the majority of these initiatives have found form through the British Standards Institute, the European Quality Award, the Malcolm Baldrige National Quality Award, the Edwards Deming Prize, or derivatives thereof. In addition, the hospitality industry has also been investing quite heavily in raising quality standards through human resource development. Such initiatives include the Investors in People Award, the Welcome Host Initiative, and various vocational qualification schemes. Oliver (1996) describes these initiatives as belonging to the total quality management movement, advocating organizational strategies and changes, which are thought to make a firm more customer friendly. In this context, "customer satisfaction is thought to be a natural outgrowth of optimal organisational design, and of instilling the appropriate organisational culture, personnel training and customer responsiveness within employee ranks. In short, it is believed that the attainment of satisfaction will be enhanced if these practices are followed" (Oliver, 1996, p. 7).

In proposing a more behavioral focus, Oliver (1996) goes on to state that such managerial practices alone cannot guarantee customer satisfaction, for the principal reason that management cannot see "inside the head of its constituents." By adopting a more behavioral focus, in contrast, "managers may be better able to see the workings of the consumer's mind, and in so doing may be better placed to consistently satisfy customer demands" (p. 7). The central tenet of any such approach is the study of consumer perceptions of service quality or that process by which individuals select, categorize, and interpret purchase and nonpurchase-related stimuli, which, in turn, may lead to either first time, repeat, or transferred patronage.

According to Van Der Wagen (1994, p. 4), individual "customers have many different perceptions which are influenced by their education, upbringing, experience and many other factors." As hospitality professionals whose future very much depends upon these customers' perceptions of actual service delivery, we must strive to gain an understanding of how we are performing in the customers' eyes. As Bank (1992, p. 14) states, "the idea is to stay ahead of the customer, to anticipate his or her needs . . . so that when he or she articulates the need you have already planned for it and are ready (ahead of the competition) to meet it." Knowledge of customer perceptions of the service offering would undoubtedly aid hospitality professionals in this process.

Simply stated, today's hospitality professional must consider the measurement of service quality an integral part of any quality improvement exercise.

## MEASURING SERVICE QUALITY IN THE HOSPITALITY CONTEXT

An integral part of any organization's attempt to instill a "quality culture" is a commitment to a process of "continuous improvement" (Witt and Muhlemann, 1995). To support this, a systematic approach to quality measurement is needed. This is especially true of businesses whose predominant product is service as, unlike their counterparts in the manufacturing sector, they have fewer objective measures of quality by which to judge their production (Hudson and Sheppard, 1998). Cronin and Taylor (1992, p. 50) concur with this viewpoint, stating that managers need to know "what aspects of a particular service best define its quality." In turn, this should enable the organization to take up a competitive position based upon its ability to deliver that which is demanded as opposed to that which the organization perceives to be in demand. The fact is, clear, sustained, and continuous quality improvement is not possible without some indication of quality performance. To know the real effect of changes over time, managers need measures to compare the quality performance of the service (Edvardsson, Thomasson, and Ovretveit, 1994).

Ramaswamy (1996) identifies three different sets of measures with which a company must be concerned:

1. *Service performance* measures are primarily internally focused and evaluate the current performance of the service and ensure that it is continuing to reliably meet the design specifications.
2. *Customer measures,* on the other hand, are both internal and externally focused, aimed at assessing the impact of the service performance on customers.
3. *Financial measures* are indicators of the financial health of the organization.

Naturally, the correlation between financial and customer measures will determine the revenue-generating potential of the service, while the relationship between service performance measures and customer measures will give some indication as to how the service is performing in the customers' eyes. In turn, this will have a direct bearing on a company's financial performance and overall market share.

It cannot be assumed, however, that a service that continues to meet internal performance standards will continue to provide the desired level of customer satisfaction. Customer-perceived measures must be independently developed and correlated with performance. These measures will direct future improvement efforts aimed at both improving operational efficiency and satisfying and retaining customers.

Although traditionally it has been easy for operators to claim that the unique characteristics of services precluded any attempt at measurement, the present-day competitive environment has forced a serious rethinking of this attitude. This is especially true of the hotel industry, where an increasing oversupply of hotel accommodation worldwide has forced managers to invest in the delivery of higher levels of service quality as a competitive strategy aimed at differentiating their product and service offering. As evidence continues to suggest that continual measurement is one way of differentiating the successful long-term quality improvement program, it has become imperative for managers to provide for its application in the hospitality context (Lewis, 1987; Getty and Thompson, 1994).

This is not to deny the complexity of the task. Indeed, as Edvardsson, Thomasson, and Ovretveit (1994) point out, managers face a number of difficulties in measuring service quality:

- First, many measurement systems are flawed, as those designing and using the system do not know enough about what is to be measured, the purpose, and how the results are to be used.
- A second problem is that managers quite often do not measure quality throughout the service chain. While some may choose to concentrate solely on internal performance measures, others may concen-

trate on external customer measures only. Of course, what is required is a balance between both and an understanding that while quality may be defined at the "moment of truth," the process of providing quality starts well before the actual interaction with the customer. More often than not, externally perceived quality ratings will reflect the level of internal performance.

- A third problem is that measuring customer perceptions may of itself increase expectations. In many cases, the very mention of quality improvement is enough to create a heightened sense of expectation on the part of the customer.
- A final pitfall is too much measurement. Organizations run the risk of tiring both customers and staff with too much measurement. Given the time and expense required to undertake such an exercise, it is imperative that it is not overdone.

These authors emphasize two issues in particular in an attempt to avoid these difficulties: identifying what should be measured and designing the most appropriate measurement instrument for gathering and analyzing the pertaining data.

In answering the first question, what to measure, Palmer (1998) suggests that organizations should set about asking the following key questions:

- What do customers consider the important features of the service?
- What level of those features do they expect?
- How do customers perceive service delivery?

By answering each of these questions the organization will be better able to establish clear goals and standards for quality improvement as well as being better placed to offer customers the right level of service quality.

The question of how to measure service quality depends upon what is to be measured. Recent years have witnessed the development of a plethora of measurement tools and techniques aimed at assessing service quality and customer satisfaction levels within the hotel sector. This is apparent in both the academic and industrial press and to the uninitiated is a veritable minefield of terminology. Such terms as SERVQUAL, SERVPERF, DINE-SERV, LODGSERV, LODGQUAL, and more recently GROVQUAL have become common parlance among academics and practitioners. Added to the full range of quantitative and qualitative methods available, it quickly becomes clear that the most critical challenge for managers is to identify and implement the most appropriate methods for measuring the quality of the service experience (Ford and Bach, 1997).

## MEASUREMENT TECHNIQUES

Today's hotel manager faces many choices when it comes to measuring customer perceptions of service quality. A full range of measurement techniques is now available for the assessment of service quality, each with its own particular strengths and weaknesses, depending upon what is being measured and why it is being measured. The difficulty is that many of these techniques are too costly, too complicated, or totally inappropriate for what is being measured.

By and large, hoteliers employ a mix of qualitative and quantitative methods, choosing to collect feedback through a combination of observation and/or communication techniques. Qualitative methods include interviews, focus groups, customer role-play, and observation research and, although highly subjective, nonetheless provide an interesting insight into the mind-set of individual customers. Quantitative techniques, on the other hand, collect information on the basis of a predetermined standard and as such are more objective and measurable in nature. In the majority of cases this information is collected by surveys, which can be administered either face-to-face (as in the case of exit surveys), indirectly (by telephone), or simply left for the customer to fill out later (as in the case of room surveys and customer comment cards). Ford and Bach (1997) provide a detailed listing of the many techniques available to managers as well as addressing the relative strengths and weaknesses of each. A summary of these techniques and others along with their principal advantages and disadvantages is provided in Table 10.1.

A number of the more popular techniques shall now be addressed in relation to their suitability to the hotel industry and, where permission has been granted, examples of each will be provided.

### Unobtrusive Observation Measures

Unobtrusive observation measures have been widely applied within the broad tourism sector and recently to assess visitor satisfaction levels with festivals and events (Seaton, 1997). According to Ford and Bach (1997), this is the simplest and least expensive technique to assess service quality in hotel operations. In short, managers are required to take a step back from operational duty in order to observe, map, and analyze the many

TABLE 10.1. Summary of Data Collection Techniques

| Techniques | Principal Advantage | Principal Disadvantage |
|---|---|---|
| Management Observation | No inconvenience to customer | Presence of observer may influence delivery |
| Employee Feedback | Employee knowledge of delivery problems | Employee bias |
| Comment Cards | Suggest company interest in customer opinions | Comments generally reflect extremes |
| Mail Surveys | Ability to gather valid and representative samples | Time lag and effect of memory retention |
| On-Site Personal Interview | Detailed guest feedback | Sample representation |
| Telephone Interviews | Representative and valid sample of target customers | Customer inconvenience |
| Critical Incident Technique | Identification of what is critical to customer | Low response rate |
| Disconfirmation Models | Directs improvement | Administration |
| Focus Groups | Information rich | Symptom identification |
| Mystery Shoppers | Consistent and unbiased | Cost |

interactions that take place daily between the organization and its customers. The principal advantage of this technique is that it can identify real-time service problems and sources of customer inconvenience, which can then be put right on the spot. Observers have a detailed knowledge of their own operations and are therefore quite adept at noticing service problems as well as the causes of these problems. Another great benefit of this method is its minimal inconvenience to the customer, with the majority of observation research being conducted without the customer's knowledge. Quite often it also gives management a greater appreciation of the pressures on frontline employees.

This method has problems, however. In the first instance, management observers require highly specialized training, which may prove both time consuming and expensive. Observation also raises a number of ethical concerns in relation to invasion of privacy. Consequently, many organizations inform both customers and employees that they are being observed for the purposes of quality improvement. Also, employees may underperform because they feel intimidated by the constant pressure of management observation. Thus there may be great benefit in extending the observation role to include frontline employees. Frontline staff may be much more critical of their own roles within the organization, and peer evaluation may be much better received by employees than "yet another ill-informed" management appraisal. This brings us to another very lucrative source of information—employee feedback.

### Employee Feedback

It is very important to realize that much of service quality as perceived by the customer is related to moments when the service supplier and the customer meet face-to-face. More than any other factor it is the quality of our people, in both the front and back of the house, which determine success as defined at this moment of truth. It only makes sense, therefore, that employee feedback of customer perceptions be sought and that employees be used as vehicles for gathering such information.

Most customers feel at ease with frontline service personnel and often like to talk about the service they have received. It is much easier to report a service failure verbally than in writing. This presents a fantastic opportunity for hoteliers to gain firsthand and up-to-the-minute customer feedback. The benefits are clear: problems that are identified can be put right immediately or at least prior to the customer's departure. This not only generates information about the quality of the guest experience, but boosts employee morale in terms of the satisfaction derived from an immediate service recovery. On the other hand, managers need to be aware of the problem of employee bias. All too often what gets reported is only a fraction of what should be reported. There is also a danger that employees will be somewhat selective with the truth.

As a result, many hoteliers are now encouraging frontline staff to solicit and record feedback during their many encounters with customers. This may be done either formally or informally through various interview approaches, as in the case of checkout or bill settlement, or by random sampling. This information may be gathered on a daily or weekly basis by means of one-to-one reporting, departmental interviews, or employee report cards (see Figure 10.3). Above all, it provides a source of instant feedback on customer perceptions which, if they are to be of any use to management, must be acted upon immediately.

### One-to-One Customer Interviews

The customer interview is perhaps one of the least employed, yet most effective techniques for achieving a deeper understanding of customer perceptions of service quality. In the main, such interviews are carefully structured and follow a closely worded script with little room for deviation. The

FIGURE 10.3. Employee Feedback Card Used by the ACCOR Hotel Group in Western Australia to Gather Feedback from Both Employees and Customers

# GUEST EXPERIENCE / EMPLOYEE FEEDBACK RECORD

**DATE:** ........... / ........... / ...........

**DEPARTMENT:**

- ☐ Front Office
- ☐ Engineering
- ☐ Housekeeping
- ☐ Other ...............
- ☐ F&B

**SECTION:** ...............................
(Eg. Room Servicing, Check In, Restaurant - breakfast)

☐ Please tick the appropriate box

**DETAILS:** MAIN PROBLEM / SUCCESS CATEGORY

- ☐ People (e.g., quality of service)
- ☐ Process/Policy (e.g., Timing of service, hotel policy)
- ☐ Equipment (e.g., Cracked plates, computer breakdown)
- ☐ Other (e.g., Hotel surroundings - noisy rooms, stained carpet)

...............................................
...............................................
...............................................
...............................................
...............................................

☐ GUEST EXPERIENCE    or    ☐ EMPLOYEE FEEDBACK

Guest Name: ...................    Employee Name: ...................
Room Number: ...................    Department: ...................

*THANK YOU FOR COMPLETING THIS FORM*
*YOUR EFFORT WILL HELP TO IMPROVE THE SERVICE WE OFFER OUR GUESTS*

*Source:* Reproduced with the permission of the ACCOR Hotel Group, Perth, Western Australia.

great benefit, of course, relates to the richness of the information that may be gathered and the fact that it is current. It also enables the company to set about building a relationship with customers that should have a knock-on effect in itself in terms of retention. The customer will feel valued and is left with an impression that the company really cares for his or her personal well-being.

The major problem with this technique is the time and expense required to conduct such interviews, not to mention the specialized training and customer intrusion issues. As a result, many companies tend to restrict the use of this technique to particular times of the year and to particular types of customer, namely their larger corporate accounts, special events, and individual complainants. Many hotels deem it essential to follow up on good and bad survey results and individual letters of complaint. For instance, the Joondalup Resort Complex in Western Australia makes it a priority to follow up on each and every function held in the resort. The resort liases with all function customers both pre- and postevent to ensure that their needs have been fully met. If a problem becomes apparent, customers are invited to a one-on-one meeting with the property manager to assess the specific nature of their dissatisfaction. Whereas once customers would have been lucky to receive a letter of apology, many managers now realize that this more personal approach allows for a greater chance of recovery and differentiation in the marketplace.

### Focus Groups

It is not uncommon for hotels to issue invitations to their customers to attend focus groups. Having their beginnings in group therapy as used by psychiatrists, these groups are designed to get customers talking in depth and at length about the organization's ability to meet their needs. More specifically, these sessions are designed to ascertain what the customer deems important in terms of quality provision. The underlying premise is that there is safety in numbers and one person's response may become a stimulus for another to contribute. This technique is rather useful in that it involves customers not only in identifying problems but also in their solution, which from a customer's point of view is highly rewarding.

Once again, expense is a problem, especially for the small- to medium-sized enterprise. Hoteliers are normally expected to meet the guest's expenses in traveling to participate in these sessions, not to mention the fee for professional facilitators. It is not unusual, though, for guests to receive an open invitation to attend weekly team improvement meetings. In fact, such invitations are frequently posted in many hotel lobbies. This may be viewed as a more open form of the quality improvement circle, where guests are actively encouraged to contribute and offer suggestions based upon direct experience. The author can testify that he has attended many such sessions and has found them most rewarding indeed.

### Critical Incident Technique

Critical incident is a technique designed to elicit details about services that "particularly dissatisfy or delight customers" (Lovelock, Patterson, and Walker, 1998, p. 137). This information may be collected during one-to-one interviews or, as is more common in the hotel industry, by means of in-house comment cards (see Figure 10.4). Comments from cards and transcripts from interviews are collated to identify common problems or sources of delight. Unlike other qualitative methods of gleaning feedback, customers are not forced to give answers to predetermined potential problems. Rather, this technique seeks to encourage them to record their most memorable incidents from the service experience. According to Hope and Muhlemann (1997) the technique is useful in a number of respects:

- It facilitates the identification of specific attributes of service which have a significant impact upon customers.
- This can be used to redesign the service delivery system around the more important customer-perceived quality attributes.

### Customer Surveys

Surveys are by far the most common and most abused data collection technique employed by the hotel sector. These surveys can be employed on a regular basis, as in the case of guest comment cards, or less regularly, as in the case of the more detailed attribution techniques now being employed. Of importance here is the validity, reliability, and practicability of the particular survey instrument.

### Customer Comment Cards

The more regular survey techniques normally take the form of simple comment cards placed on dining room tables and in guest bedrooms. They can range from the very simple (see Figure 10.5) to the much more complicated (see Figure 10.6). Customers are normally invited to rate the quality of individual attributes of the service experience on a predetermined scale, as well as the overall quality of the service received. In the majority of cases

FIGURE 10.4. An Example of a Critical Incident Card Used by Rydges Hotel, Perth, Western Australia

Impressions are important to us. That's why we'd like to hear what you think about your stay with us. And if you have any suggestions on how you think we could improve things, we'd like to hear them, too. Just jot down your thoughts here, then drop it off at the reception desk. Thank you.

_____

_____

_____

_____

_____

_____

_____

_____

Your name: _____

Room number: _____ Date: _____

*Note:* This card adopts a largely unstructured approach to assessing guests' perceptions of service quality. Reproduced with the permission of Rydges Hotel, Perth, Western Australia.

customers are also invited to offer individual comments on any aspect of the service not covered by the survey.

The major advantage of this scheme is its simplicity in terms of data collection. Once placed, comment cards require no further employee effort or time in terms of administration. As such they are a very cheap means of highlighting repeated service problems and, in particular, problems that hoteliers would otherwise never become aware of. If positive feedback is provided they also present management with an excellent opportunity to acknowledge it to staff, which in turn acts as an excellent incentive to improve performance. Such cards, depending upon where they are placed,

FIGURE 10.5. Typical Comment Card Taken from the Western Australian Restaurant Sector

# YOUR COMMENTS COUNT

DATE: _____ TIME: _____

CAFE: _____

| | 🙂 | 😐 | 🙁 |
|---|---|---|---|
| *QUALITY OF FOOD* | | | |
| *EMPLOYEE COURTESY* | | | |
| *FOOD TASTE* | | | |
| *SPEED OF SERVICE* | | | |
| *MENU / VARIETY* | | | |
| *CLEANLINESS* | | | |
| *VALUE* | | | |
| *HYGIENE* | | | |
| *FOOD PRESENTATION* | | | |
| *AMBIENCE / COMFORT* | | | |

ANY OTHER COMMENTS: - - - - - - - - - - - - - - - - - - - -
- - - - - - - - - - - - - - - - - - - - - - - - - - - - - - - - - - - -
- - - - - - - - - - - - - - - - - - - - - - - - - - - - - - - - - - - -
- - - - - - - - - - - - - - - - - - - - - - - - - - - - - - - - - - - -

*Note:* This card uses a combination of structured and unstructured approaches to assess guests' perceptions.

FIGURE 10.6. Excerpt from a More Detailed Comment Card Used by the Hyatt Regency, Perth, Western Australia

---

## RESTAURANTS

Which restaurant did you dine in during your stay?

(select one) _____

| EXPECTATIONS | Not met | Met | Exceeded | N/A |
|---|---|---|---|---|
| Friendliness of staff | 1 | 2 | 3 | 4 |
| Timeliness of meal | 1 | 2 | 3 | 4 |
| Quality of food | 1 | 2 | 3 | 4 |
| Menu variety | 1 | 2 | 3 | 4 |
| Selection of beverages | 1 | 2 | 3 | 4 |
| Value for money | 1 | 2 | 3 | 4 |
| Atmosphere/Ambience | 1 | 2 | 3 | 4 |

Any comments you would like to make regarding our restaurants.

_____

_____

_____


Would you come back to this restaurant?        q   Yes              q   No

## CHECK OUT

| EXPECTATIONS | Not met | Met | Exceeded | N/A |
|---|---|---|---|---|
| Checked out efficiently | 1 | 2 | 3 | 4 |
| Accuracy of account | 1 | 2 | 3 | 4 |
| Account easy to understand | 1 | 2 | 3 | 4 |
| Account timely | 1 | 2 | 3 | 4 |

Any comments you would like to make regarding your check out.

_____

_____

_____

_____

---

*Note:* This card uses a combination of both direct disconfirmation and unstructured approaches to assess guests' perceptions of service quality. Reproduced with the permission of the Hyatt Regency Hotel, Perth, Western Australia.

also convey a warm, caring attitude to patrons, which is highly conducive to establishing an ongoing relationship with them. Depending upon the simplicity of design they may actually be a pleasure to fill in.

A major disadvantage, however, is their very low return rate. As they rely totally on voluntary customer participation, they are more often than not ignored as clutter. According to Simpson (1997, p. 83), "so many companies have got onto the bandwagon of customer feedback that there is now a customer backlash from being inundated with surveys, question-naires, checklists and the like. They are not responding." It is not uncom-mon therefore to record a response rate as low as 20 percent, which of course is next to meaningless.

In the majority of cases, respondents are either bored, have been de-lighted, or are highly dissatisfied with the service encounter. Thus, those that are collected may not reflect general customer feeling. In recognition of this fact many hoteliers are now offering incentives to guests to encour-age greater participation. Such incentives include free meals, weekend breaks, and/or room discounts during the customer's next stay.

Another serious problem with this technique is the time-lag factor. At best the cards are analyzed weekly, which normally means that by the time managers have gotten around to rectifying recorded problems the custom-er has already moved on. Where appropriate, therefore, and regardless of return rate, cards should be analyzed daily. A common practice in the restaurant sector is for shift leaders to analyze results at the end of a shift. Information regarding service problems is then passed on to the next shift leader so that problems can be resolved within the day.

*Attribution Techniques*

According to Palmer (1998), quality is so complex a concept that it cannot satisfactorily be measured by a series of ad hoc studies. This, and the increasing importance of service quality as a means of gaining compet-itive advantage, has led to the recent development and application of a series of more detailed survey techniques aimed at measuring customer-perceived service quality with the hospitality industry.

The majority of these more detailed quantitative studies have adopted the confirmation-disconfirmation paradigm, which seeks to explore the relationship between a customer's prepurchase expectations and percep-tions of service performance. As consumers evaluate service performance, they typically cannot help but compare that performance to what they expected. In turn these expectations provide a baseline for the assessment of a customer's level of satisfaction. These models contend that service quality can be conceptualized as the difference between what a consumer expects to receive and their perceptions of actual delivery. They hold that product and service performance exceeding some form of standard leads to satisfaction, while performance falling below this standard results in dissatisfaction (Wilkie, 1994; Wells and Prensky, 1996; Oliver, 1996). According to Mowen (1995), this expectancy disconfirmation approach helps explain consumer perceptions of service quality as well as consumer satisfaction judgments.

Researchers have adopted both inferred and direct disconfirmation techniques. The inferred approach seeks to estimate the size of any gap between the customer's expectations and the actual performance received. Expectations and perceptions are measured separately, producing a relative measure of how well the service has performed compared to what the consumer expected. Direct disconfirmation, on the other hand, provides an absolute measure of performance. It is a measure of how the service has performed on the basis of the customer's absolute level of satisfaction or dissatisfaction.

Preeminent among these studies has been the work of Parasuraman, Zeithaml, and Berry (1985) and the development of their SERVQUAL instrument. Their research has concentrated on the belief that service quality is measurable, but only in the eyes of the consumer. They take the view that service is of high quality when customers' expectations are confirmed by subsequent service delivery.

They postulate that, as services are less tangible than goods, the dimensions on which customers form expectations may also be different. Initial qualitative research has led to the identification of five dimensions (tangibles, reliability, responsiveness, assurance and empathy—referred to previously as RATER) on which customers evaluate service quality. If expectancies are disconfirmed on any of these dimensions, satisfaction gaps result, and the customer is likely to record a poor rating of the service. Over the years these researchers have developed their initial qualitative studies into the more comprehensive statistical tool known as SERVQUAL, which is now widely used to measure service quality throughout the services sector.

SERVQUAL has been extensively researched to validate its psychometric properties and while it has attracted criticism for its conceptualization of quality measurement issues, it has nonetheless been applied in a wide variety of sectors (Lewis, 1987; Lee and Hing, 1995; Ryan and Cliff, 1997; Lam, Wong, and Yeung, 1997). It takes the form of a two-part twenty-two-item questionnaire (see Appendix, p. 186), which seeks to estimate customers' preconsumption expectations of service as well as postconsumption perceptions of actual service received. Customers are asked to complete each section of the survey using a seven-point Likert scale that extends from 1 (strongly disagree) to 7 (strongly agree). Measures of service quality can be derived by subtracting the expectation scores from perception scores, which can also be weighted to take account of the relative importance of each quality dimension. In turn, these importance scores allow managers to focus attention where it is likely to have most impact or where it is most needed. The scores across all the questionnaires are summed and averaged to find a score for each question. The results of the questions within each dimension are then averaged to obtain a score for each dimension, which can then be used to highlight how well an organization is performing in light of customer expectations.

The benefits derived from this approach are clear and may be summarized as follows:

- SERVQUAL gives management a clear indication of how the company is performing in the customer's eyes both individually and en masse.
- It helps prioritize customer needs, wants, and expectations by identifying what is most important in the customer's eyes. As stated, this information can be gleaned from the weighting of individual dimensions.
- It allows the organization to set an expected standard of performance that can then be communicated to all staff and patrons.
- It can also identify the existence of any gaps between customers and providers and thereby helps focus improvement efforts by directing organizational energies at closing these gaps.

Each of these benefits can be clearly illustrated by the example shown in Table 10.2, taken from a comparative study conducted by the author in the Northern Ireland tourism sector. The information provided gives a clear indication of how the company is performing across all dimensions.

TABLE 10.2. SERVQUAL Scores

| Dimension | Perceptions | Expectations | Difference Score |
|---|---|---|---|
| Tangibles | 6.37 | 5.83 | 0.54 |
| Assurance | 6.07 | 5.82 | 0.25 |
| Reliability | 6.38 | 6.28 | 0.10 |
| Responsiveness | 5.45 | 6.10 | -0.65 |
| Empathy | 6.66 | 6.08 | 0.58 |

*Source:* O'Neill, 1997.

In addition to prioritizing what is important from the customer's point of view, it also identifies a clear gap in relation to the responsiveness of the service provided. In turn this directed organizational improvement efforts in relation to wait and delivery times.

Over the years, there have been many adaptations of the original SERVQUAL tool to suit the specific operational characteristics of the hospitality environment (Getty and Thompson, 1994; Knutson, Stevens, and Patton, 1995; Walker, 1996; Dowell, Hing, and Leiper, 1998). As a result, such terms as LODGQUAL, LODGSERV, DINESERV, and GROV-QUAL have become common in the industry. Each of these instruments has sought to develop and build upon the original and more generic SERVQUAL tool. In the case of LODGQUAL, Getty and Thompson (1994) identified three basic dimensions of service quality in the lodging industry. The tangibles and reliability dimensions are as previously defined. The authors identified a third dimension, however, contact, which was a composite of SERVQUAL's responsiveness, empathy, and assurance. Their results suggest that these three dimensions are "indistinguishable and, in general, represent the patron's contact experience with the employees" (Getty and Thompson, 1994, p. 8). LODGSERV (Knutson et al., 1990) is also built on the same five dimensions as SERVQUAL but contains questions specifically tailored to the lodging industry. Further work by the authors led to the development of DINESERV, which was tailored to better capture the uniqueness of the dining experience.

From an academic viewpoint, the original SERVQUAL instrument has been challenged on a number of fronts (Palmer, O'Neill, and Beggs, 1998). Questions have been raised about the dimensions of SERVQUAL and whether they are consistent across industries, its psychometric properties, and how expectations are formed (Babakus and Boller, 1992; Brown, Churchill, and Peter, 1993; Zeithaml, Berry, and Parasuraman, 1993). While these criticisms have generated quite substantial debate among academics, they are not addressed in any great detail in this chapter. Industrialists, it seems, are more concerned with the more practical methodological issues that present difficulty from an administration point of view. For example, some researchers have suggested better wording for some of the scale items (Bolton and Drew, 1991). Customers find it hard to differentiate between many of the scale items, particularly when "negative forms of questions are used" (Hope and Muhlemann, 1997, p. 288). For example, consider the following: "the company strives to get it right the first time" and "the company gets it right the first time."

There has also been debate about whether it is practical to ask consumers about their expectations of a service immediately before consumption and their perceptions of performance immediately after. Customers may become tired or distressed as a result of being asked to complete both surveys. Some analyses have therefore used combined single scales to measure gaps (Carman, 1990; Babakus and Boller, 1992). It has been suggested that expectations may not exist or be clear enough in respondents' minds to act as a benchmark against which perceptions are assessed (Iacobucci, Grayson, and Omstrom, 1994). Consequently customers have a tendency to circle "strongly agree" or "very important" for all aspects. Furthermore, it is argued that expectations are only formed as a result of previous service encounters, that is, perceptions feed directly into expectations (Kahneman and Miller, 1986).

For all of these reasons many researchers now believe that a more direct approach to the measurement of service quality is now needed. It is felt that performance-only-based measures of service quality may be an improved means of measuring the service quality construct (Churchill and Surprenant, 1982; Bolton and Drew, 1991; Cronin and Taylor, 1992). This has led to the development and application of a more direct form of disconfirmation technique such as SERVPERF. Like SERVQUAL, this approach requires the customer to rate a provider's service performance on a five-point Likert scale ranging from (1) strongly disagree to (5) strongly agree. Unlike SERVQUAL, however, it does not seek to estimate difference scores; rather, it seeks to assess consumers' postconsumption perceptions only. As such, it is an absolute rating of customer attitudes toward service quality.

According to Hope and Muhlemann (1997) this approach overcomes some of the problems raised regarding SERVQUAL, namely: raising expectations, administration of the two parts of the questionnaire, and the statistical properties of difference scores. Taking a single measure of service performance is seen to circumvent all of these issues. It is felt, however, that from an operational point of view, much useful information is lost when performance-only measures are taken. This can be clearly demonstrated through the example shown in Table 10.3.

Following the administration of SERVQUAL, it is clear that tangibility is the dimension of the service encounter furthest from meeting customer expectations. It can also be seen that the reliability dimension recorded the highest expectation rating, which is in line with other studies that the author has conducted and which no doubt confirms the relative importance of reliable service to the majority of customers.

From an operational standpoint this information highlights the need for quality improvement efforts in all areas, but most specifically in relation to the more tangible aspects of the service encounter. If a performance-only measure were taken, tangibles would still top the list of quality improve-

TABLE 10.3. Inferred and Direct Disconfirmation Scores

| Dimension | Perceptions | Expectations | Difference Score |
|---|---|---|---|
| Tangibles | 2.15 | 4.64 | -2.49 |
| Assurance | 6.74 | 4.85 | 1.89 |
| Reliability | 6.49 | 5.82 | 0.67 |
| Responsiveness | 6.21 | 4.26 | 1.95 |
| Empathy | 5.96 | 4.62 | 1.34 |

*Source:* Gabbie and O'Neill, 1997.

ment, but the order of the other dimensions would change, placing reliability as the second most important factor from the customer's point of view. As a consequence, the prioritization of any organizational improvement effort may be wrong and even misdirected.

Having worked with both techniques, the author believes they are beyond the concern of the majority of hotel operators, who are more interested in the practicalities of the tool and its ability to provide timely and relevant customer feedback and assist with quality improvement. It is not surprising to note therefore that neither technique has been widely applied within the hospitality industry. They have mostly been used as part of some academic research exercise. It should also be borne in mind that many industrialists do not have the required level of expertise to administer and/or analyze the data from such quantitative techniques. As a result, they are required to bring in an outside body who normally charges quite a large consulting fee. Thus, cost is also a factor.

## CONCLUSION

Galileo once wrote "count what is countable, measure what is measurable, and what is not measurable make measurable" (Edvardsson, Thomasson, and Ovretveit, 1994, p. 178). No business today can afford to ignore the customer. There is simply too much choice within the wider competitive environment. If customers are not already, then they must become the focal point of all organizational effort. More than at any other time in recent business history their satisfaction is critical to future corporate survival. In turn, this will be determined by an organization's ability to deliver consistently on the service quality front.

Gone are the days when organizations could differentiate on the basis of their product offerings alone. Gone are the days when organizations determined their own levels of service and quality. Gone also are the days when the provision of customer service was seen as something that only the "service industries" did. What is clear is that whether production or service oriented, organizations from all economic sectors are now turning to service quality as the only remaining means of differentiating their business offering, turning one-time customers into longer-term clients. This requires an approach to quality improvement that concentrates on the continual measurement of service quality as perceived by the customer. In short, what gets measured gets done, completed, and continually improved upon.

### *APPENDIX: SERVQUAL INSTRUMENT*

Please complete Part A by indicating your expectations of hotels *in general.* Then complete Part B indicating your perceptions of this hotel *in particular.* Please answer on a scale from 1 (strongly disagree with the statement) to 7 (strongly agree).

[PART A]

Directions: please complete the following questionnaire pertaining to service quality. If you feel the features mentioned in each statement are essential in your judgment of the hotel, please circle 7. However if you feel the features mentioned are of little importance, please circle number 1.

|     |     | Strongly Disagree | Strongly Agree |
| --- | --- | --- | --- |
| (1) | An excellent hotel will have modern-looking equipment, e.g., dining facility, bar facility, crockery, cutlery, etc. | 1...2...3...4...5...6...7 | |
| (2) | The physical facilities, e.g., buildings, signs, dining room decor, lighting, carpet, etc., at an excellent hotel will be visually appealing. | 1...2...3...4...5...6...7 | |
| (3) | Staff at an excellent hotel will appear neat, e.g., uniform, grooming, etc. | 1...2...3...4...5...6...7 | |
| (4) | Materials associated with the service, e.g., pamphlets, statements, table wine, serviettes will be visually appealing in an excellent hotel. | 1...2...3...4...5...6...7 | |
| (5) | When an excellent hotel promises to do something by a certain time, it will do so. | 1...2...3...4...5...6...7 | |
| (6) | When patrons have a problem, an excellent hotel will show genuine interest in solving it, e.g., an error in a bill. | 1...2...3...4...5...6...7 | |
| (7) | An excellent hotel will perform service right the first time. | 1...2...3...4...5...6...7 | |
| (8) | An excellent hotel will provide its services at the time it promises to do so. | 1...2...3...4...5...6...7 | |
| (9) | An excellent hotel will insist on error-free service. | 1...2...3...4...5...6...7 | |
| (10) | Staff at an excellent hotel will tell patrons exactly when services will be performed. | 1...2...3...4...5...6...7 | |

| (11) | Staff at an excellent hotel will give prompt service to patrons. | 1...2...3...4...5...6...7 |
|---|---|---|
| (12) | Staff at an excellent hotel will always be willing to help patrons. | 1...2...3...4...5...6...7 |
| (13) | Staff at an excellent hotel will never be too busy to respond. | 1...2...3...4...5...6...7 |
| (14) | The behavior of staff at an excellent hotel will instill confidence in patrons. | 1...2...3...4...5...6...7 |
| (15) | Patrons of an excellent hotel will feel safe in their transactions. | 1...2...3...4...5...6...7 |
| (16) | Staff at an excellent hotel will be consistently courteous with patrons. | 1...2...3...4...5...6...7 |
| (17) | Staff at an excellent hotel will have the knowledge to answer patrons' requests. | 1...2...3...4...5...6...7 |
| (18) | Staff at an excellent hotel will give patrons individualized attention. | 1...2...3...4...5...6...7 |
| (19) | An excellent hotel will have opening hours convenient to all of its patrons. | 1...2...3...4...5...6...7 |
| (20) | An excellent hotel will have staff who give its patrons personal attention. | 1...2...3...4...5...6...7 |
| (21) | An excellent hotel will have the patrons' best interests at heart. | 1...2...3...4...5...6...7 |
| (22) | The staff of an excellent hotel will understand the specific needs of their patrons. | 1...2...3...4...5...6...7 |

|  |  | Strongly Disagree | Strongly Agree |
|---|---|---|---|
| **[PART B]** | | | |
| (1) | The hotel has modern-looking equipment. | 1...2...3...4...5...6...7 | |
| (2) | The physical facilities at the hotel are visually appealing. | 1...2...3...4...5...6...7 | |
| (3) | Staff at the hotel appear neat. | 1...2...3...4...5...6...7 | |
| (4) | Materials associated with the service are visually appealing. | 1...2...3...4...5...6...7 | |
| (5) | When the hotel promised to do something by a certain time, it did it. | 1...2...3...4...5...6...7 | |
| (6) | When patrons have problems, the hotel shows a genuine interest in solving them. | 1...2...3...4...5...6...7 | |
| (7) | The hotel performs the service right the first time. | 1...2...3...4...5...6...7 | |
| (8) | The hotel provides its services at the time it promises to do so. | 1...2...3...4...5...6...7 | |
| (9) | The hotel insists on error-free service. | 1...2...3...4...5...6...7 | |
| (10) | Staff at the hotel were able to tell patrons exactly when services would be performed. | 1...2...3...4...5...6...7 | |
| (11) | Staff at the hotel give prompt service to the patrons. | 1...2...3...4...5...6...7 | |
| (12) | Staff at the hotel are always willing to help patrons. | 1...2...3...4...5...6...7 | |
| (13) | Staff at the hotel are never too busy to respond to patrons. | 1...2...3...4...5...6...7 | |
| (14) | The behavior of staff instills confidence in patrons. | 1...2...3...4...5...6...7 | |
| (15) | Patrons of the hotel feel safe in their transactions. | 1...2...3...4...5...6...7 | |
| (16) | Staff at the hotel are consistently courteous with patrons. | 1...2...3...4...5...6...7 | |

| | | |
|---|---|---|
| (17) | Staff at the hotel have the knowledge to answer patrons. | 1...2...3...4...5...6...7 |
| (18) | The hotel gives patrons individualized attention. | 1...2...3...4...5...6...7 |
| (19) | The hotel has opening hours convenient to all of its patrons. | 1...2...3...4...5...6...7 |
| (20) | The hotel has staff who give its patrons personalized attention. | 1...2...3...4...5...6...7 |
| (21) | The hotel has the patrons' best interests at heart. | 1...2...3...4...5...6...7 |
| (22) | The staff at the hotel understand the specific needs of their patrons. | 1...2...3...4...5...6...7 |

# REFERENCES

Babakus, E. and Boller, G. (1992). An Empirical Assessment of the SERVQUAL Scale. *Journal of Business Research,* 24 (May): 253-268.

Bank, J. (1992). *The Essence of Total Quality Management.* London: Prentice Hall.

Berry, L.L. (1983). Relationship Marketing. In L.L. Berry et al. (eds.), *Emerging Perspectives in Services Marketing.* Chicago: American Marketing Association.

Berry, L.L. (1997). Multiple Method Listening: The Building of a Service Quality Information System. Proceedings of the Academy of Marketing Conference (Marketing Without Borders), Manchester Metropolitan University, July 8-10.

Berry, L.L., Parasuraman, A., and Zeithaml, V. (1985). Quality Counts in Services Too. *Business Horizons,* 28 (1): 44-52.

Berry, L.L., Parasuraman, A., and Zeithaml, V. (1988). The Service Quality Puzzle. *Business Horizons,* 28 (5): 35-43.

Bitner, M.J. (1990). Evaluating Service Encounters: The Effects of Physical Surroundings and Employee Responses. *Journal of Marketing,* 54 (April): 69-82.

Bolton, R. and Drew, J.H. (1991). A Multistage Model of Customers' Assessments of Service Quality and Value. *Journal of Consumer Research,* 17 (4): 375-384.

Brown, T., Churchill, G., and Peter, J.P. (1993). Research Note: Improving the Measurement of Service Quality. *Journal of Retailing,* 69 (Spring): 127-139.

Carman, J.M. (1990): Consumer Perceptions of Service Quality: An Assessment of the SERVQUAL Dimensions. *Journal of Retailing,* 66 (1): 33-55.

Christopher, M., Payne, A., and Ballantyne, D. (1991). *Relationship Marketing: Bringing Quality, Customer Service and Marketing Together.* Oxford: Butterworth Heinemann.

Churchill, G.A. and Suprenant, C. (1982). An Investigation into the Determinants of Customer Satisfaction. *Journal of Marketing Research,* 19: 491-504.

Cook, S. (1997). *Customer Care,* Second Edition. London: Kogan Page.

Cronin, J.J. and Taylor, S.A. (1992). Measuring Service Quality: A Re-examination and Extension. *Journal of Marketing,* 56 (July): 55-68.

Crosby, P.B. (1984). *Quality Without Tears.* New York: New American Library.

Dowell, R., Hing, N., and Leiper, N. (1998). GROVQUAL: A New Research Tool for Measuring Excessive Service in Hospitality. Working Paper for the Australian Tourism and Hospitality Research Conference, Griffith University, Goldcoast, Queensland, Australia, February 11-14.

Edvardsson, B., Thomasson, B., and Ovretveit, J. (1994). *Quality of Service: Making It Really Work.* London: McGraw-Hill.

Fitsimmons, J. and Maurer, G. (1991). A Walk Through Audit to Improve Restaurant Performance. *Cornell Hotel and Restaurant Administration Quarterly,* 31 (4): 94-99.

Ford, R.C. and Bach, S.A. (1997). Measuring Hotel Service Quality: Tools for Gaining the Competitive Edge. *Florida International University Hospitality Review,* 15 (1, Spring): 83-95.

Gabbie, O. and O'Neill, M. (1997). SERVQUAL and the Northern Ireland Hotel Sector: A Comparative Analysis. *Managing Service Quality,* 7 (1): 43-49.

Garvin, D.A. (1987). Competing on the Eight Dimensions of Quality. *Harvard Business Review,* 65 (6): 101-109.

Getty, J.M. and Thompson, K.N. (1994). The Relationship Between Quality, Satisfaction and Recommending Behaviour in Lodging Decisions. *Journal of Hospitality and Leisure Marketing,* 2 (3): 3-22.

Gronroos, C. (1983). *Strategic Management and Marketing in the Service Sector,* Report No. 83-104, Swedish School of Economics and Business Administration, Helsingfors.

Gronroos, C. (1984). *Service Management and Marketing.* Lexington, MA: Lexington Books.

Gronroos, C. (1988). Service Quality: The Six Certeria of Good Perceived Service Quality. *Review of Business,* 9 (3): 10-13.

Gronroos, C. (1990). *Service Management and Marketing: Managing the Moments of Truth in Service Competition.* Lexington, MA: Lexington Books.

Gwynne, A.L., Devlin, J., and Ennew, C.T. (1998). Service Quality and Customer Satisfaction: A Longitudinal Analysis. *The British Academy of Marketing Annual Conference,* Sheffield Business School, Sheffield Hallam University, July 8-10, 1998: 186-191.

Hope, C. and Muhlemann, A. (1997). *Service Operations Management.* Prentice Hall.

Hudson, S. and Shephard, G.W.H. (1998). Measuring Service Quality at Tourist Destinations: An Application of Importance-Performance Analysis to an Alpine Ski Resort. *Journal of Travel and Tourism Marketing,* 7 (3): 61-77.

Iacobucci, D., Grayson, K.A., and Omstrom, O.L. (1994). The Calculus of Service Quality and Customer Satisfaction: Theoretical and Empirical Differentiation and Integration. In T.A. Swartz, D.E. Bowen, and S.W. Brown (Eds.), *Advances in Services Marketing and Management,* Third Edition (pp. 1-68), Greenwich, CT: JAI Press.

Juran, J.M. (1982). *Upper Management and Quality.* New York: Juran Institute.

Kahneman, D. and Miller, D.T. (1986). Norm Theory: Comparing Reality to Its Alternatives. *Psychological Review,* 93: 136-153.

Knutson, B.J. (1988). Frequent Travellers: Making Them Happy and Bringing Them Back. *Cornell Hotel and Restaurant Administration Quarterly,* 29 (1): 83-87.

Knutson, B.J., Stevens, P., and Patton, M. (1995). DINESERV: Measuring Service Quality in Quick Service, Casual/Theme and Fine Dining Restaurants. *Journal of Hospitality and Leisure Marketing,* 3 (2): 35-44.

Knutson, B.J., Stevens, P., Wullaert, C., Patton, M., and Yokoyama, F. (1990). The Service Scoreboard: A Service Quality Measurement Tool for the Hospitality Industry. *Hospitality Education and Research Journal,* 14 (2): 413-420.

Lam, T., Wong, A., and Yeung, S. (1997). Measuring Service Quality in Clubs: An Application of the SERVQUAL Instrument. *Australian Journal of Hospitality Management,* 4 (1): 7-14.

Lee, Y.L. and Hing, N. (1995). Measuring Quality in Restaurant Operations: An Application of the SERVQUAL Instrument. *International Journal of Hospitality Management,* 14 (3-4): 293-310.

Lewis, R.C. (1987). The Measurement of Gaps in the Quality of Hotel Services. *International Journal of Hospitality Management,* 6 (2): 83-88.

Lovelock, C.H., Patterson, P.G., and Walker, R.H. (1998). *Services Marketing.* Sydney: Prentice Hall.

McAlexander, J.H., Kaldenberg, D.O., and Koenig, H. (1994). Service Quality Measurement. *Journal of Health Care Marketing,* 14 (3, Fall): 34-39.

Morgan, M. (1996). *Marketing for Leisure and Tourism.* London: Prentice Hall.

Mowen, J.C. (1995). *Consumer Behaviour,* Fourth Edition. Englewood Cliffs, NJ: Prentice Hall.

Oliver, R.L. (1980): A Cognitive Model of the Antecedents and Consequences of Satisfaction Decisions. *Journal of Marketing Research,* 17 (November): 460-469.

Oliver, R.L. (1981). Measurement and Evaluation of Satisfaction Processes in Retail Settings. *Journal of Retailing,* 57: 25-48.

Oliver, R.L. (1993). Cognitive, Affective, and Attribute Bases of the Satisfaction Response. *Journal of Consumer Research,* 20: 418-430.

Oliver, R.L. (1996). *Satisfaction: A Behavioral Perspective on the Consumer.* London: McGraw-Hill.

O'Neill, M. (1997). Investing in People: A Perspective from the Northern Ireland Tourism Sector. *Managing Service Quality,* 7 (6): 292-306.

Palmer, A. (1998). *Principles of Services Marketing,* Second Edition. London: McGraw-Hill.

Palmer, A., O'Neill, M.A., and Beggs, W.R. (1998). Time Delay Effects of Service Quality Measurement: An Exploratory Empirical Study, Academy of Marketing Annual Conference (Adding Value Through Marketing), Sheffield Hallam University, July 8-10, 1998.

Parasuraman, A., Zeithaml, Y.A., and Berry, L.L. (1985). A Conceptual Model of Service Quality and Its Implications for Future Research. *Journal of Marketing,* 49 (Fall): 41-50.

Parasuraman, A., Zeithaml, V.A., and Berry, L.L. (1988). SERVQUAL: A Multiple Item Scale for Measuring Consumer Perceptions of Service Quality. *Journal of Retailing,* 64 (1): 12-37.

Ramaswamy, R. (1996*). Design and Management of Service Processes: Keeping Customers for Life* (pp. 362-363). Reading, U.K.: Addison Wesley.

Ryan, C. and Cliff, A. (1997). Do Travel Agencies Measure Up to Customer Expectations? An Empirical Investigation of Travel Agencies' Service Quality as Measured by SERVQUAL. *Journal of Travel and Tourism Marketing,* 6 (2): 1-28.

Saleh, F. and Ryan, C. (1991). Analysing Service Quality in the Hospitality Industry Using the SERVQUAL Model. *The Service Industries Journal,* 11 (July): 324-343.

Seaton, A. (1997). Unobtrusive Observational Measures As a Qualitative Extension of Visitor Surveys at Festivals and Events: Mass Observation Revisited. *Journal of Travel Research,* 35 (4): 25-30.

Simpson, S.N. (1997). *Service Into Profit.* Perth, Australia: TAFE Publications of Western Australia.

Sung, H.S., Yeong, H.L., Yonghee, P., and Geon, C.S. (1997). The Impact of Consumer Involvement on the Consumers' Perception of Service Quality— Focusing on the Korean Hotel Industry. *Journal of Travel and Tourism Marketing,* 6 (2): 33-52.

Tenner, A.R. and DeToro, I.J. (1992). *Total Quality Management: Three Steps to Continuous Improvement.* Cambridge, MA: Addison-Wesley.

Tse, D.K. and Wilton, P.C. (1988). Models of Consumer Satisfaction Formation: An Extension. *Journal of Marketing Research,* 25 (May): 204-212.

Van Der Wagen, L. (1994). *Building Quality Service with Competency Based Human Resource Management.* Chatswood, Australia: Butterworth-Heinneman.

Walker, R.H. (1996). Towards Identifying How Visitors to Tasmania Define and Assess Service Quality in the Hospitality Industry. *Australian Journal of Hospitality Management,* 3 (2): 27-39.

Wells, W. and Prensky, D. (1996). *Consumer Behavior.* New York: John Wiley.

Wilkie, W. (1994). *Consumer Behavior,* Third Edition. New York: John Wiley.

Witt, C. and Muhlemann, A. (1995). Service Quality in Airlines. *Tourism Economics,* 1 (1): 33-49.

Zeithaml, V.A., Berry L., and Parasuraman, A. (1993). The Nature and Determinants of Customer Expectations of Service. *Journal of the Academy of Marketing Science,* 21 (1): 1-12.

Zeithaml, V.A., Parasuraman, A., and Berry, L. (1990). *Delivering Quality Service: Balancing Customer Perceptions and Expectations.* New York: The Free Press.

Zemke, R. and Schaaf, D. (1990). *The Service Edge.* New York: Penguin.

# Chapter 11

# Managing Service Failure Through Recovery

Beverley Sparks

## *INTRODUCTION*

The tourism and hospitality industry offers a range of services, including accommodation, food and beverage, transport, tours, and attractions. Like all service industries, the services provided within the tourism and hospitality sector have several things in common, which distinguish them from the products offered by manufacturing and other commercial sectors. For example, services are relatively intangible, and they are characterized by simultaneous production and consumption. Thus, it is difficult to observe tourism and hospitality services in advance and even harder to "try before you buy." The provision of services is often immediate and spontaneous. Successful service provision requires a matching of expectations and behaviors, a task that is difficult to achieve under conditions of time pressure and customer variability. For all of these reasons, achieving zero defects is quite difficult and, inevitably, service failures sometimes occur.

This chapter focuses upon the topic of service failure and recovery, an area that has only received limited attention in the hospitality and tourism literature. To get a detailed understanding of this complex topic, a facet analysis is presented and discussed. A model illustrating the process of service failure, recovery, and outcomes is depicted, and implications for services management, marketing, and research are discussed.

## *FACET ANALYSIS*

Service provision, failure, and recovery are multifaceted processes. In an effort to gain a deeper understanding of the various components of these processes, a facet analysis has been conducted and is presented in Table 11.1. This involves an attempt to identify and systematize the differ-

## TABLE 11.1. Facets and Types of Elements

| First-level facet | Second-level facet | Third-level facet | Examples |
|---|---|---|---|
| FAILURE | Omission | | Tour is canceled |
| | Commission | Quantity | Too few seats at table |
| | | Quality/manner | Dirty room |
| | | Timing | Flight delay |
| | | Location | Lost luggage |
| | | Agency | Chef's night off |
| | | Cost | Wrong price |
| CONTEXT | Cultural | | Norms regarding forms of address |
| | Organizational | Policies | Policy about handling service breakdowns |
| | | Structure and size | Small family business versus large bureaucracy |
| | | Management philosophy | The customer is always right |
| | | Human Resource Management | Training programs |
| | Physical | Architecture, temperature, furnishing, music, tidiness | Poor soundproofing |
| | Psychosocial | Number, groupings, relationships of people present | Large, noisy party |
| | Financial | High price/low price | Hidden costs |
| | Temporal | Daily, weekly, seasonal | Time of day, season, day of week, peak/off peak |
| PERSONAL | Psychological | Mood | |
| | | Values | |
| | Demographics | Education | |
| | | Age | |
| | | Gender | |
| | | Race | |
| | | Occupation | |
| PROCESS | Overt | Verbal | |
| | | Nonverbal | |
| | Covert | Attribution theory | |
| | | Distributive, interactive, and procedural judgments | |
| RESPONSE | Strategy | Recovery | Replacement, compensation, apology |
| | | Nonrecovery | Denial, avoidance |
| CONSEQUENCES | Immediate | Customer satisfaction | |
| | | Customer complaints | |
| | Long term | Word of mouth | |
| | | Loyalty | |

ent aspects of a target phenomenon. It includes a breakdown of the service failure process, the context in which the failure occurs, personal factors influencing failure and recovery, process factors, responses to failure, and consequences of failure and recovery. Each of these broad facets is broken down into more specific second-level subfacets and, where appropriate, third-level facets and examples are given.

## CAUSES OF SERVICE FAILURE

The topic of service failure has received limited attention in the literature, and no clear definition of precisely what "failure" means is evident. This contrasts with the broader services marketing and hospitality literature, where considerable focus has been given to issues of service quality or customer satisfaction (see Bojanic and Rosen, 1994; Brown, Fisk, and Bittner, 1994; Knudson et al., 1990). As discussed in other chapters, the general consensus that emerges from this literature is that customer satisfaction and service quality should be defined in terms of customers' perceptions. Hence, for the purposes of this chapter, service failure or breakdown will be defined as that which does not meet the customer's expectations. It is the customer's perception of service failure that is critical, not whether the service provider was responsible, nor whether the perceptions are fair and reasonable.

As shown in Table 11.1, failure can occur due to elements of the organization, other customers, or the actual customer, or because of some combination of or interaction between these agents. In addition, failures may be categorized as occurring due to error of either omission or commission. Failure as a result of omission means that some part of the service offering is not given. For instance, a particular service is not available. In contrast, failure as a result of commission occurs when the service is delivered but does not meet the expected standards. Although not shown in Table 11.1, service failures usually involve either core or peripheral activities (Iacobucci, Grayson, and Ostrom, 1994). The core service breakdowns may include occurrences such as a hotel room not being ready, or a steak being cooked well done when requested rare. Peripheral activities that may contribute to a perceived breakdown of service include a lack of interpersonal skills (e.g., friendliness) on the part of the service provider. Finally, failures may vary across a range of other dimensions including severity, duration, frequency, and avoidability. The following discussion is organized around the causes of service failure, and other dimensions of failure are mentioned in passing only.

## Omission

Service failures sometimes occur due to nonavailability. For instance, certain dishes are advertised on a restaurant's menu but are no longer available. Alternatively, failure may occur if critical details of the service are not provided to the customer at the time of sale. For example, a customer books a hotel room and on arrival finds the property is in the midst of renovation and was not informed. A cancelled flight or a room service meal that does not arrive are other examples of service failures due to omission.

## Commission

The largest proportion of failures arise when a service is delivered but does not meet the customer's expectations. Six types of service failure errors of commission can be distinguished, as described in the sections that follow.

### Quantity

Service failures frequently involve incorrect quantities. For instance, the wrong number of seats are reserved for a restaurant booking or the wrong number of coffees are served. In most instances, failures of excessive quantity are inconvenient, but are less serious than failures that involve insufficient quantity.

### Quality of the Product

In tourism and hospitality settings, most service failures relate to the quality of service received. As indicated previously, failures of service quality may relate to either core or peripheral aspects of service. First, core aspects include all that is central to the service, such as the meal served at a restaurant, the safe transport between two airports provided by an airline, or the provision of accommodation at a hotel. Customers are likely to perceive service to have broken down if the steak is tough or their flight is unsafe. In the case of a hotel, cleanliness, bed comfort, and functioning of appliances within the room are often key indicators of the core product quality. Research on service quality has found that reliability of the core service is an especially important determinant of customer evaluations (see Parasuraman, Berry, and Zeithaml, 1991).

Peripheral aspects include all that is tangential to the core service, particularly the interpersonal relations between the service provider and customer. The service encounter between customer and provider can be conceptualized as a largely ritualized event based on shared norms appropriate to the situation (e.g., politeness, smiling). Within the service encounter, it can be expected that the service provider and the customer will engage in a range of behaviors determined partly by the situation. Central to the encounter is the use of interactional and communication strategies, which can enhance or detract from the effectiveness of the service delivery. If these peripheral activities are not carried out effectively the customer may perceive a breakdown in the service offering. Examples of factors that could contribute to a breakdown include a moody or unhelpful receptionist or waiter, ignoring the customer during the waiting process, or deflecting responsibility and sending the customer to another department (Kelley, Hoffman, and Davis, 1993). Similarly, Keaveney (1995) found that many service failures were attributed to some aspect of the service employees' behavior or attitudes such as being uncaring, impolite, or unresponsive. In each case it is the quality of the service that has suffered.

## Timing

A common cause of service failure relates to timing issues. Most timing problems can be categorized as either too slow (delays or wait times) or too fast (inappropriate timing). For instance, in a study of restaurant patrons, 38 percent of respondents indicated failures as attributable to time delays (Sparks, 1998). Timing failures also include waiting in line to check in or out of a hotel. As mentioned, not only do delays contribute to failures, but poor timing in general is also an important problem. For instance, a timing failure occurs in a restaurant when waiters bring out the main course before the customers have finished their appetizer.

## Location

Service may fail due to what may be termed location issues. For instance, a common failure in aircraft services is missing luggage. Bejou, Edvardsson, and Rakowski (1996) report lost luggage as a major failure cited by customers in a study of airline passengers. Similarly, luggage or room service being delivered to the wrong room in a hotel is likely to be construed as a failure. Other complaints voiced by customers include taxi drivers who take a longer route than necessary to get to a hotel or get lost trying to find the assigned hotel. In each case, the service has been provided, but not in the expected location.

## Agency

Sometimes a service may fail if the normal or expected provider is not there to deliver it. For instance, a regular customer at a restaurant who always has the same server may experience a failure simply because that person is not present. Another example could be a couple selecting a particular restaurant because of the great things they have heard about the chef, only to find it is that particular chef's night off. Similarly, customers who always use a particular agent to manage their travel plans may experience a failure if that person is not available.

## Cost

Another common problem involves pricing or cost. A failure may occur if an account has been incorrectly added up. Similarly, misquoted charges for a service, such as a hotel room, are quite possible. Extra charges of which the customer was unaware may also give rise to a service failure of this type. In a study conducted by Keaveney (1995) billing problems were cited as a major category of service failures.

## SOURCES OF SERVICE FAILURE

This section examines three potential courses of failure: the organization, the customer, and other customers. In reality, many service failures occur because of a combination of actions attributable to more than one of these sources.

### Organizational Factors

Sometimes organizational factors may contribute to a service failure. Organizations frequently contribute to service breakdowns by creating false expectations in their customers' minds and/or their unwillingness to invest in the resources necessary to deliver the expected service. Indeed, Kelley, Hoffman, and Davis (1993), in a study of the retail industry, found failure occurred for a variety of reasons that can be classified as organizationally driven. For instance, policies were perceived by customers as inequitable, or service was slow or unavailable due to understaffing or poor training. In a study conducted on the restaurant industry, unclear policies, such as restaurants not accepting a particular credit card, led to perceptions of failure (Hoffman, Kelley and Rotalsky, 1995).

Other management decisions, for example, the number of staff per shift, may affect service delivery and recovery. Similarly, a lack of training or a failure to take responsibility for the recovery process may add to the severity of a service failure. For example, consider the following story, which deals with an airline company's policy on baggage damage claims:

A traveler took a plane from one city to the next, collected his luggage, including a guitar, and drove four hours to his home. On unpacking, he discovered damage to his guitar, which had been marked "fragile." On calling the airline he was told to send a letter and a quote for repairs or replacement to a city address in another state. He took this advice and sent the documentation. After four weeks and no response, he phoned the airline company and was told to call another number, and then yet another number. Finally he spoke to a claims officer who informed him he should have reported the damage within seventy-two hours and that he needed documentation proving he flew on that flight. Furthermore, although he was not likely to be able to make a claim, he was informed that if he wanted to "pursue the matter," he needed to bring the guitar to the airport where he landed (a four-hour drive) to arrange an inspection of the damaged item.

In this case, conflicting information and continual barriers, including being passed from one company representative to another, served to increase the customer's dissatisfaction with the company.

### Customer Actions

The customer can also contribute to service failure by, for instance, making an erroneous booking or by misunderstanding a special offer. In addition, as service becomes more automated (e.g., self-checkout), there is a greater probability of customers themselves contributing to a service failure situation. For instance, with electronic airline ticketing, customers need to ensure they have photo identification with them to check in and get their boarding passes. If the customer fails to have such identification, it can cause a serious failure in the service system.

### Other Customers

Although not well documented, evidence exists to suggest other customers can contribute to service failures. For instance, noisy customers "partying on" until the early hours of the morning in the next hotel room may well mean that the service promise of a pleasant night's sleep is not met. Similarly, airlines report problems with customers who consume too much alcohol and then prove a nuisance, detracting from other customers' experience of their flight. In addition, mixing nonsmoking customers with smoking customers may result in failed service. As Zeithaml and Bitner (1996) have pointed out, other customers may cause delays, display disruptive behavior, or cause unpleasant crowding. As an example, the following story illustrates how other customers may exacerbate a service failure situation.

> A traveler reported an incident following a long-haul flight (seventeen hours). The traveler was required to transfer to another plane on arrival and proceeded to the check-in point for seat allocation. On arrival, most counters had long queues, so the traveler lined up with the other customers. A check-in counter in the next line opened and a customer from the rear of the queue pushed forward to take the front position. Several customers complained and voiced their annoyance.

In this instance, a fellow customer violated norms of polite behavior and caused other customers to experience even further delays.

## CONTEXTUAL FACETS OF SERVICE FAILURE

Under this heading, consideration is given to several facets of the situation or context in which the service failure occurs. These contextual factors may be relevant to the failure in a variety of ways: they may contribute to the failure, moderate the impact of the failure, affect the response to the failure, and so on. Hence, the context in which service takes place will influence not only the service delivery but also the recovery process. Relevant contextual subfacets include cultural factors, organizational factors, physical conditions, psychosocial factors, financial factors, and temporal conditions.

### Cultural Factors

All service provision occurs within a cultural setting. Cultural factors may impact on perceptions of failure and on acceptable recovery tactics. For example, cultural background may influence expectations regarding service and may determine the type of complaint made. Also, tourists may be reluctant to complain about substandard service as they may feel less self-assured or competent in a foreign country. The effectiveness of a recovery tactic may also be reduced when dealing with customers from foreign countries, especially if language barriers are present. Indeed, one Australian general manager of a hotel reported:

> Japanese customers rarely complain when they stay at our hotel. However, if something isn't up to standard you certainly hear about it from the travel agent once the customer has returned home. . . .

And there is an expectation that the problem is properly fixed. As an example, one tour agent who received a complaint that one of our spa baths wasn't operating expected that we immediately go through the entire (400-room) hotel and check each spa. This is done in the interest of future customers. (personal communication, Greg Cox, General Manager, Parkroyal Surfers Paradise)

Hence, cultural factors may contribute to service failure and influence the service recovery process.

### Organizational Factors

Most tourism and hospitality services are delivered within a broader organizational context. Experiences associated with obtaining a room at a hotel, air travel, eating at a restaurant, or visiting a theme park are all influenced by organizational structures, procedures, and policies. Management decisions on levels of autonomy and discretion given to frontline staff will clearly moderate the effectiveness of service recovery processes.

Other elements of the organization that may affect the recovery process include the overall "climate" of the organization. Indeed, evidence suggests that positive service climate is associated with higher levels of customer satisfaction (Schneider, White, and Paul, 1998) and it is possible that climate is also correlated with service failure and recovery. A climate that encourages service staff to take control of the situation and implement a service recovery plan may well lead to higher levels of satisfaction.

Schlesinger and Heskett (1991) argue that many organizations, including restaurants, airlines, and hotels, employ principles of traditional mass production in running their businesses. As a result, they argue that the service system itself leads to a range of failures and inhibits effective recovery. These authors found that many service systems left no room for employee discretion, which resulted in disaffected staff and increased employee turnover. More important, such factors led directly to an increase in failures and a lack of concern with recovery. Thus, an organization's service system and human resource policies, including selection, training, and levels of pay, have important implications for the processes of service delivery and recovery (see also Boshoff, 1997).

Brymer (1991) and others have argued that service providers need to be more empowered by organizations. Empowerment is often defined in terms of how much discretion and autonomy frontline personnel are given (Kanter, 1977; Kelley, 1993).

Several different levels or forms of empowerment may be distinguished (Kelley, 1993; Bowen and Lawler, 1992; Brymer, 1991). The influence of each of these levels of empowerment upon customers' evaluations may be mediated by perceptions of the consideration being shown, and feelings of control over the outcome of the interaction. With full, or what Brymer (1991) refers to as "flexible" empowerment, there is considerable latitude in decision making, with very broad guidelines and limits. One possible alternative to full empowerment is to provide frontline staff with training in the implementation of a set of guidelines that specify the action to be taken and compensation to be offered in the event of service breakdown. Brymer (1991) refers to this as "limited" empowerment, in that it allows the staff member to make some decisions but under tighter control. As Bowen and Lawler (1992) note, many customers value "no surprises" in service delivery, and they like to know what to expect when they visit a service business.

Hart, Heskett, and Sasser (1990) argue that the best way to recover from service failure is for frontline workers to identify and solve problems, even if this means breaking rules. Hence, it is suggested that effective service recovery requires latitude in decision making and, ultimately, support from management to take whatever action is necessary to fix the problem. Evidence to support this contention comes from the work of Sparks and Bradley (1997), who found that fully empowered employees were clearly preferred over the other alternatives, but only when the service provider used an accommodating (personalized) communication style.

### Physical Conditions

The physical environment can be influential in a variety of ways. It may, for example, facilitate or constrain effective service delivery and recovery. It may make customers feel anxious or at ease. Bitner (1992) discusses how the physical environment encourages approach or avoidance behavior. She argues that the environment can facilitate approach behaviors that encourage customers to remain and interact with service personnel. Hence, the environment may influence the willingness of customers who have experienced service failure to complain or report failures. In another study, Bitner (1990) found that the tidiness of a travel agent's office influenced the manner in which failures were perceived. More specifically, she found that people who were exposed to a tidy or organized travel agent environment were less likely to expect the failure to occur again than those who were exposed to an untidy or disorganized environment. Thus, cues in the physical environment can influence customers' attributions and perceptions in a service failure situation. Similarly, signs at an airport might assist or hinder customers in finding the correct check-in counter and potentially contribute to failure situations. Failure may also result from climatic factors, for instance a restaurant that is overly air-conditioned may create an unpleasant environment and detract from customer experiences.

## Psychosocial Factors

Psychosocial factors, by which is meant the number and kind of people present and the interactions that occur between them, may also influence the perceptions of failure and the process of recovery. For instance, the recognition and perceived seriousness of a failure may well be influenced by factors such as the number of people dining or touring in a party. In addition, it may be that a person is more likely to complain in the company of others than alone. The actions taken by a service provider in response to a service failure may well differ depending upon whether the failure is being dealt with in relative privacy or on public display. In addition, relationship variables such as whether the individual is a regular or new customer may influence the propensity to complain about a failure and also what is done about the failure.

## Financial Factors

The financial dimension of the service, including how much is paid, how it is paid, and when it is paid may also be a moderating factor upon perceptions of failure. It has been found that customers' expectations are influenced by price, and the higher the price, the greater the expectations (Parasuraman, Berry, and Zeithaml, 1991). Similarly, customers' perceptions of a failure may be influenced by the relative cost of a service. For example, a customer's "zone of tolerance" (see next section) may be much narrower when staying in a hotel that costs $500 per night versus $80 per night. Whether the service exchange involves a ninety-day world tour or an afternoon's bus tour of a city, customers expect value for money, and their experience of the service is typically evaluated within the context of "how much is being paid to whom."

## Temporal Conditions

Time issues can also influence likely failures as well as opportunities to recover a failure. For instance, the time of day may increase the potential for a service failure. In a hotel that caters to business clientele, the hours between 7 and 8 a.m. may be an especially busy checkout time, leading to longer wait times, queuing, and service provider stress. Time also plays a role in a seasonal sense, with peak seasons resulting in greater crowding, which leads to congestion and increased wait times. The opportunity for error at a theme park is likely to increase during school holidays. Crowds result in people having to wait longer for rides. Similarly, recovery processes are likely to be hindered by crowds and busy periods.

## PERSONAL FACTORS
## OF SERVICE FAILURE

A range of factors relating to the individuals involved, both the customer and service provider, are likely to influence whether the service delivery is perceived as a failure and whether action taken constitutes a satisfactory recovery process. These personal factors include the parties' demographic background, personality, attitudes and values, abilities, and current physical and emotional state. A brief discussion of some of these factors follows.

### Zone of Tolerance

As mentioned earlier, service failure occurs when the delivery does not meet a customer's expectations. A range of reasons for service failure have been suggested; however, not all customers will perceive the same actions as failures. Parasuraman, Berry, and Zeithaml (1991) propose that customers have what is termed a "zone of tolerance," that is, beliefs regarding what constitutes both adequate and desired levels of service expectations. The "space" between the adequate and desired service expectations is the zone of tolerance. This space can expand or contract, resulting in differing evaluations of service delivery. The zone width may vary between customers and from one situation to another.

### Psychological Factors

Past experience can influence how recovery tactics are perceived. For instance, Kelley and Davis (1994) have reported that regular customers (those who are more committed to the firm) hold higher expectations about the service recovery effort of the firm. Similarly, as a customer's experience increases it may also serve to narrow the zone of tolerance. For instance, a regular customer may have higher expectations and a narrower tolerance level.

Other psychological factors such as the customer's or service provider's mood may contribute to the service failure or the recovery process. Mood has been shown to influence consumer actions and evaluations, and Gardner (1985) reports that customers in a good mood are easier to please and report more positive evaluations. A personality factor that may affect how people perceive the failure and recovery process is called locus of control (Rotter, 1966). Sparks and Bradley (1998) developed a *service locus of control* (SLOC), which identified control over events as having three sources: internal, belonging to a powerful other (providers of service), or luck. Customers who rank high on the powerful others scale may not complain as they believe events are out of their control and other forces determine the outcome.

In addition, the importance of the event to a person may influence whether something is seen as a service failure. Customers may pay far more attention to the service delivery when organizing a restaurant meal for a group of friends out to celebrate a birthday than when stopping off for a casual meal on the way home from work. The level of importance may, therefore, lead to quite different perceptions of service delivery. The zone of tolerance is likely to be narrower in the case of an important event.

## Demographics

A range of demographic variables such as age, education, and sex may impact upon the recovery process. For example, older customers may expect a more formal service delivery style than do younger customers. To date, some studies have investigated these demographic variables in conjunction with complaining behaviors. However, little support for the predictive power of these variables is evident (Bearden and Oliver, 1985; Bolfing, 1989; Singh, 1990).

## PROCESSES

Before outlining the ways in which providers respond to service failures, it is necessary to consider some of the overt (observable, behavioral) and covert (unobservable, hidden) processes that take place during, and immediately after, the service encounter.

## Overt

The service encounter, its antecedents, and its consequences are characterized by a range of overt actions by both the provider and customer. These overt actions can include both verbal and nonverbal actions that are communicated between the parties. As Bitner, Booms, and Tetreault (1990) note, in many instances failures are a result of not effectively delivering the core service. However, much of customers' dissatisfaction is caused by the manner in which the provider responds to the failure.

Hence, when errors do occur, the key to the recovery process lies in the action taken by the service provider, such as demonstrating effort to fix the problem (see Sparks and Bradley, 1997), showing sincerity about the problem, or being receptive to the customer's needs. Johnston's (1995) research has also shown that three of the most important actions in the recovery process are clear indicators of attentiveness, care about the problem, and responsiveness. These actions can be evidenced in the verbal and nonverbal messages given by service personnel. For example, a service provider can use the customer's name, engage in small talk, seek the customer's input, and even change the service delivery to accommodate the customer's unique needs.

### Covert

At all points in the service encounter/failure/recovery chain, the participants are engaged in a variety of covert cognitive and affective processes, as they appraise and evaluate events that occur. In the brief discussion that follows, emphasis is given to a small subset of such processes, namely, those that relate to forming judgments about fairness. These judgments ultimately affect levels of customer satisfaction. The most extensively used approaches to understanding how these evaluations take place are attribution and justice theories.

### Attribution Theory

When the delivery of a service does not match customers' prior expectations or normative standards, customers may engage in attributional processes to make sense of what has occurred (Bitner, 1990; Harvey and Weary, 1984). According to attribution theory (Hewstone, 1989; Weiner, 1982), causes may be of two types—internal and external. Internal causes include factors inherent to the service provider, such as the amount of effort put into the delivery of the service, the strategies used to deal with service situations, and the skill level demonstrated. External causes include factors outside the service encounter, including the activities of other people such as suppliers, or bad luck. Research into the fundamental attribution error (Heider, 1958) indicates that in general, customers will attribute causes for service breakdowns to features that are internal to the service provider (for example, the provider's inexperience or the organization's poor training programs) rather than to luck or organizational policy. Past research indicates that the value of customer attributions depends upon the range of information available regarding the cause of the problem, including the frequency of the problem, perception of whether the problem is preventable or due to bad luck, and the extent to which the service provider tried to solve the problem (see Bitner, 1990; Folkes, 1984).

## Justice Theory

Another framework used to evaluate the service recovery process is that of justice. What is perceived to be fair and reasonable in the circumstances will influence the level of customer satisfaction. Service and organizational research studies (see for instance, Bies and Moag, 1986; Clemmer, 1993; Goodwin and Ross, 1990; Sparks and Callan, 1996; Tyler, 1994) have confirmed that customer satisfaction is not merely based upon the ultimate outcome of the service recovery but also upon the procedures used to reach an outcome, as well as the interactions along the way. Clemmer and Schneider (1996) make the point that in services marketing, what is important is the need to focus on processes and relationships rather than outcomes, due to the intangible nature of services and the key role played by service personnel. An important point to emerge from these studies is that while it is likely that some form of compensation is important to levels of customer satisfaction, the desire to establish and maintain a positive relationship with the firm is also likely to influence feelings of satisfaction. Hence, the effectiveness of service recovery techniques used by tourism and hospitality firms may rely upon customers' evaluations of both the intervention process and the outcomes of this exchange.

*Procedural.* Procedural justice primarily addresses means used to achieve an outcome (see Lind and Tyler, 1988). It is argued that procedural justice will affect satisfaction and fairness judgments independently of outcomes. Issues of procedural justice can include actions such as process control and decision control. Process control refers to whether a customer has an opportunity for input into how the situation is dealt with and is often referred to as "voice." Decision control refers to the extent to which a customer has control over the actual outcome. Procedural justice can also be influenced by factors such as waiting time, flexibility, and efficiency of the recovery process. Thus, the actions that have been discussed as possible service recovery responses may be evaluated differently depending upon how they are perceived by customers in terms of procedural fairness.

*Interactional.* How the firm manages its response to a customer who experiences a service failure is likely to be a key determinant of the customer's satisfaction levels and perceptions of the company (Bitner, Booms, and Tetreault, 1990). As many services are largely intangible, it is the perceived quality of the interaction between customer and service provider that influences judgments about satisfaction with a service. A key determinant of service quality and customer satisfaction evaluations is service provider empathy, that is, concern demonstrated by the service provider (Zeithaml and Bitner, 1996; Johnston, 1995). Hocutt, Chakraborty, and Mowen (1997) found that following a service failure incident, customers were most satisfied when service personnel displayed high levels of empathy and responsiveness. Similarly, in a scenario study of hotels, Sparks and McColl-Kennedy (1998) found the amount of concern a service provider displayed was especially important to perceptions of satisfactory service recovery.

*Distributive.* Distributive justice is generally understood to focus on the actual objective outcome of the service recovery. This could include financial compensation such as a refund or discount for the defective service. Research primarily undertaken in the organizational behavior field and based on equity theory (Adams, 1965) reveals that an outcome will be evaluated in terms of its perceived equity. It is argued that a person will evaluate the outcome based upon a ratio of inputs to outputs. It is possible that an outcome may even be perceived as too good, or too different from what others receive and, as a result, be perceived as inequitable (Adams, 1965; Leventhal, Weiss, and Long, 1969). Similarly, other research has suggested that the form and value of the compensation should match the explanation given for service failure (Sparks and Callan, 1996). Thus, it appears that the amount of compensation and under what conditions such compensation should be provided remains in doubt.

## RESPONSE

### Recognition of Service Failure

For service recovery to take place, it is first necessary that the service provider recognize that a problem has occurred. Service failures frequently go undetected. For example, a customer's soup may be cold, but unless this is brought to the attention of the server, it is not known. Similarly, a service provider may ask a customer how things are but does not get a truthful answer. This type of behavior is quite common in restaurant settings when a waiter asks the customer how the meal is and gets a standard "it's fine" response, irrespective of the quality. Hence, the recognition of service failure often depends upon a customer voicing dissatisfaction. Indeed, it is argued by many (for example, Andreason, 1984, 1985; Ritchins, 1983) that up to two-thirds of customers may not voice their dissatisfaction with a failure. In addition, service providers may not recognize a situation as a failure if they believe corrective action has already been taken. As an example, consider a situation in which a person has booked a flight from one destination to another. Upon arrival to check in for the flight, airline personnel inform the customer that the flight is canceled and she has been reallocated to a flight one hour later. In this situation the provider offers no apology but simply an alternative flight, and there is no apparent recognition of the inconvenience caused.

## Nonrecovery Actions

### Denial and Avoidance

One response option open to a service provider is to deny or largely ignore the service failure. This may not be as uncommon as one might think. Bitner, Booms, and Tetreault (1990), in a study of critical incidents, found unsatisfactory service encounters were largely related to service providers' inability or unwillingness to respond to service failure situations. A provider may respond to a disappointed customer with an argument that challenges the existence or legitimacy of the customer's concern and may not actually invoke any further recovery tactics. An example of this was reported by two tourists, the first an American tourist in London, and the second an Australian business traveler:

> The tourist was staying at a moderate-range small hotel, and at breakfast requested decaffeinated coffee. The waiter replied, "We're not a five-star hotel, you know" and offered regular coffee.

> Similarly, when a business executive was traveling by plane from Australia to Thailand she found her earphones were not operating. On calling the flight attendant, the man looked, shrugged his shoulders, and then acted as if nothing was wrong.

At other times service providers may simply avoid the disgruntled customer, choosing to remain "back of house." More commonly, perhaps, service providers may simply avoid responding to the complaint, choosing to change the topic to an aspect of the service that has been satisfactory.

### Service Recovery Actions

Service recovery is the process of dealing with a service failure situation with the aim of restoring the customer's satisfaction. Recovery techniques usually involve attempts to rectify the service breakdown but may also entail providing customers with explanations about the service failure, apologizing, making offers of compensation, and being courteous in the process (see for example, Bitner, 1990; Blodgett, Hill, and Tax, 1997;

Goodwin and Ross, 1990; Hoffman, Kelley, and Rotalsky, 1995; Sparks and Callan, 1996). As many of these responses are enacted by frontline service providers, customers tend to base their evaluations largely on the behavior of these staff (Bowen and Schneider, 1988; Surprenant and Solomon, 1987). The choice of recovery actions taken is likely to depend upon a range of factors already considered, including the context, process, and people involved, together with the seriousness of the failure. For instance, it is unlikely that customers would expect a full refund of their restaurant account just because an addition error had occurred.

## Fix the Problem

Wherever possible, it is desirable to rectify the original problem encountered by the customer. Sometimes this is not feasible, such as when a flight is delayed, a tour bus breaks down, or a restaurant meal arrives late. However, as an example, the following anecdote illustrates how fixing the problem can lead to highly satisfied customers:

> A couple who had requested a double room checked into a hotel and were allocated a room, only to find two single beds. The couple decided to go down to reception and discuss the matter with the front desk staff. The staff member checked the rooms available and offered to relocate the guests to another room with a double bed. The desk attendant gave a key to the couple and suggested they go and see whether they liked the room. On entry, the couple found the room was a suite.

The action of fixing the problem, giving some control to the customers and providing a better room, resulted in very satisfied customers.

## Apology

An apology for a failure is another way to recover the customer's confidence in the firm. Apology can range from a simple statement of regret to more extended "confessions of responsibility for negative events which include remorse" (Tedeschi and Norman, 1985, p. 299). For most customers, an apology is the minimum requirement for recovering a service failure. The manner in which an apology is delivered is relevant, and some expression of sincerity usually helps the recovery process. Hence, coupling an apology with statements of concern or empathy is important.

## Explanations

When a failure has occurred, one option is to offer an explanation. Firms offer explanations in an effort to increase customer understanding of

the problem or to diffuse customer anger. Explanations can be predomi-
nantly internal ("it was our fault") or external ("the problem was beyond
our control"), and presumably, these explanations are included in the
evidence considered by customers in making attributions. An example of
an external explanation includes a pilot of an aircraft announcing to passengers "we're in a holding pattern awaiting clearance to land. This is due
to heavy congestion at the air terminal. We will be landing just as soon as
clearance is provided. We expect to be around fifteen minutes late due to
this situation." Research has shown that when employees offer an external
explanation for service failure, the firm is judged to have less control over
the breakdown (Bitner, 1990).

The effectiveness of explanations as a means of service recovery is still
unclear and to some degree underresearched. Tax, Brown, and Chandrashekaran (1998) report that the provision of information had both positive
and negative outcomes for customer perceptions. It seems the manner in
which the information is perceived makes a considerable difference. For
instance, when information was perceived as an excuse to mitigate an
organization's accountability, it was seen as negative. In contrast, information that increased understanding about the problem and led to a quick
resolution was perceived favorably. Similarly, Sparks and Callan (1995)
found that accepting the responsibility (that is, giving an internal explanation) and being prepared to back this up with some form of compensation
(of a value kind) was evaluated very favorably in a service failure situation. However, when the breakdown is clearly outside the firm's control, a
symbolic offer (such as a couple of drink vouchers) was judged more
favorably than a value offer.

## Customer Input

One recovery tactic is to involve the customer in the service recovery
such that the customer feels some control over the process. Bies and
Shapiro (1988) and Lind, Kanfer, and Earley (1990) report that process
control, or voice, influences perceptions of the fairness of the recovery.
Voice procedures involve customers having an opportunity to express their
views or provide input to the decision, whereas customers who do not
have this opportunity are said to be involved in "mute" procedures (Bies
and Shapiro, 1988). The opportunity for individuals to express their feelings about an apparent injustice (to have voice) is also important in influencing levels of satisfaction, especially when it is accompanied by
some tangible compensation (Goodwin and Ross, 1990). Previous research (Lind, Kanfer, and Earley, 1990) has demonstrated that the beneficial effects of voice emerge for two reasons. The first is instrumental; that

is, people assume that the opportunity to express a view will help them control their outcomes. The second benefit is called "group value"; that is, people value voice because it suggests their views are worth hearing and hence, that they are members of an important status group (see Lind, Kanfer, and Earley, 1990). In contrast, failure to consider customers' inputs (voice) may result in feelings of limited control over what happens, a lack of a sense of fairness, and low overall satisfaction.

Tourism and hospitality firms can do several things to encourage customer input. First, service providers can be trained to encourage customers to provide feedback about their experiences on the spot. Second, it is possible to encourage customer input through less personal methods such as complaint or suggestion boxes, toll-free customer service numbers, or survey feedback forms. The key is to invite input from customers so as to recognize the source of their inconvenience, and to prevent its occurrence in the future. Furthermore, Blodgett, Wakefield, and Barnes (1995) found customers are more likely to report a problem if it is clear the firm is willing to fix the problem. They argue that explicit factors such as a service guarantee or service warranty help to cultivate such an environment. These authors (1995) underscore the importance of addressing the problems voiced by clients. Failure to do so is expected to result in further dissatisfaction from the customer's perspective.

## Compensation

Another service recovery action is to provide the customer with financial compensation such as a refund or discount. What appears to customers to be appropriate compensation is still underresearched. Goodwin and Ross (1990) found that customers preferred to receive a tangible outcome, even a token refund, when there was a breakdown in service delivery. Other researchers (for example, Bitner, 1990) report that the presence of an offer of compensation leads the customer to attribute greater control to the firm and to believe the cause is less stable (i.e., a temporary lapse in service). Research reported by Sparks and Callan (1996) found that an offer was perceived more or less favorably depending upon other factors such as the explanation provided for the breakdown. Blodgett, Wakefield, and Barnes (1995) found that compensation only made a positive difference in satisfaction when accompanied by high levels of courtesy and respect. This implies that if the recovery process involves a rude service provider, then no amount of financial compensation will make up for the service failure. In contrast, Johnston (1995) did not find any evidence to support the need for "atonement" in a service recovery process.

## CONSEQUENCES

Once a service recovery tactic has been used and evaluated, the customer is likely to have formed feelings of satisfaction or dissatisfaction. The definition of satisfaction is covered elsewhere. However, it is important to note that previous studies have clearly demonstrated a link between the actions taken by service firms in response to a service failure and resulting satisfaction levels. It should be noted that, in addition to satisfaction, there is a number of other potential consequences, both immediate and long term, of the service recovery process.

### *Immediate Outcomes*

#### *Direct Complaint Behavior*

When a failure occurs, one option open to the customer is to complain directly. Such complaints are often made to the frontline staff who are easily accessible, but may be made to a supervisor, or in written form, through customer feedback surveys. As already discussed, the manner in which complaints are handled is often a key factor in how the recovery is perceived.

#### *Satisfaction*

A key concern of the service recovery process is customer satisfaction. Within the service context, customer satisfaction is concerned with judgments about an event or encounter. Evidence from a range of studies (e.g., Bitner, 1990; Bolton and Drew, 1991; Cronin and Taylor, 1992) suggests customer satisfaction is inextricably linked not only to judgments of service quality, but also to repurchase intentions and customer loyalty. Bitner's (1990) research demonstrated a direct path between customer satisfaction and the evaluations of service quality.

### *Long-Term Outcomes*

Some outcomes of the failure and recovery process are more long-term in nature. The information communicated by a satisfied or dissatisfied customer may be ongoing and may have wide ramifications. Similarly, the long-term loyalty of customers is likely to be affected by failure and recovery processes, especially where there is opportunity to change service providers (that is, engage in switching behavior). For instance, it is relatively easy to change from one restaurant to another.

## Word-of-Mouth Actions

One outcome of the recovery process may be that positive or negative word of mouth (WOM) is communicated. Generally, WOM communications are comments made by personal sources such as business colleagues, friends, or relatives. While positive WOM is clearly desired, negative WOM is most damaging. Unfortunately, negative WOM is reasonably common, especially among aggrieved customers. As an example, Blodgett, Hill, and Tax (1997) reported that customers who feel they have been treated with courtesy and respect are more likely to repatronize the firm and spread positive WOM. In contrast, those who received rude service indicated they engaged in an increased level of negative WOM. Sparks and Bradley's (1997) research study on service breakdown in a hospitality setting found that customers who express higher levels of satisfaction with the service recovery process are less likely to engage in negative WOM.

## Loyalty to Firm

Service failures, if not properly handled, can have devastating effects on the firm. Indeed, Keaveney (1995) found people most frequently switched firms due to service failures. Similarly, Dube and Maute (1996) reported on the importance of dealing effectively with customers' complaints to prevent brand switching in services. Other research (Gilly, 1987; Sparks and Bradley, 1997) has found that customers who are more satisfied with the service recovery response are more likely to consider using the service firm again. Others (Zeithaml, Parasuraman, and Berry, 1996) have demonstrated that among customers who experience service problems, those who receive satisfactory resolution are more likely to remain loyal to the firm than are those who experience unsatisfactory resolution. Hence, effective service recovery significantly improves behavioral reuse intentions.

## AN ILLUSTRATIVE MODEL OF THE SERVICE BREAKDOWN AND RECOVERY PROCESS

The discussion thus far provides an organized list of the discrete facets of the service failure/recovery process, but is of little help in "fitting the pieces together." To further understand these phenomena, it is necessary to develop a model that specifies the dynamic, temporal relationships between the various facets. Figure 11.1 provides such a model. Organization-

FIGURE 11.1. Diagrammatic Overview of the Service Failure and Recovery Process

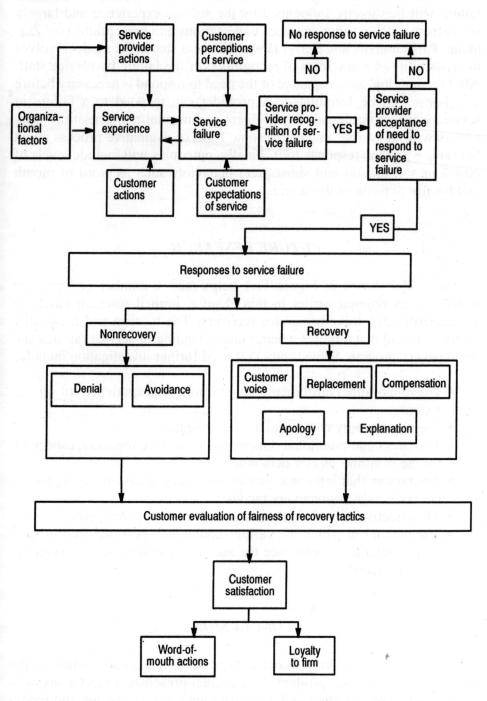

al factors, service provider actions, and customer actions are the three factors that are most likely to influence the service experience. A service failure will be directly influenced by the service experience and largely result from a discrepancy between expectations and perceptions (see Zeithaml, Parasuraman, and Berry, 1996). The next step in the model involves the possibility of some form of recognition of the failure by service staff. After recognition, an acceptance of the need to respond is necessary before a response can be formulated. A provider can respond to a failure in several ways, from denial of a problem to financial compensation. Customers will, of course, engage in some form of evaluative process about the failure and the response to it. Finally, outcomes will include levels of customer satisfaction and subsequent behaviors such as word of mouth and loyalty or reuse of the service.

## *FUTURE RESEARCH*

The model shown in Figure 11.1 helps raise a number of important issues. As mentioned earlier in this chapter, limited research has been conducted on the topic of service recovery. The tourism and hospitality sector is a field that requires a better understanding of service failures and the recovery process. Some topics that need further investigation include:

- The role of other customers as contributors to experiences of service failure
- The reasons why customers do not complain
- The stress and emotional dimensions of service recovery, especially for the frontline service personnel
- The factors that influence service providers' decisions to invoke recovery versus nonrecovery tactics
- The effectiveness of alternative service recovery strategies
- The manner in which the various contextual, personal, and process factors interact to influence the success or otherwise of service recovery attempts

## *CONCLUSION*

Service failure is likely to occur because of the unique nature of the hospitality and tourism product. This chapter presented a facet analysis to make explicit the factors likely to impact upon service failure and recovery. Several types of service failures have been distinguished, and the contextual, personal, and process dimensions of service failure and recovery have been elucidated. While a range of options is available for recovering from service failure, ultimately what matters are the subjective evaluations customers make of these recovery tactics. The effectiveness of many tactics is likely to depend upon other facets of the service delivery/failure/recovery system. A framework for understanding the service failure and recovery process as well as associated outcomes has been proposed. This model may be useful to service managers and marketers in helping to pinpoint the sources of service failures and the range of possible recovery strategies. Further research is required to develop a deeper understanding of the many facets of the service recovery process.

## REFERENCES

Adams, J.S. (1965). Inequity in Social Exchange. In L. Berkowitz (Ed.), *Advances in Experimental Social Psychology, 2* (pp. 267-299). New York: Academic Press.

Andreason, A.R. (1984). Consumer Satisfaction in Loose Monopolies: The Case of Medical Care. *Journal of Public Policy and Marketing, 2*: 122-135.

Andreason, A.R. (1985). Consumer Responses to Dissatisfaction in Loose Monopolies. *Journal of Consumer Research, 12* (September): 135-141.

Bearden, W.O. and Oliver, R.L. (1985). The Role of Public and Private Complaining in Satisfaction with Complaint Resolutions. *Journal of Consumer Affairs, 19* (Winter): 222-240.

Bejou, D., Edvardsson, B., and Rakowski, J.P. (1996). A Critical Incident Approach to Examining the Effects of Service Failures on Customer Relationships: The Case of Swedish and US Airlines. *Journal of Travel Research, 35* (1): 35-40.

Bies, R.J. and Moag, J.S. (1986). Interactional Justice: Communication Criteria of Fairness. In R. Lewicki, M. Bazerman, and B. Sheppard (Ed.), *Research on Negotiation in Organizations 1* (pp. 57-79). Greenwich, CT: JAI Press.

Bies, R.J. and Shapiro, D.L. (1988). Voice and Justification: Their Influence on Procedural Fairness Judgments. *Academy of Management Journal, 31* (3): 676-685.

Bitner, M.J. (1990). Evaluating Service Encounters: The Effect of Physical Surroundings and Employee Responses. *Journal of Marketing, 54* (2): 69-82.

Bitner, M.J. (1992). Servicescapes: The Impact of Physical Surrounds on Customers and Employees. *Journal of Marketing, 56* (2):69-82.

Bitner, M.J., Booms, B.H., and Tetreault, M.S. (1990). The Service Encounter: Diagnosing Favourable and Unfavourable Incidents. *Journal of Marketing, 54* (January): 71-84.

Blodgett, J.G., Hill, D.J., and Tax, S.S. (1997). The Effects of Distributive, Procedural and Interactional Justice on Postcomplaint Behavior. *Journal of Retailing, 73* (2): 185-210.

Blodgett, J.G., Wakefield, K.L., and Barnes, J.H. (1995). The Effects of Customer Service on Consumer Complaining Behavior. *Journal of Services Marketing, 9* (4): 31-42.

Bojanic, D.C. and Rosen, L.D. (1994). Measuring Service Quality in Restaurants: An Application of the SERVQUAL Instrument. *Hospitality Research Journal, 18* (1). 3-14.

Bolfing, C.P. (1989). How Do Customers Express Dissatisfaction and What Can Service Marketers Do About It? *The Journal of Services Marketing, 3* (Spring): 5-25.

Bolton, R.N. and Drew, J.H. (1991). A Multistage Model of Customers' Assessment of Service Quality and Value. *Journal of Consumer Research, 17* (4): 375-384.

Boshoff, C. (1997). An Experimental Study of Service Recovery Options. *International Journal of Service Industry Management, 8* (2): 110-130.

Bowen, D.E. and Lawler, E.E. (1992). The Empowerment of Service Workers: What, Why, How and When. *Sloan Management Review, 33* (3): 31-39.

Bowen, D. and Schneider, B. (1988). Service Marketing and Management: Implications for Organizational Behavior. In L.L. Cummings and B.M. Staw (Eds.), *Research in Organizational Behavior, 10* (pp. 43-80). Greenwich, CT: JAI Press.

Brown, S.W., Fisk, R.P., and Bitner, M.J. (1994). The Development and Emergence of Services Marketing Thought. *International Journal of Service Industry Management, 5* (1): 21-48.

Brymer, R.A. (1991). Employee Empowerment: A Guest Driven Leadership Strategy. *The Cornell H.R.A. Quarterly, 32* (1): 58-68.

Clemmer, E.C. (1993). An Investigation into the Relationship of Fairness and Customer Satisfaction with Services. In R. Copranzano (Ed.), *Justice in the Workplace* (pp. 193-207). Hillsdale, NJ: Lawrence Erlbaum Associates.

Clemmer, E. and Schneider, B. (1996). Fair Service. In T.A. Swartz, D.E. Bowen, and S.W. Brown (Eds.), *Advances in Services Marketing and Management Research and Practice, 5* (pp. 127-151). Greenwich, CT: JAI Press.

Cronin, J.J. Jr. and Taylor, S.A. (1992). Measuring Service Quality: A Re-Examination and Extension. *Journal of Marketing, 56* (3): 55-68.

Dube, L. and Maute, M. (1996). The Antecedents of Brand Switching, Brand Loyalty and Verbal Responses to Service Failure. In T.A. Swartz, D.E. Bowen, and S.W. Brown (Eds.), *Advances in Services Marketing and Management Research and Practice, 5* (pp. 127-151). Greenwich, CT: JAI Press.

Folkes, V.S. (1984). Customer Reactions to Product Failures: An Attributional Approach. *Journal of Consumer Research, 10* (March): 398-409.

Gardner, M.P. (1985). Mood States and Consumer Research: A Critical Review. *Journal of Consumer Research, 12* (3): 281-300.

Gilly, M.C. (1987). Post Complaint Processes: From Organizational Response to Repurchase Behavior. *Journal of Consumer Affairs, 21* (Winter): 293-313.

Goodwin, C. and Ross, I. (1990). Consumer Evaluations of Responses to Complaints: What's Fair and Why? *The Journal of Consumer Marketing, 7* (2): 39-47.

Hart, C.W.L., Heskett, J.L., and Sasser, W.E. (1990). The Profitable Art of Service Recovery. *Harvard Business Review, 68* (4): 148-156.

Harvey, J.H. and Weary, G. (1984). Current Issues in Attribution Theory and Research. *Annual Review of Psychology, 35:* 427-459.

Heider, F. (1958). *The Psychology of Interpersonal Relations.* New York: Wiley.

Hewstone, M. (1989). *Causal Attribution: From Cognitive Processes to Collective Beliefs.* Oxford: Basil Blackwell.

Hocutt, M.A., Chakraborty, G., and Mowen, J. (1997). The Impact of Perceived Justice on Customer Satisfaction and Intention to Complain in Service Recovery. In M. Brucks and D.J. MacInnis (Eds.), *Advances in Consumer Research, 24* (pp. 457-463). Provo, UT: Association for Consumer Research.

Hoffman, K.D., Kelley, S.W., and Rotalsky, H.M. (1995). Tracking Service Failures and Employee Recovery Efforts. *Journal of Services Marketing, 9* (2): 49-61.

Iacobucci, D., Grayson, K.A., and Ostrom, A.L. (1994). The Calculus of Service Quality and Customer Satisfaction: Theoretical and Empirical Differentiation and Integration. In T. Swartz, D.E. Bowen, and S.W. Brown (Eds.), *Advances in Services Marketing and Management, 3* (pp. 1-67). Greenwich, CT: JAI Press.

Johnston, R. (1995). Service Failure and Recovery: Impact, Attributes and Process. In T.A. Swartz, D.E. Bowen, and S.W. Brown (Eds.), *Advances in Services Marketing and Management Research and Practice, 4* (pp. 211-228). Greenwich, CT: JAI Press.

Kanter, R.M. (1977). *Men and Women of the Corporation.* New York: Basic Books.

Keaveney, S.M. (1995). Customer Switching Behavior in Service Industries: An Exploratory Study. *Journal of Marketing, 59* (April): 71-82.

Kelley, S.W. (1993). Discretion and the Service Employee. *Journal of Retailing, 69* (Spring): 104-126.

Kelley, S.W. and Davis, M.A. (1994). Antecedents to Customer Expectations for Service Recovery. *Journal of the Academy of Marketing Science, 22* (1): 52-61.

Kelley, S.W., Hoffman, K.D., and Davis, M.A. (1993). A Typology of Retail Failures and Recoveries. *Journal of Retailing, 69* (4): 429-452.

Knudson, B., Stevens, P., Wallaert, C., Patton, M., and Yokoyama, F. (1990). LODGSERV: A Service Quality Index for the Lodging Industry. *Hospitality Research Journal, 14* (2): 277-284.

Leventhal, G.S., Weiss, T., and Long, G. (1969). Equity, Reciprocity and Reallocating Rewards in the Dyad. *Journal of Personality and Social Psychology, 13*: 300-305.

Lind, E.A., Kanfer, R., and Earley, P.C. (1990). Voice, Control, and Procedural Justice: Instrumental and Noninstrumental Concerns in Fairness Judgments. *Journal of Personality and Social Psychology, 59* (5): 952-959.

Lind, E.A. and Tyler, T.R. (1988). *The Social Psychology of Procedural Justice.* New York: Plenum Press.

Parasuraman, A., Berry, L., and Zeithaml, V. (1991). Understanding Customer Expectations of Service. *Sloan Management Review, 32* (3):39-48.

Ritchins, M.L. (1983). Negative Word of Mouth by Dissatisfied Customers: A Pilot Study. *Journal of Marketing, 47* (1): 68-78.

Rotter, J.B. (1966). Generalized Expectancies for Internal versus External Control of Reinforcement. *Psychological Monographs, 80* (1): (Whole No. 609).

Schlesinger, L.A. and Heskett, J.L. (1991). The Service Driven Company. *Harvard Business Review, 69* (5): 71-81.

Schneider, B., White, S.S., and Paul, P.C. (1998). Linking Service Climate and Customer Perceptions of Service Quality: Test of a Causal Model. *Journal of Applied Psychology, 83* (2): 150-163.

Singh, J. (1990). Identifying Consumer Dissatisfaction Response Styles: An Agenda for Future Research. *European Journal of Marketing, 24* (6): 55-72.

Sparks, B.A. (1998). Service Failures and Justice in a Restaurant Setting. Working Paper, Griffith University, Queensland, Australia.

Sparks, B.A. and Bradley, G.L. (1997). Antecedents and Consequences of Perceived Service Provider Effort in the Hospitality Industry. *Hospitality Research Journal, 20* (3): 17-34.

Sparks, B.A. and Bradley, G.L. (1998). Service Locus of Control in the Hospitality Industry. *HSMAI/EUROCHRIE Conference on Hospitality Sales and Marketing Proceedings* (pp. 39-43). Stavanger: Norwegian Hotel School.

Sparks, B.A. and Callan, V.J. (1995). Dealing with Service Breakdowns: The Influence of Explanations, Offers and Communication Style on Consumer Complaint Behavior. *Proceedings of the World Congress 7th Bi-annual Marketing Science Conference, 7* (2), (9): 106-115.

Sparks, B.A. and Callan, V.J. (1996). Service Breakdowns and Service Evaluations: The Role of Customer Attributions. *Journal of Hospitality and Leisure Research, 4* (2): 3-24.

Sparks, B.A. and McColl-Kennedy, J.R. (1998). Justice Strategy Options for Increased Customer Satisfaction in a Service Recovery Setting. Working Paper, Griffith University, Queensland, Australia.

Surprenant, C.F. and Solomon, M.R. (1987). Predictability and Personalisation in the Service Encounter. *Journal of Marketing, 51* (2): 86-96.

Tax, S.S., Brown, S.W., and Chandrashekaran, M. (1998). Customer Evaluations of Service Complaint Experiences: Implications for Relationship Marketing. *Journal of Marketing, 62* (2): 60-76.

Tedeschi, J.T. and Norman, N. (1985). Social Power, Self Presentation and the Self. In B.R. Schlenker (Ed.), *The Self and Social Life* (pp. 293-322). New York: McGraw-Hill.

Tyler, T.R. (1994). Psychological Models of the Justice Motive: Antecedents of Distributive and Procedural Justice. *Journal of Personality and Social Psychology, 67* (5): 850-863.

Wiener, Y. (1982). Commitment in the Organization: A Normative View. *Academy of Management Review,* 7 (3): 418-428.

Zeithaml, V.A. and Bitner, M.J. (1996). *Services Marketing.* New York: McGraw-Hill.

Zeithaml, V.A., Parasuraman, A., and Berry, L.L. (1996). The Behavioral Consequences of Service Quality. *Journal of Marketing, 60* (April): 31-46.

# Chapter 12

# Empowering Service Personnel to Deliver Quality Service

## William N. Chernish

### *NEED FOR MOTIVATION AND EMPOWERMENT*

Motivation, leadership, empowerment, workers, and service quality are all inextricably intertwined in any organization that seeks to satisfy guests, customers, and others whom it serves. When the organization operates within the hospitality, tourism, and leisure sector, much or all of its output will necessarily be an intangible service rather than a hard product. The service will likely be perishable, delivered directly to the consumer, and not subject to the types of quality assurance measures that may be used when manufacturing, distributing, and selling a product.

In light of these characteristics, the service delivery and the quality of the service and level of customer satisfaction will be highly dependent upon the employee who interfaces with the customer. It is that employee who represents the organization and its reputation many times in the course of doing business. Carlzon referred to this interface and interaction as "moments of truth" (Carlzon, 1989). For the service to be delivered in the appropriate manner and with the expected level of quality, employees must be prepared and must have sufficient reason to perform according to, or above, standards.

### *Basic Philosophy of Empowerment*

Several authors have examined and developed tools and techniques for creating organizations and assisting people to become self-empowered and act upon it. Many of the theories and techniques have their basis in contemporary organizational psychology and motivation theory. Factors distinguishing traditional motivation from the evolving notions of empowerment focus on changes in organizational structures and processes, and on preparing employees and managers to accept new ways of doing business and new ways of modeling behavior.

The introduction and application of the principles of empowerment are designed to increase employee motivation and control by reducing the number and types of bureaucratic constraints. The concept results in greater employee independence to act, prevent, or resolve problems, and deliver appropriate service and guest satisfaction. This freedom and self-control is thought to result in greater worker satisfaction and higher organizational morale.

### Industry Characteristics

The hospitality, tourism, and leisure industry segments are characterized by factors that distinguish them from production-oriented and hard-product businesses. The manufacture of traditional goods, whether on an assembly line or otherwise, permits the inspection, testing, and verification of quality before shipment, sale, and consignment to the ultimate customer. In the manufacturing sector, various techniques have been developed to apply statistical, total quality, continuous quality improvement, and other tools to the assurance of quality before shipment. Where the product does not meet appropriate standards, or is unlikely to meet standards, shipment may be postponed for further testing and adjustments (Bowen and Lawler, 1992; Petrick and Furr, 1995).

Rather than manufacturing tangible products, the hospitality, tourism, and leisure industry focuses upon the sale and delivery of rooms, meals, and transportation services for immediate consumption. This delivery involves the active participation of employees in interacting with the guests. There is limited or no opportunity for inspection and testing of service delivery, and the employee is the representative of the organization. When coupled with the fact that many hospitality, tourism, and leisure employees are paid relatively low wages, the managerial challenge for service integrity is significant (Albrecht and Zemke, 1985; Lashley, 1997; Moon and Swaffin-Smith, 1998).

Managers facing such challenges may have limited ability to change products or services offered, to utilize different facilities or processes, or to change the location of their business operations. The variable most under managers' influence is the employees of the organization. Managers must find better ways for employees to do their jobs, and must find ways to encourage those employees to perform at or above expectations and service standards. Motivation and empowerment are two approaches to this challenge.

In an industry where service quality is important, it becomes essential that those delivering that service be able to do so in an effective, efficient, and customer-satisfying manner. This implies that employees must be motivated to do a job, and further be given the tools and the latitude to act on that motivation—to be empowered to provide the appropriate level of creation, inspection, and delivery of service quality.

In a business or industry where employees create as well as deliver a service, employers must place great faith and trust in the frontline customer service employee. It is that employee who provides the interface between customer and the organization, and who has a great deal of control over the quality of the delivery and the customer experience. The hospitality industry—restaurant and other food service, lodging, travel and transportation, entertainment, and related sectors—all share those characteristics and share the need for employees who act to provide the appropriate level of service and guest experiences. These characteristics make the concept of empowerment appropriate and useful for the travel, tourism, and hospitality industry.

## MOTIVATION

### Definitions of Motivation

Employee motivation has been a subject of managerial study for more than half a century, beginning with Roethlisberger and Dixon's (1939) work at Western Electric. One can also find early work in motivation theory in the "hedonic calculus" of Jeremy Bentham in 1789 (Steers, Porter, and Bigler, 1996).

"Motivation" is generally related to the Latin *movere*, which means "to move," and as used in contemporary management also means to entice employees to move in a direction and manner that meet the organization's goals (Jones, 1955; Atkinson, 1964; Vroom, 1964; Campbell and Pritchard, 1976). Further study of the definitions laid out by those researchers identify three common characteristics, which are concerned with (1) what energizes human behavior, (2) what directs or channels such behavior, and (3) how this behavior is maintained or sustained (Steers, Porter, and Bigler, 1996). The implication is that the behavior is directed *toward* something, and that the something is consistent with the goals of the organization.

Later work in motivation provides more definitive theories of ways in which managers can better understand the needs and movement of workers. The works of Maslow (1968), Herzberg (Herzberg, Mausner, and Snyderman, 1959), and McClelland (1961) are considered essential contributions to the "content theory" of motivation, while the work of Vroom (1964) and Porter and Lawler (1968) are classified as "process theories."

## Content Theories of Motivation

Maslow and Herzberg are probably the most widely recognized names associated with content motivation. Maslow developed a "hierarchy of needs," which describes how people's needs guide behavior. Maslow contends that an individual has needs which are arranged hierarchically, and that the fundamental needs must be met before upper-level needs may begin to drive behavior. Maslow's theory contends that only unsatisfied needs can influence behavior; those that are satisfied do not motivate (Maslow, 1968; Steers, Porter, and Bigler, 1996) (see Table 12.1).

TABLE 12.1. Motivation—Maslow's Hierarchy of Needs

| Need and Definition | Organizational Assurance |
| --- | --- |
| Self-actualization: realization of one's potential | Major components are competence and achievement, implying the necessity for adequate training and tools to control the environment of the workplace, and to achieve organizational goals. |
| Self-esteem: desire for self-respect and respect of others | That organizations take appropriate measures to balance needs for profits and people |
| Social: associations and friendships, interaction with others | By developing opportunities for social interactions, informal activities, and employee gatherings |
| Safety: job security, safe working conditions, freedom from physical or mental harm | Development of safety programs and methods of participatory decision making, especially when organizational change is required |
| Basic: physiological; water, air, food | Providing a work setting which is conducive to meeting human needs, including food, rest, refreshment |

*Sources:* Maslow, 1943; Frunzi and Savini, 1997.

Herzberg developed the motivator-hygiene theory based upon research involving accountants and engineers. On the basis of his study, he identified factors that were called "motivators," including variables such as achievement, recognition, and work itself as well as responsibility, advancement, and growth (Steers, Porter, and Bigler, 1996). A separate set of factors was also identified, which Herzberg referred to as "hygiene" factors (see Table 12.2). This set of factors focused on extrinsic non-job-related factors such as company policies, supervisory style, pay, and coworker relations. Herzberg held that elimination of the dissatisfying hygiene factors would only bring workers to a neutral position, and that motivation would occur only when the hygiene factors were all present, and then the "motivators" could be brought into play (Herzberg, Mausner, and Snyderman, 1959; Steers, Porter, and Bigler, 1996).

Managers in the hospitality industry may apply the theories of Maslow and Herzberg in many ways, some of which may seem obvious. The work of both researchers suggests that employees will be unwilling to make additional contributions to their job or the organization unless some basic conditions are met. Thus, inadequate pay, unsafe working conditions, work schedules that conflict with child care needs, or an onerous supervisor will serve to inhibit employee motivation to meet service standards and therefore reduce the overall level of customer satisfaction (Raleigh, 1998). Managers and executives can also adjust organizational conditions to promote employee satisfaction by providing a favorable environment where employees can move toward self-actualization (Johnson, 1997).

TABLE 12.2. Herzberg's Motivator-Hygiene Theory Factors

| Motivation Factors | Hygiene Factors |
| --- | --- |
| Opportunity for growth and advancement | Working conditions |
| Achievement or accomplishment | Money, status, and recognition |
| Recognition for accomplishment | Interpersonal relationships |
| Challenging or interesting work | Supervision |
| Responsibility for work | Company policies and administration |

*Sources:* Herzberg, Mausner, and Snyderman, 1959; Herzberg, 1968.

### Process Theories of Motivation

Vroom developed the "expectancy theory" for work situations. His model is based on the assumption that individuals make conscious and rational choices about work behavior. Application of the Vroom model may be based on the notion of outcomes and valences. The *outcomes* are consequences anticipated by a worker following certain behavior, while *valences* refer to the extent to which those outcomes appear to be attractive. The expectancy theory would explain employee behavior as being that which would bring about the greatest expectation of individual value based on accomplishment, acceptance by peers, fatigue, and similar factors (Vroom, 1964). Porter and Lawler have refined the Vroom model and hold that efforts by an individual may not necessarily result in good job performance because of an individual's inability to accomplish necessary tasks, or that there may not be a good understanding of the tasks necessary to complete the job in a satisfactory manner (Steers, Porter, and Bigler, 1996).

### Other Theories of Motivation

The work of Maslow, Herzberg, Porter, and Lawler has provided a useful framework within the structure of process and content. Managers, however, have not easily adapted to the findings of these behaviorists. In a more traditional setting, managers have taken a less reasoned approach. One has proven effective under some circumstances that were prevalent in the past. One of the earliest theories to find its way into the management literature was that of Frederic Winslow Taylor, based on his work at the Midvale Steel Company in Pennsylvania at the start of the twentieth century. Taylor is generally recognized for his part in developing the scientific management school. In his work, Taylor recognized that responsibility for providing an adequate work environment, tools, and training belonged to managers, not workers (Urwick, 1956). Taylor understood that it was necessary to provide basic factors, such as Maslow's basic needs and Herzberg's hygiene factors, before additional efforts to motivate workers would be effective.

McGregor, Ouchi, and others have set forth useful management motivation models. McGregor is best known for his recognition that some managers may categorize workers as either Theory X or Theory Y people. In that categorization, Theory X workers dislike work and will avoid it when possible, have little ambition, tend to shun responsibility, want security, and therefore require managers to use coercion, control, and threats of punishment to attain organizational objectives (Hodgetts, 1996). McGregor's

Theory Y holds that people find work as natural as resting or playing, will exercise self-direction and self-control, will associate commitment to objectives with rewards for achievement, will seek responsibility, and will use imagination and creativity to solve problems. Theory Y also holds that most of the potential of the workforce is only partially utilized (McGregor, 1960; Hodgetts, 1996).

Ouchi, who studied Japanese organizations, has also added an international dimension to the theories of motivation. He has provided tools for adapting the Japanese model to other cultural environments with his Theory Z. Ouchi sets out certain dimensions that characterize Japanese management. In some sense, the characteristics of that model are applicable in a broader, global setting: lifetime employment, consensual decision making, collective responsibility, slow evaluation and promotion, informal control, nonspecialized career paths, and holistic concerns for people have been historically present in the Japanese organization (Ouchi, 1991). Although some of these characteristics are changing, managers can view the elements that contribute to success and apply them to the motivation of hospitality, tourism, and leisure employees (Albrecht, 1988; Siu, Tsang, and Wong, 1997).

## EMPOWERMENT

### Definitions of Empowerment

Empowerment takes the theories of employee motivation and places them in a larger setting, one that also considers organizational processes, communication, and organizational boundaries. Empowerment involves making clear to workers that they have both the authority and resources for getting work done correctly and then holding them responsible for that work (Hodgetts, 1994, 1996). Blanchard stresses that people in an organization already have the power to do the job through their knowledge and motivation, and that empowerment is merely the process of "letting the power out" (Blanchard, Carlos, and Randolph, 1996; Lashley, 1996).

One prominent example of the application of empowerment in the hotel industry comes from the Ritz-Carlton group. The chain takes special care to fully train each employee in its philosophy, divided into "Credo," "Three Steps of Service," and "The Ritz-Carlton Basics." Each employee has a wallet-size card to remind him or her of those elements. Employees are taught that "We Are Ladies and Gentlemen Serving Ladies and Gentlemen." This stresses a sense of equality and the level of behavior expected.

The Credo states:

> The Ritz-Carlton Hotel is a place where the genuine care and comfort of our guests is our highest mission.
>
> We pledge to provide the finest personal service and facilities for our guests who will always enjoy a warm, relaxed yet refined ambience.
>
> The Ritz-Carlton experience enlivens the senses, instills well-being, and fulfills even the unexpressed wishes and needs of our guests.

The steps of service provide further general guidance to all employees, and make clear that each is responsible for the guest experience. Moreover, each employee has the ability to remedy problems and may commit hotel assets toward ensuring the Credo and philosophy are carried out.

Hodgetts provides a different viewpoint in stating that "The basic ideas of empowerment include: (1) giving employees greater authority to make decisions, (2) maintaining an open and decentralized communication system, (3) drawing people from many different departments in solving complex organizational problems, and (4) rewarding and recognizing those who assume responsibility and perform well" (Hodgetts, 1993). Empowerment gives autonomy over the *way* in which work is done and reemphasizes the need for accountability (Carr, 1994).

### Different Concepts and Applications of Empowerment

Blanchard has laid out a straightforward model for organizational empowerment in which he contends that "empowerment isn't magic. It consists of a few simple steps and a lot of persistence" (Blanchard, Carlos, and Randolph, 1996, p. 115). Application of the Blanchard model lies in three keys: sharing information with everyone, creating autonomy through boundaries, and replacement of the old hierarchy with self-directed work teams.

Blanchard's "first key is to share information with everyone" (Blanchard, Carlos, and Randolph, 1996, p. 27). Managers have traditionally shared only the information with employees that the managers believed the employees needed to know. This approach rations information, and permits the manager to act as a broker of a resource. Lower-level employees are not provided all available information, and are frequently provided insufficient information to be effective at minimal levels. Blanchard's approach permits employees to decide what information is necessary for effective operation and makes that information available to them. An extension of the total sharing of information is contained in the concept of "open-book management," in which employees at all levels are given access to information, and are also provided training and education to best use the information for their, and for the organization's, benefit (Stack, 1992; Case, 1996).

Blanchard's "second key is to create autonomy through boundaries" (Blanchard, Carlos, and Randolph, 1996, p. 39). He refers to boundaries as those things that mark the limits and define the areas in which employees are free to operate without direct managerial supervision. These boundaries may be defined by goals, policies, and general guidelines. The areas that are specifically cited include:

1. Business purpose
2. Organizational values
3. Image of the future
4. Organizational goals, including what, when, where, and how individuals and the organization do things
5. Roles of people
6. The organizational structure and its supporting systems (Blanchard, Carlos, and Randolph, 1996).

Blanchard's "third key is to replace the hierarchy with self-directed work teams" (Blanchard, Carlos, and Randolph, 1996, p. 57). The essence of this concept is that workers at the lowest possible level can form teams which can produce more and better service than can the same individuals working alone (see Table 12.3). Self-directed teams consist of groups of employees who have responsibility for an entire product, service, or process (Blanchard, Carlos, and Randolph, 1996). Such teams are not necessarily without a manager, though the role of the manager may rotate and that manager may be selected by the team itself. To achieve and ensure that self-directed work teams can occur, Blanchard suggests that employees must be sufficiently trained and educated to work independently, and that managers must teach team members that the teams can become less dependent on hierarchical management and direction.

## BRINGING TOGETHER MOTIVATION AND EMPOWERMENT

Motivation implies providing the incentive for individuals to move toward organizational goals (Perry, 1997). Empowerment implies the need to move people toward meeting goals, and providing additional tools and the environment and circumstances necessary for that motivation to work

TABLE 12.3. Adaptation of Blanchard's Three Keys to Empowerment

| | Key 1 | Key 2 | Key 3 |
|---|---|---|---|
| **Motivational Elements from Empowerment** | Sharing information with everyone | Creating autonomy through boundaries | Replace hierarchy with self-directed work teams |
| | Lets people understand the current situation in clear terms | Builds upon information sharing | Empowered teams can do more than empowered individuals |
| | Begins to build trust throughout the organization | Clarifies the vision (big picture) with input from everyone | People don't start out knowing how to work in self-directed teams |
| | Breaks down traditional hierarchical thinking | Helps translate vision into roles and goals (little pictures) | Dissatisfaction is a natural step in the process |
| | Helps people be more responsible | Defines values and rules that underlie desired actions; when values are clear, decision making is easier | Everyone has to be trained in team skills |
| | Encourages people to act like owners of the organization | Develops structures and procedures that empower people | Commitment and support have to come from the top |
| | | Reminds us that empowerment is a journey | Teams with information and skills can replace the old hierarchy |

*Source:* Blanchard, Carlos, and Randolph, 1996.

freely, effectively, and successfully. Motivation is therefore an essential, but not exclusive, element of empowerment. Empowerment in hospitality, tourism, and leisure settings requires bringing together all those elements: motivation, information, and the structural considerations necessary for effective team interactions (VanDerWall, 1998).

A hospitality employer may wish to introduce the Blanchard approach to empowerment, and might implement the three keys through a program involving employee training and structural adjustments over time. Servers and other front-of-house employees might be taught appropriate service standards, behavioral expectations, and how to better understand the business and profit aspects of the organization. Back-of-house employees might participate in similar educational efforts where the customers are internal: the servers and others who have the direct guest interface. Structural changes will also be necessary to permit employees to act differently.

The owner will have to provide additional information, delegate authority to make decisions to the lowest practical level, and provide some incentive to encourage employees to work in self-directed teams and to behave in different ways (McDonald, 1997; Wilson, 1998).

Empowerment as a concept was first introduced into the manufacturing sector, yet is readily adaptable to many segments of the hospitality, tourism, and leisure industries. Managers in some segments will find a more hospitable environment than in others. Some characteristics that contribute to or tend to impede application of empowerment in hospitality are shown in Table 12.4.

TABLE 12.4. Factors Enabling or Inhibiting Empowerment in Hospitality, Tourism, and Leisure Organizations

| **Empowerment Enabling Factors** | |
| --- | --- |
| Service orientation | Service delivery occurs at the "moment of truth," meaning that the frontline employee is responsible for service and service quality to the customer. |
| Distributed workplaces | Many aspects of the hospitality, tourism, leisure industry are distributed at various locations, making it necessary for employees to operate with a high degree of independence. |
| Lack of close oversight | The distribution of employees, and the fact that employees interact directly with guests and customers, frequently makes close supervision difficult or impractical. |
| Traditions of the industry | Industry traditions of providing "service to the guest" encourages frontline employees to take necessary initiatives to deliver appropriate levels and quality of service. |
| **Empowerment Inhibiting Factors** | |
| Low wage, high turnover | Many industry jobs require minimal formal education and experience, and are relatively poorly compensated. Entry-level employees may not find sufficient motivation to become empowered, or have sufficient experience to do so. |
| Lack of training | Persons filling jobs in the hospitality, tourism, and leisure industry frequently receive little or minimal technical training, and seldom receive the training necessary to understand their larger roles in an organization, thereby making empowerment difficult to achieve. |
| Pressure for profits | As is the case with many organizations, firms in the industry frequently operate with very thin margins and find significant pressures to increase short-term profitability at the expense of investment in training, education, or organizational change necessary for empowerment. |

Travel, tourism, and hospitality owners, executives, and managers who seek improved organizational performance, profitability, and guest or customer satisfaction may seek to empower their employees to meet those objectives. Within the industry, each manager will have to examine critically the organizational situation and the degree to which the organization is willing to cede authority to lower-level managers, supervisors, or first-line employees. Many of the characteristics of the industry actually favor empowerment, while others serve to inhibit it. Each can be overcome over time, with the appropriate commitment.

Bowen suggests that employees are not suddenly empowered because managers tell them they are or because companies publicize a culture of empowerment (Bowen and Lawler, 1995). Lawler, Mohrman, and Ledford (1992) further suggest that empowerment exists when companies implement practices that distribute power information, knowledge, and rewards throughout the organization.

Not all employees and not all managers favor the implementation of empowerment programs. Employees may feel that they are being expected to do more without additional reward. Managers and owners may feel that their authority is being removed and that they will be stripped of decision-making ability by staff (Potochny, 1998). The challenge to managers is to implement programs wisely in order to create a powerful tool to increase revenue and improve customer service.

For an organization to implement a program of employee empowerment, some factors must be present and visible. These may be identified as "tools for implementation of empowerment."

### Tools for Implementation of Empowerment

1. *Executive leadership:* As is the case with most organizational initiatives, the introduction of empowerment activities requires a commitment from the top of the organization. If an organization chooses to conduct business in the same manner as in the past, there is little reason to believe that the results will be different. This change requires a demonstrated commitment and a willingness to change in order to introduce new methods (Stutts, 1986; Sparrowe, 1995).

2. *Policies in place for empowerment to work:* The boundaries and autonomy described by Blanchard must be established to provide the flexibility and independence for employees to act freely to their full capacity.

3. *Training to bring individual competencies to necessary levels:* For employees to be empowered, they must have the tools necessary to do their jobs. These tools, skills, and knowledge, must include ap-

propriate technical skills, interpersonal and managerial skills, and team skills necessary for success in an interdependent environment.

4. *Information sharing:* Blanchard and others have emphasized the need for free dissemination of information and for the skills necessary to use that information. This implies the development of systems and procedures to develop and share information and knowledge directly related to the workplace and to the economic environment in which the organization operates (Stack, 1992; Blanchard, Carlos, and Randolph, 1996; Case, 1996).

5. *Organization and structural change to permit successful operations:* The fundamental systems of an organization must be reviewed and revised to permit employees to become empowered and to operate in an empowered manner. This may require development and implementation of policies, rules, reporting relationships, and lines of organization to permit uninhibited operation of self-directed work teams and empowered employees (Sanson, 1995; Belasco, 1996; Hayes, 1998).

## Other Benefits of Empowerment

Effective empowerment is expected to permit frontline employees to deliver higher quality customer service and to be able to respond more quickly to guest service challenges. Empowerment programs may also have a positive effect on other aspects of organizational operations: better relationships among employees and between employees and management, lower turnover, and higher employee morale (Potochny, 1998; Rowe, 1998). Bowen and Lawler (1995) also cite the potential for greater and sustainable competitive advantage in the marketplace with an empowered employee force.

## CONCLUSION

Empowerment of workers in the hospitality, tourism, and leisure industries can provide firms with a competitive advantage and a way of motivating employees and increasing levels of customer service and potential profit. The path to empowerment is one which requires significant commitment and investment, but one which literature and experience tells us will be repaid.

## REFERENCES

Albrecht, K. (1988). *At America's Service.* Homewood, IL: Dow Jones-Irwin.

Albrecht, K. and R. Zemke (1985). *Service America!* Homewood, IL: Dow Jones-Irwin.

Atkinson, J.W. (1964). *An Introduction to Motivation.* Princeton, NJ: Van Nostrand.

Belasco, J. (1996). Can an HR Department Empower a Change Process. *Journal for Quality and Participation* 19(1): 52-54.

Blanchard, K., J. Carlos and A. Randolph (1996). *Empowerment Takes More Than a Minute.* San Francisco: Berrett-Koehler.

Bowen, D.E. and E.E. Lawler (1992). The Empowerment of Service Workers: What, Why, How, and When. *Sloan Management Review* (Spring): 31-39.

Bowen, D.E. and E.E. Lawler (1995). Empowering Service Employees. *Sloan Management Review* 36(1): 73-84.

Campbell, J.P. and R.D. Pritchard (1976). Motivation Theory in Industrial and Organizational Pyschology. In *Handbook of Industrial and Organizational Psychology,* ed. M.D. Dunnette (pp. 263-296). Chicago: Rand McNally.

Carlzon, J. (1989). *Moments of Truth.* New York: HarperCollins.

Carr, C. (1994). Empowered Organizations, Empowering Leaders. *Training and Development Journal* 34(4): 47-59.

Case, J. (1996). *Open-Book Management: The Coming Business Revolution.* New York: HarperBusiness.

Frunzi, G.L. and P.E. Savini (1997). *Supervision: The Art of Management.* Upper Saddle River, NJ: Prentice Hall.

Hayes, J. (1998). ECR Confab: Win Customers with Better, Smarter Choices. *Nation's Restaurant News* 32(13): 8.

Herzberg, F. (1968). One More Time: How Do You Motivate Your Employees? *Harvard Business Review* 46(January-February): 53-62.

Herzberg, F., B. Mausner, and B.B. Snyderman (1959). *The Motivation to Work.* New York: Wiley.

Hodgetts, R.M. (1993). *Blueprints for Continuous Improvement: Lessons from the Baldridge Winners.* New York: American Management Association.

Hodgetts, R.M. (1994). Quality Lessons for America's Baldridge Winners. *Business Horizons* 23(6): 5.

Hodgetts, R.M. (1996). *Modern Human Relations at Work.* Fort Worth, TX: Dryden Press, Harcourt Brace College Publishers.

Johnson, E. (1997). Human Resources Motivation: Beyond Employee of the Month. *Lodging* 22(7): 33.

Jones, M.R. (Ed.) (1955). *Nebraska Symposium on Motivation.* Lincoln, NB: University of Nebraska Press.

Lashley, C. (1996). Research Issues for Employee Empowerment in Hospitality Organizations. *International Journal of Hospitality Management* 15(4): 333-346.

Lashley, C. (1997). Employee Empowerment in Hospitality Services. *Journal of College & University Foodservice* 3(3): 33-62.

Lawler, E.E., S.A. Mohrman, and G.E. Ledford (1992). *Employee Involvement and Total Quality Management: Practices and Results in Fortune 1000 Companies.* San Francisco: Jossey-Bass Publishers.

Maslow, A.H. (1943). A Theory of Human Motivation. *Psychology Review* 50(2): 378-379.

Maslow, A.H. (1968). *Motivation and Personality*. New York: Harper & Rowe.

McClelland, D.C. (1961). *The Achieving Society*. Princeton, NJ: Van Nostrand.

McDonald, T. (1997). Real Issues: Getting in the Spirit: Improve Your Job by Putting Your Soul to Work. *Successful Meetings* 46(7): 22.

McGregor, D. (1960). *Human Side of Enterprise*. New York: McGraw-Hill.

Moon, C. and C. Swaffin-Smith (1998). Total Quality Management and New Patterns of Work: Is There Life Beyond Empowerment? *Total Quality Management* 9(2/3): 301-310.

Ouchi, W.G. (1991). *Theory Z: How American Business Can Meet the Japanese Challenge*. Reading, MA: Addison Wesley.

Perry, P.M. (1997). Motivating Interest: Sure-Fire Ways to Make Employees Work Harder and Smarter. *Restaurants USA* 17(2): 36-38.

Petrick, J.A. and D.S. Furr (1995). *Total Quality in Managing Human Resources*. Delray Beach, FL: St. Lucie Press.

Porter, L.W. and E.E. Lawler (1968). *Mangerial Attitudes and Performance*. Homewood, IL: Richard D. Irwin.

Potochny, D.K. (1998). Employee Empowerment: Key to Efficient Customer Service. *Nation's Restaurant News* 32(32): 46.

Raleigh, P. (1998). Employee Turnover and Theft Is Not Inevitable. *Nation's Restaurant News* 32(18): 46, 114.

Roethlisberger, F. and W.J. Dixon (1939). *Management and the Worker*. Cambridge, MA: Harvard University Press.

Rowe, M. (1998). Why Service Still Stinks. *Lodging Hospitality* 54(2): 22-26.

Sanson, M. (1995). Fired Up! Some of the Industry's Best Motivators Share Strategies for Helping Managers and Staff to Do Their Very Best. *Restaurant Hospitality* 79(2): 53-64.

Siu, V., N. Tsang, and S. Wong (1997). What Motivates Hong Kong's Hotel Employees? *Cornell Hotel & Restaurant Administration Quarterly* 38(5): 44-49.

Sparrowe, R.T. (1995). The Effects of Organizational Culture and Leader-Member Exchange on Employee Empowerment in the Hospitality Industry. *Hospitality Research Journal* 18(3): 95-109.

Stack, J. (1992). *Great Game of Business*. New York: Doubleday.

Steers, R.M., L.W. Porter, and G.A. Bigler (1996). *Motivation and Leadership at Work*. New York: McGraw-Hill.

Stutts, A.T. (1986). Productivity: A Review for the Hospitality Manager. *FIU Hospitality Review* 4(1): 38-47.

Urwick, L.F. (Ed.) (1956). *The Golden Book of Management*. London: Newman Neame Limited.

VanDerWall, S. (1998). Balance of Power: Authority or Empowerment? How You Can Get the Best of Both in the "Interdependent" Organization. *HR Magazine* 43(7): 190-191.

Vroom, V.H. (1964). *Work and Motivation*. New York: Wiley.

Wilson, K. (1998). Why the Owner-Operator System Still Works. *Nation's Restaurant News* 32(13): 32, 62.

Maslow, A.H. (1987) *Motivation and Personality*. New York: Harper & Row.

McClelland, D.C. (1961) *The Achieving Society*. Princeton, NJ: Van Nostrand.

Meyer, J.P. (1977) Real Money Comes in the Spirit: Impact Your Impact and Your Skill to Work. *Success in Progress*, 6(7), 82.

Mintzberg, H. (1980) *Mind in the Enterprise*. New York: McGraw-Hill.

Moore, T. and R. Griffin-Shin (1995) Total Care Quality Management and New Patterns of Work. In *Human Life Cycle and Improvement*, *Quality Care Practice*, January 10, 26, 30, 310.

Orsburn, J.D. (1990) *Quality E-Teams: Creating an Effective Core Value Top Line and Effective Bottom Line, 6(7)*. Addison Wesley.

Peters, T. (1992) *Mind in the Enterprise System*. New York: McGraw-Hill, Macmillan and Schuster Publisher.

Porter, L. and D.S. Fowler (1990) *Employee Motivation Behavior*. New York: Harper & Row.

[several illegible entries]

Schlesinger, L. and D.J. Dennis (1990) Service Leadership and the Bottom Line. In *Human Life Cycle*. New York.

Stone, M. (1992) Why Service We Work. *Fortune*, 6(7).

Spencer, M. (1990) *Total Life Cycle Chain Reaction*. New York: Harper. *Principles for Learning, Measurement and Success, 6(7), 12, 310.* Your Organization, *Employee Performance*, 6-38.

Stone, M.A. (1990) and S. Wolf (1992) ...Social Media Analysis, In *Employees' Choice Chain, R.C. Ashurman, Editor. Harper. Germany, 307, 11-40.*

Spreitzer, K.J. (1995) Total Chain of Organizational Culture: An Leader Member Exchange on Employee Empowerment in the Hospitality Industry. *Hospitality Research Journal, 18(3), 27-44.*

Shackleton, (1992). *Service Game in Business*. New York: Prentice.

Steers, R.M., L.W. Porter and Gregory Bigley (1996). *Motivation and Leadership at Work*. New York: McGraw-Hill.

Sloan, A.P. (1988) Productivity. *Analysis for the Hospitality Manager, 6(3). Hospitality Review*, 6(1), 38-42.

Upwick, L.F. (1947, 1996) *The Golden Book of Management*. London: Institute Named Impact.

VanDerWall, S. (1998) *Recognition Programs Aim to Boost Morale, How You Can Get the Best of Health in the Interval Period*. "Organization" HR Magazine. 43(3), 190-191.

Vroom, V.H. (1964) *Work and Motivation*. New York: Wiley.

Wilson, K. (1989) Why We Own Operational Systems. *HR News, Society for Human Resource Management, 6, 8.* "See More Team Charging Year."

# Chapter 13

# Service Guarantee: An Organization's Blueprint for Assisting the Delivery of Superior Service

Jay Kandampully

## INTRODUCTION

Tourism and the various components of tourism services have become an integral part of everyone's social pattern of consumption. In both developed and developing countries, social life has incorporated some aspects of hospitality, tourism, and leisure service consumption. This can take many forms, such as vacation, holiday, travel, recreation and eating out, etc. Consequently, tourism as a social phenomenon has gained recognition and acceptance in almost all social systems around the world. Williams and Shaw (1992) indicate that more than 637 million tourists were expected to cross international boundaries by the year 2000, and according to the World Tourism Organization (1999), tourism is currently the world's largest industry, earning over US$444.7 billion in 1998. Thus we can expect continued growth in tourism.

Growth in hospitality, tourism, and leisure services globally has posed an ongoing challenge to its managers. Relentless advances in technology have rendered ever-shorter life cycles to products and services (Achrol, 1991), ultimately diminishing their customer appeal. Products and services deemed satisfactory by the customer today will undoubtedly prove unsatisfactory to the same customer tomorrow. Hence, it is imperative that products and services demonstrate continuous enhancement of value through innovation and improvement. Today quality no longer constitutes a competitive weapon but is, in fact, the basic core offering expected by customers of every organization. The global economy has succeeded in elevating the role of quality to center stage in every business function. Thus, an organization's ability to continuously enhance the value of the service offering now constitutes the decisive factor in the pursuit of success.

Managers today have realized that traditional approaches to management are inadequate if they are to keep abreast of an increasingly competitive market. To maintain market leadership, managers need to adopt new approaches that will not only enable improvements to be made, but that will also support simultaneous improvement and innovation of the organization's systems, procedures, and people on a continuous basis.

From a customer's perspective, it is the service element (customer-employee interaction) that effectively increases the value of a hospitality, tourism, and leisure organization's product/service offering. Moreover, in almost all of these organizations, products and services cannot be sold in isolation, but are commonly offered in combination. Not only does one support the other, but it is this combination that significantly increases the value to the customer. Consequently, customers' perception of the services offered are vital to all hospitality, tourism, and recreational organizations. This warrants continuous improvement and innovation of systems, procedures, and people to ensure that customers receive superior value for their patronage.

## SERVICE PROMISE

Empirical findings from Berry, Parasuraman, and Zeithaml (1994) demonstrate that service reliability is at the heart of excellent service and is considered the core attribute of good service by most customers. Breaking the service promise is the single most important way in which service companies fail their customers (Berry, Zeithaml, and Parasuraman, 1990). In most service businesses, customers are required to pay before the service is delivered. In other words, service is first sold, then produced and consumed simultaneously. For example, the customer buys a flight ticket first, with the full expectation of receiving all that is promised. Consistency of service refers to the absence of variation in the output from one occasion to another as well as in comparison with what is promised in the first instance (Chase and Bowen, 1991). So, to the service customer, consistency and reliability are synonymous. Consistency implies that the customer receives the same treatment, and the same level of service—time and time again. The authors point out that in the majority of service interactions, customers are unable to pretest the service reliability prior to purchase, with the result that the customer is unsure of the reliability of the particular service being offered.

According to Zeithaml (1981), services offer only a limited number of cues to customers wishing to make a purchasing decision. Therefore, consumers perceive a greater risk when buying services than when buying products (Zeithaml, 1981; Eiglier and Langeard, 1977). For organizations in the tourism and hospitality industry, developing strategies that reduce the risk consumers associate with using their services is important. One such strategy is to offer a service guarantee. This guarantee has a dual role: informing customers what to expect, and ensuring that the services delivered are commensurate with that standard (Maher, 1991). A service guarantee offers an organization the opportunity to take immediate corrective action, which is crucial in converting dissatisfied customers into satisfied ones (Bredin, 1995). The service guarantee serves as an organization's commitment to ensuring its guests are happy (Evans, Clark, and Knutson, 1996).

The main theme in the literature regarding service guarantees is that they can help firms learn from their mistakes, which directly reduces the risk of customers being exposed to a repeat of the same service failure. This is achieved through the conduit of customer information. Service guarantees trigger the flow of information back to the company as immediate feedback (Ettorree, 1994), enabling the organization to learn quickly about customers' changing expectations (Bredin, 1995). As customers become less inhibited about complaining (Firnstahl, 1989), information flows more freely. Moreover, by using service guarantees, firms are able to learn from complaints (Bredin, 1995), they are forced to respond to customer feedback (Rose, 1990), and they are able to measure quality failures as they happen (Gooley, 1993) as well as critically analyze the data in a meaningful way (Martin, 1995). Thus, service guarantees enhance a company's opportunity to continuously improve systemwide and have the capacity to transform dissatisfied customers into loyal ones.

## GAINING CUSTOMER TRUST

Indeed, this customer focus, the strategic management decision to add value to the firm's offering, underlies the success of almost all leading hospitality, tourism, and recreational organizations. The long-term sustainability of this market leadership is every organization's aim. Gaining and sustaining the customer-supplier relationship as a long-term commitment has thus become a prerequisite for leading organizations. Moreover, gaining and sustaining customers' trust in the organization extends beyond the marketing function.

The outcome of a service encounter is seldom subject to a guarantee, rendering a customer's perceived risk intangible, which is an inherent feature of interaction with a service organization. The encounter cannot be reworked or returned and, more important, the customer's payment is given with the tacit understanding and expectation of receiving a good result. In every service transaction, customers (unable to see or pretest the outcome) are thus at risk. Service managers need to recognize, acknowledge, and reduce this customer risk and by so doing, create a unique opportunity to differentiate themselves from their competitors. To minimize this risk, many leading hospitality, tourism, and leisure organizations have recognized and implemented the strategy of offering a service guarantee.

## BLUEPRINT FOR SUPERIOR SERVICE

A service guarantee essentially constitutes an organization's service standard, a "blueprint" for service, defining the organization's service promise to its internal and external customers simultaneously. This means that the service guarantee maintains both marketing and operational functions. As a marketing function, the service guarantee informs customers of the specific service standards they can expect to receive. Operationally, the service guarantee represents the blueprint of the organization's service standard, its promise (external standard) to be maintained. Thus, service guarantees simultaneously affect and enhance an organization's marketing effectiveness and operational competency, both internally and externally (see Figure 13.1).

Moreover, I argue that a clear and customer-focused service guarantee will force an organization to do several things better than it has ever had to do them before. A service guarantee enhances an organization's ability to:

- Reinforce the service promise
- Indicate the level (standard) of expected service, to both customers and employees
- Receive immediate customer feedback
- Respond to customer feedback
- Identify failure points in the service system
- Reward customers/employees
- Continuously assess and revise standards

- Undertake training and education to complement changes
- Adopt empowerment programs
- Encourage employee involvement and ownership
- Enhance internal service quality
- Develop structures and systems to support service
- Anticipate changes in the marketplace

The focus of the service guarantee is to bring the customer loop right to every employee in the company—thus, the employees can literally hear the customer speaking to them through these guarantees. Additionally, the service guarantee presents the organization with an opportunity to take immediate corrective action, this being crucial in converting dissatisfied customers into satisfied ones. Leading on from this point, it can be argued that one of the significant benefits of the service guarantee is the myriad information received from customers as immediate feedback, which, in turn, rapidly informs the organization of its customers' changing expectations. Not only does the service guarantee enable an organization to learn from customers' complaints, but it effectively compels the organization to respond to customer feedback.

Thus, the service guarantee assists an organization to create a customer-driven standard of service (see Figure 13.2). Understanding customers'

FIGURE 13.1. Service Guarantee: The Impact on Marketing and Operational Functions

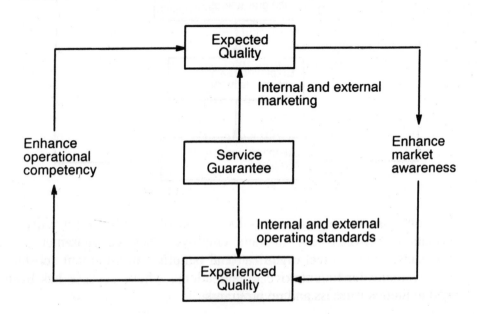

FIGURE 13.2. A Mechanism to Develop and Implement Guarantees for Creating Superior Service

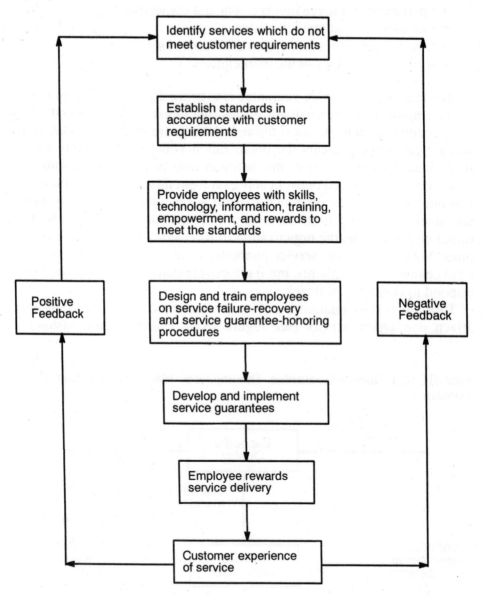

wants increases the organization's likelihood of establishing a unity of expectations between customer and employee. Service guarantee programs substantially affect organizational benefits, an argument substantiated by many leading service organizations, whose success has been linked to their service guarantee programs.

Kandampully and Butler (1998) proposed the employment of service guarantees and reward systems, which will not only enhance the customer feedback mechanism, but may be effectively utilized to initiate a process of recovery, correction, and innovation. Service management literature suggests that service guarantees force the organization to create an "error discovery" system (Hart, 1988), particularly where customers have encountered a negative service experience.

According to Hart, Schlesinger, and Maher (1992), a guarantee forces an organization to acknowledge and understand the reasons underlying failure. It can therefore be argued that guarantees assist organizations to identify negative service experiences, initiate recovery and corrective action (staff training, procedural changes), and subsequently make innovations in service delivery. The focus here is not merely to solicit complaints, but to ensure that the problem is corrected in the first instance, and that action is taken to prevent its reoccurrence. Guarantees also enable firms to maintain records of negative incidents, from which training issues can be identified. Additionally, guarantees encourage customers to communicate positive comments and specific personal requirements. Moreover, it is possible that customers' specific requests may be adopted as value-adding service concepts.

Although it is important to learn of customers' negative experiences, it is equally important that an organization learns of customers' positive experiences for the purpose of informing and rewarding the internal customers (Kandampully and Butler, 1998). This will directly affect employee morale, which has the potential to immeasurably increase the probability of augmented service and quality (Stevens, 1996). The success of hospitality, tourism, and leisure organizations depends, to a large extent, on the commitment of their frontline staff, so these organizations must place a premium on attracting and rewarding employees with exceptional social skills (Zemke, 1988). For all service organizations, developing and maintaining long-term relationships with customers and employees is of particular importance (Kandampully and Duddy, 1999), and linking service guarantees with reward systems assists an organization to recognize and compliment its patrons and employees.

## ELEMENTS OF AN EFFECTIVE
## SERVICE GUARANTEE

There is little debate in current literature as to what constitutes an effective service guarantee. According to Hart (1988), an effective guarantee contains certain elements without which it lacks power and credence and results in greater damage to the organization's image. Hence, guarantees should have the following qualities:

1. *Easy to understand and communicate:* It should be written in simple, concise language that pinpoints the promise. The service guarantee must be understood by both employees and the customer. Written guarantees must use plain language to avoid confusion and misinterpretation. Employees need to know what the guarantee contains without referring to a manual; therefore a simple, precise statement is best.
2. *Unconditional:* It should promise customer satisfaction unconditionally. The more conditions placed upon the customer, the less credible the guarantee becomes. Conditions only place barriers in the customer's way when they wish to communicate their displeasure.
3. *Meaningful:* The guarantee should promise features that are important to the customer, not the organization. This ensures that the organization researches what is meaningful to the customer before developing the guarantee. Areas that are important to the customer include having the telephone answered quickly, receiving service that is nonthreatening, dealing with employees who are knowledgeable and efficient, etc.
4. *Easy to invoke:* Customers who are already dissatisfied should not have to jump through hoops to invoke a guarantee. Any impediment to making a complaint will only exacerbate their anger and frustration. "No hassles" (but not "no questions asked") allows quick resolution of the problem but does not preclude the opportunity to enquire about the failure points, thereby allowing the firm to correct the system.
5. *Easy and quick to collect:* Customers should not have to work hard to collect a payout from a guarantee. Any form of compensation should be immediate, without a lengthy, formal procedure. Empowerment of staff with responsibility, authority, knowledge, training, and trust will allow all employees to authorize compensation.

Promising significant payout in the service guarantee has three effective results: (1) it communicates to the customer that the firm is serious about its commitment, (2) it encourages the customer to complain, and (3) it motivates the company to make immediate changes in the system to prevent further payouts.

## IMPLICATIONS

Offering a service guarantee implies that an organization is committed to quality service and desires to continually make improvements to its service. However, the implementation of a guarantee has other implications.

A service guarantee becomes a proactive method of providing the organization with information on whether the service being offered is pleasing the customer. Analysis of this information will determine any changes in customer expectations and will enable changes to the service to meet customer demand.

Dissatisfied customers can do great harm to an organization. The 3/39 rule states that one satisfied customer will tell three other people, but a dissatisfied one will tell thirty-nine others. This also is true for dissatisfied customers who complained and became victims of a poorly designed and written service guarantee.

Hospitality, tourism, and leisure organizations should always underpromise and overdeliver a service. Overpromising and underdelivering will ensure that a customer will be dissatisfied.

Empowerment of employees with knowledge, training, and trust will prove essential to effectively manage the service guarantee. Employee empowerment provides the customer with an instant solution to problems, and the employees themselves will develop an attitude of "whatever it takes to please the customer."

Employees will also be forthcoming with their problems with the system rather than hiding them. Once they realize that the system is not intended to punish employees, they will accept ownership of their work and take every measure to improve it.

## EMPLOYEE PARTICIPATION AND EMPOWERMENT

Service management literature has repeatedly emphasized the importance of the human element in the delivery of superior service (Solomon et al., 1985) and the dual role of service personnel in the maintenance of operational and marketing tasks in the organization (Bitner, Booms, and Tetreault, 1990). Many services are designed to assist, service, or fulfill customers' personal needs, and it is in such situations that the customer commonly seeks to establish and maintain a relationship with the service provider (Parasuraman, Berry, and Zeithaml, 1991). Further, research shows that, although reliability is the most important dimension in meeting customer expectations, the human elements often serve to bridge any gaps that may occur as service failures.

Associated with service guarantees is the issue of employee participation and empowerment. Lawler (1992) believes that organizations in which employee involvement/empowerment is the norm will prove superior, as empowerment has a direct effect on four organizational performance variables: cost, productivity, quality, and speed in responding to customer requests. One of the underlying assumptions of those advocating empowerment is that employees' values will be in line with those of the organization. Organizations must be prepared to allow employees the freedom to act and to make decisions based on their own judgment. For example, if a hotel receptionist is empowered, then that receptionist must be able to decide how best to deal with the needs of the customer and should be accountable and responsible for dealing with customer complaints. However, unless employees are authorized, informed, trained, and empowered to respond immediately to customers' requests, guarantees will not prove successful. Employees need to be given responsibility, authority, and information so that their decisions will be in line with the organization's goal. Additionally, managers will have to trust their employees to act on behalf of the organization and should reward the employees regularly for their initiatives and efforts. Evans, Clark, and Knutson (1996) state that employee training and empowerment are the two keys to successful implementation of a service guarantee program.

## PITFALLS ASSOCIATED WITH SERVICE GUARANTEES

Service guarantees that are poorly designed or incorrectly implemented can cause problems for both customers and the organization. These pitfalls are discussed in the following sections.

### Customers Who Cheat

The expectation that customers will abuse the promise has prevented managers from implementing a service guarantee, but only a very small percentage of customers are dishonest. Establishing a good information management system to record past claims can prevent this problem.

### The Organization Fails to Learn from Dissatisfied Customers and Fails to Correct Errors

If the organization fails to learn and to make changes, not only will the dissatisfied customers tell others of their poor experience, but payouts will continue to occur for the same failures. Having a service recovery system means accepting that service errors will occur; however, the organization preplans for such situations and establishes systems to detect errors as and when they happen so that immediate corrective action can be taken. By learning from the failure the organization can prevent future failures, not only by the person who was involved with the service delivery but every employee in the organization.

### The Groundwork Has Not Been Done

An organization must have the following:

1. Consistency in meeting the standards stated in the service guarantee, or it will lose considerable sums of money.
2. Fully empowered employees. The firm's employees must have the authority to implement the policy and solve customer's problems on the spot. The guarantee will soon lose its effectiveness if a long, complex procedure must be followed. Therefore, training and support from the managers are necessary. Hampton Inn (Promus Corporation, USA) employees are "empowered to do whatever it takes to satisfy the customer" (Sowder, 1996, p. 57). If managers do not support employees' decisions, then the employees too will be dissatisfied. Unhappy employees do not create satisfied customers.
3. A reward system that motivates employees (to take additional responsibility) and customers (to inform the organization of both positive and negative service outcomes) alike.
4. A system designed to equip employees with information and training so that they are able to respond to customer needs.

### Competitors Are First in Offering Service Guarantees

Obviously the first organization in the industry to implement a guarantee gets publicity from the guarantee launch and therefore gains the competitive edge.

### Service Guarantee That Excludes Too Many Customers

Exclusions and conditions in the fine print have been utilized to discourage complaints and payouts in the past. If customers are discouraged from complaining, then the organization will not learn from its mistakes and will not make the appropriate changes.

### Service Guarantee That Tarnishes the Company's Image

Guaranteeing parts of the service that are basic features, such as clean and hygienic rooms, should not be necessary. In fact, to do so would make customers suspect that these are areas in which the company regularly fails. In Japan a written guarantee may provoke suspicion, as the culture assumes implied guarantees from every firm.

## SERVICE GUARANTEES
## IN THE FAST-FOOD SECTOR

### McDonald's

McDonald's offers an explicit unconditional service guarantee on the quality of the food as well as the speed of their service. It is the aim of McDonald's to deliver an order within sixty seconds. A customer who has to wait more than three minutes will receive a complementary item (e.g., drink or fries), and for a wait of more than five minutes the customer will be given vouchers for his or her next visit. Customers who are dissatisfied with their current meal will have the problem fixed immediately and will receive their next meal free.

### Kentucky Fried Chicken

Kentucky Fried Chicken appears to have an implicit guarantee, in that they have internal standards with which they wish to comply. They aim to deliver an order within sixty seconds, and nobody should wait more than five minutes. Payouts are management's responsibility and can range from complementary items to vouchers to the value of the meal. In June 1998, they had a special promotion called the "service challenge," which was to deliver all food orders within sixty seconds or provide free fries.

According to Maher (1992), guarantees should not be judgment calls; "prompt delivery" or "courteous service" are open to interpretation. Statements such as "lunch in five minutes" or "you will have a room," on the other hand, set a standard to be lived up to.

## SERVICE GUARANTEES IN THE HOTEL SECTOR

### Hampton Inn

The Hampton Inn of Memphis, Tennessee, offers a 100 percent satisfaction guarantee for guests who are not satisfied with the quality of their stay at the hotel. Employees at all levels from general manager to house-keeper are empowered to do whatever it takes to satisfy guests. According to Sowder (1996), the unconditional guarantee offered by Hampton Inn is not merely a program; instead, it represents how the hotel makes decisions and runs its business.

## SERVICE GUARANTEES IN THE TRAVEL SECTOR

*Citytravel*

Citytravel (a subsidiary of Citycorp) guarantees the lowest price in the market. A customer who is aware of a lower price offered by a competitor can inform Citytravel through a toll-free number. Following confirmation of this through their computer fare index, Citytravel will offer the lower fare to the customer or refund the money (Hart, 1988). Citytravel believes that by doing this, they gain the opportunity to demonstrate their superior service to their customers.

## CONCLUSION

A service guarantee serves as a standard, expressed explicitly to both customers and employees, for what is being promised by the firm and what standard the customers may expect of them. Service guarantees allow customers to communicate directly with employees. Additionally, the service guarantee presents the firm with an opportunity to take imme-diate corrective action, which is crucial to converting dissatisfied custom-ers into satisfied ones. Consequently, it can be argued that one of the significant benefits of the service guarantee is the immediate feedback of customer information, which informs the firm of customers' changing expectations. Not only does the service guarantee enable a firm to learn from customers' complaints, it effectively compels the organization to respond to customer feedback immediately. In realizing the cost involved with each failure, the company has an additional opportunity to learn from the mistake and so eliminate the possibility of further similar mistakes.

In essence, the service guarantee assists an organization to create a customer-driven standard of service. Services management literature sug-gests that well-managed service guarantee programs substantially affect organizational benefits, which is confirmed by many leading service orga-nizations, whose success has been linked to their service guarantee pro-grams.

# REFERENCES

Achrol, R.S. (1991). Evolution of the Marketing Organization: New Forms for Turbulent Environments, *Journal of Marketing*, 55 (October): 77-93.

Berry, L.L., Parasuraman, A., and Zeithaml, V.A. (1994). Improving Service Quality in America: Lessons Learned, *Academy of Management Executive*, 8 (2): 32-45.

Berry, L.L., Zeithaml, V.A., and Parasuraman, A. (1990). Five Imperatives for Improving Service Quality, *Sloan Management Review*, (Summer): 29-38.

Bitner, M.J., Booms, B.H., and Tetreault, M.S. (1990). The Service Encounter: Diagnosing Favorable and Unfavorable Incidents, *Journal of Marketing*, 54 (January): 71-84.

Bredin, J. (1995). Keeping Customers, *Industry Week*, 244 (18, October 2): 2.

Chase, R.B. and Bowen, D. (1991). Service Quality and the Service Delivery System: A Diagnostic Framework. In Brown, S.W., Gummesson, E., Edvardsson, B., and Gustavsson, B. (Eds.), *Service Quality*, Lexington, MA: Lexington Books, pp. 157-178.

Eiglier, P. and Langeard, E. (1977). Services As Systems: Marketing Implications. In *Marketing Consumer Services: New Insights*. Cambridge, MA: Marketing Science Institute, Report 77-115: pp. 83-102.

Ettorree, B. (1994). Phenomenal Promises That Mean Business, *Management Review*, 83 (3, March): 18-23.

Evans, M.R., Clark, J.D., and Knutson, B.J. (1996). The 100-Percent, Unconditional Money-Back Guarantee, *Cornell Hotel and Restaurant Administration Quarterly*, 37 (6): 56-61.

Firnstahl, T.W. (1989). My Employees Are My Service Guarantee, *Harvard Business Review*, 67 (4): 28-34.

Gooley, T. (1993). On Time or Else, *Traffic Management*, 32 (1): 31-34.

Hart, C. (1988). The Power of Unconditional Service Guarantees, *Harvard Business Review*, 66 (July-August): 55-62.

Hart, C., Schlesinger, L., and Maher, D. (1992). Guarantees Come to Professional Firms, *Sloan Managment Review*, 33 (3, Spring): 19-29.

Kandampully, J. and Butler, L. (1998). Service Guarantee: A Strategic Mechanism to Enhance Feedback, *The International Journal of Business Transformation*, 1 (4, April): 240-244.

Kandampully, J. and Duddy, R. (1999). Relationship Marketing: A Concept Beyond the Primary Relationship, *Marketing Intelligence and Planning*, 17 (7): 315-323.

Lawler, E.E. III. (1992). *The Ultimate Advantage: Creating the High Involvement Organization*, San Francisco: Jossey Bass.

Maher, D. (1991). Service Guarantees Double-Barrelled Standards, *Training*, 28 (6): 22-25.

Maher, D. (1992). Service Guarantees, *Manage*, (May): 22-24.

Martin, F. (1995). Putting Your Money Where Your Mouth Is, *Retail Insights*, Autumn, xv-xvi.

Parasuraman, A., Berry, L.L., and Zeithaml, V.A. (1991). Understanding Customer Expectations of Service, *Sloan Management Review,* 32 (Spring): 39-48.

Rose, M.D. (1990). No Strings Attached, *Chief Executive,* (July/August): 30-33.

Solomon, M.R., Surprenant, C., Czepiel, J.A., and Gutman, E.G. (1985). A Role Theory Perspective on Dynamic Interactions: The Service Encounter, *Journal of Marketing,* 49 (Winter): 99-111.

Sowder, J. (1996). The 100% Satisfaction Guarantee: Ensuring Quality at Hampton Inn. *National Productivity Review,* 15 (2): 53-66.

Stevens, T. (1996). Service with Soul, *Industry Week,* 245 (3).

William, A.M. and Shaw, G. (1992). Tourism Research, *American Behavioral Scientist,* 36 (2): 133-143.

World Tourism Organization. (1999). *International Tourism Receipts, Statistics and Economic Measurement of Tourism,* Madrid: World Tourism Organization.

Zeithaml, V. (1981). How Consumer Evaluation Processes Differ Between Goods and Services. In Donnelly, J.H. and George, W.R. (Eds.), *Marketing of Services,* Chicago: American Marketing, pp. 186-191.

Zemke, R. (1988). Delivering Managed Service. In Bitner, M.J. and Crosby, L.A. (Eds.), *Designing A Winning Service Strategy.* AMA Services Marketing Conference Proceedings. Chicago: AMA, pp. 5-6.

# Chapter 14

# Managing and Marketing
# Internal and External Relationships

## Linda J. Shea

### *INTRODUCTION*

The dynamic nature of the hospitality, tourism, and leisure industry has fueled the quest for improved service quality among all internal and external stakeholders. Travel agents, tour guide operators, chambers of commerce, tourism boards, hotel and restaurant suppliers, advertising agencies, and other constituents strive for competitive advantages to meet customer needs and achieve their profit or nonprofit goals. These and other organizations in the industry understand the importance of partnerships with others in the channel of distribution system. They know their employees should provide quality service, and they want to meet customers' expectations. But who is responsible for the management and marketing of these interdependent relationships? Too often, this relationship building is left to chance. Deliberate strategies are needed for encouraging the synergistic effect among individual employees, customers, and intermediaries in the delivery of service quality.

This chapter presents strategies for building and maintaining relationships with various internal and external markets, including employees, stockholders, customers, suppliers, retailers, and other intermediaries. The chapter begins with the definition and discussion of relationship marketing—its importance and components. This is followed by a look at several common relationships and strategies for building and maintaining long-term associations. It is then demonstrated how the management and marketing of these relationships directly and/or indirectly narrow the gaps of service quality. Finally, basic guidelines for managing and marketing to internal and external markets are presented.

## RELATIONSHIP MARKETING

Relationship marketing is a process of strengthening ties between the organization and its customers, intermediaries, suppliers, and employees. Building relationships involves economic, social, and structural components (Zeithaml and Bitner, 1996). Economically, relationships are built by delivering consistent service quality, meeting and exceeding expectations, and facilitating mutually beneficial financial transactions—all resulting in profit gains for both parties. While economic transactions essentially occur between organizations, social transactions occur between individual people. Socially, relationships are built and maintained by taking a personal interest in individuals involved in these transactions. The social dimension provides an additional reason to continue doing business. Structurally, long-term relationships are strengthened through customization of the service transaction. This component contributes to a dependency on the part of the recipient. These components can be applied to all relationships important to the hospitality, tourism, and leisure organization.

### Relationship with Employees

Because of the inseparability of the service from the provider, service quality begins with quality employees. In their boundary-spanning roles, hospitality service employees are the connection between the organization and the customers. Customer evaluation of the service and the organization are based on interactions with service employees, not physical assets (Carlzon, 1987). Jan Carlzon, former CEO of Scandinavian Airline Systems, emphasized the importance of this employee-customer contact. He calculated that over one year, 10 million customers had an average of five employee contacts lasting about fifteen seconds each. That means that perception of the company is created during these 50 million "moments of truth," and determines the success or failure of the company.

A staff of untrained, underpaid, unmotivated employees is unlikely to generate satisfied customers. Building, maintaining, and retaining the workforce requires a deliberate and competent management and marketing effort. In addition to using appropriate recruiting and job training methods, and offering a meaningful benefit package to employees, several strategies can build lasting relationships with employees. These strategies are based on the concept of internal marketing, or marketing the job to employees as customers. Furthermore, the strategies are interdependent.

the product through the channels to the consumer. Contrarily, services are often produced, sold, and consumed in the same location. Therefore, distribution focuses on getting the consumer to the service. Most hospitality organizations cannot rely solely on sales staff and reservation systems to distribute their services. Instead, they are realizing the need for intermediaries, partnerships, and alliances and are seeking new, creative ways of developing these relationships.

The primary distribution systems in lodging and food service are chains, franchisers, and management companies. Franchising, the most prevalent distribution format, has realized substantial growth during the last decade in lodging, fast food, health clubs, and travel industries. Franchisees pay fees or royalties to franchisers. The benefits accrued from this type of relationship include the use of brand names and their reputations and access to unique products and services, management formats, physical designs, and process methods. These relationships are contractual in nature and should be negotiated according to the mutual interest of both parties.

Important intermediaries in hospitality, tourism, and leisure services are travel agents, tour operators, tour wholesalers, incentive planners, and central reservation systems. They are commonly linked in various combinations. The most prevalent intermediary in the industry is the travel agent. Using sophisticated electronic booking systems, agents can provide customers with up-to-date information on tourist destinations, hotel properties, and air and ground transportation. They can buy packages from tour wholesalers and they can book clients with tour operators.

Additional partnerships are formed with suppliers of food products, furniture, equipment, linens, uniforms, and myriad other distributors. Relationships must also be built with other support agencies, such as advertising agencies, chambers of commerce, and convention bureaus. Also characteristic in hospitality industries are partnership arrangements with competitors. For instance, when hotels are fully booked, they may send overflow to nearby properties. Complementary firms design packages comprising transportation, restaurant, and event components.

## Management of Channels

Channel management carries with it some inherent conflict. What is beneficial to one channel member may be detrimental to another. Care must be taken to balance and control these conflicts. For example, while travel bookings on the Internet are currently insignificant, this may increase in the future and threaten the role of agents.

Guidelines listed at the end of the chapter relative to all types of internal and external relationships are particularly applicable to these types of partnerships and alliances. Additional recommendations for enhancing relationships with channel members are as follows.

### Focus on Long-Term Benefits Over Costs

When analyzing relationships with these groups, it is important to look at the broader, long-term picture. Although agents and others work on a fee basis, it is tempting for firms to consider cutting costs by eliminating ties or dependencies without considering the benefits lost. Travel agents book only 25 percent of all hotel rooms, but are responsible for the sale of 90 percent of all airline tickets and 95 percent of cruises (Schulz, 1994). Intermediaries can distribute hospitality and tourism services more efficiently. They have greater access to customers and are experienced in serving their needs.

### Promote Benefits Aggressively

Intermediaries are bombarded with information from innumerable competitors. Providing an experience creates a stronger impact than providing more reading material. Hotels, airlines, and tourist destinations link to provide "fam" trips (at almost no cost to agents) to familiarize agents with their services. Inviting a concierge for a meal forms a better impression than sending a menu. These options are more likely to establish a social component in the relationship and thereby strengthen it.

### Base Recommendations on Service Quality

Some businesses consider entering into formal or informal agreements based on the potential for reciprocity. The ability of a local restaurant to send a number of customers to a nearby hotel property in exchange for reciprocal recommendations may seem attractive initially; however, if the quality of the restaurant is poor or inconsistent, the hotel property would reap greater benefits by ignoring the opportunity. The property would, in effect, be exchanging current customers for new customers along with the additional costs. Instead, partnerships should be based on compatibility of market segments' consistency of quality.

### Recognize Your Own Strengths and Weaknesses

Hospitality firms need to be mindful of what they do well and stick with their competencies. Vertical integration of the distribution system offers potential for cost savings. Consider, for instance, establishing in-house catering, travel agents, or advertising departments in place of independents. Each of these activities requires a specific set of skills and experiences that may fall outside the range of a firm's competencies. Without expertise in a different type of business activity, more costs and more headaches result.

### Look for Innovative Distribution Connections

The past decade witnessed dramatic changes in the way hospitality firms distribute products. One such innovative strategy is retail partnerships. Taco Bell, Subway, Pizza Hut, and other franchisers are linking with large retailers such as Wal-Mart, Kmart, and convenience store chains such as Cumberland Farms to move closer to the customer. These are examples of horizontal marketing systems, whereby organizations at the same level (e.g., retailing) combine to reach new markets. Airlines, hotels, and auto rental companies offer discounts to teacher associations, auto rescue clubs, and other groups which promote them as a benefit to their members. This gives these hospitality firms access to members of those organizations. Distributing through Web sites on the Internet is yet another recent innovative advance (Connolly, Olsen, and Moore, 1998). Best Western claims to reach nearly three-fourths of customers who do not use travel agents with this method (Vis, 1995). These examples illustrate the diverse options available for developing mutually beneficial relationships.

### RELATIONSHIP MARKETING AND SERVICE QUALITY

The management and marketing of internal and external markets directly and indirectly serves to narrow the gaps in service quality (Parasuraman, Zeithaml, and Berry, 1985). Gap 1 represents the difference between customer expectations of service and company perceptions of customer expectations. Effective internal marketing includes gathering customer information from employees whose boundary-spanning roles allow them to tap into customer expectations. It establishes clear lines of communication up the chain of command. Suppliers also initiate consumer surveys and can share valuable information concerning expectations. Effective relationship marketing to external customers means knowing what they expect. All of these activities directly impact the extent of the gap and, executed properly, serve to narrow it.

Gap 2 is created when company perception of customer expectations is translated into service designs and standards. Clearly, building solid customer relationships at the structural level narrows this gap. As described previously, it means the service is custom designed to the needs of a client. When systems are devised in this manner, no guessing is involved; hence, there is less error in the translation than in a hit-or-miss approach.

The service performance gap (Gap 3) involves the transfer of service design to service delivery. The gap is potentially created by several employee-related problems and issues. Effective internal marketing, training, and empowerment all encourage effective delivery of service and reduce the performance gap. Furthermore, strong relationships with customers at the social and structural levels diffuse the reliance on price for leveling fluctuating demand. Finally, close management of the advertising function can ensure that customers are informed of their roles in the delivery transaction.

Gap 4 is the difference between service delivery and communication about service to customers. The causes for this gap include ineffective communication among internal and external markets and overpromising. Advertising should be used to communicate roles of customers as well as employees, not only to themselves, but to educate each of them about the roles of the other. Key to this communication is avoidance of the natural tendency to make unreasonable promises. When these rules are followed as part of relationship management and marketing, this gap is significantly reduced.

Gap 5 is defined as the difference between perceived and expected service. Since this gap is a function of the first four gaps, it is indirectly affected by the implementation of strategies to reduce the preceding gaps. Customized service strategies directly narrow this gap, as they represent the opportunity to exceed customer expectations.

## ADDITIONAL GUIDELINES FOR MANAGING AND MARKETING KEY RELATIONSHIPS

The following guidelines use basic marketing principles to build, maintain, and strengthen relationships of all types discussed previously.

### Communicate a Marketing Orientation

The interdependency of channel relationships mandates common goals. The achievement of service quality relies heavily on a consumer orientation. In the spirit of the marketing concept, all parties involved in the delivery of service must embrace this philosophy. It is important for managers, frontline employees, suppliers, agents and brokers, stockholders, and of course customers to receive this message. Communication to employees could be achieved through recruitment material, orientation training, or newsletters. Customers can be reached through advertisements, stockholders could be made aware through the annual report, and intermediaries can be informed through promotional material and interactions with sales associates or other personnel.

### Communicate the Organization's "Product Position"

Establishing and communicating a clear and unambiguous position promotes the integration of internal and external markets. It sends a distinct message to all channel members regarding the way in which an organization wants to be perceived and differentiated from other competitive organizations. It affords channel participants the opportunity to create unique packages and programs for solidifying that position. This strategy is particularly important in today's market, with the trend toward family branding of hotels. Marriott, Holiday Inn, and Howard Johnson all have established several hotel brands under their names. They need to further educate consumers, suppliers, and intermediaries about the relative positions of their properties, so the appropriate consumers can be directed to them.

### Target Customers

It is nearly impossible to build lasting relationships through service quality when trying to please all customers at once. Without knowing who the customer is or should be, attempts at devising a marketing plan are futile. When you factor in all other intermediaries and channel members, each with their own marketing plans, it is easy to see the resulting confusion and chaos. Instead, segments of consumers with common needs must be identified. Suppliers and intermediaries in the hospitality and tourism industry can design more accurate and precise specifications if they know who they are serving and if they are all endeavoring to serve the same segment of customers.

### Solicit Feedback

Monitoring systems are a must to determine employee, customer, and other distribution channel members' expectations. Four Seasons Hotel CEO

Isadore Sharp points out the importance of having an organizational culture to support the delivery of consistent, reliable service—particularly for the high-end deluxe properties. He claims the element of luxury comes from the "people part of the experience" (Gillette, 1998, p. 59). This, he says, requires frequent (once-a-month) monitoring of employees. Berry, Parasuraman, and Zeithaml (1994) also suggest asking employees for feedback, since the employee sees more of the service delivery than customers, and they see it from a different angle. They further suggest employees assume the role of "manager for a day" to provide input for changes.

Customer feedback should be encouraged as well. These systems can include formal broader-based periodic surveying, or continuing feedback systems such as tabletop surveys in a restaurant. This can be supplemented by less formal short-term, on-the-spot methods. Provisions for complaining should be established to make it convenient and easy for customers. For instance, in addition to the tabletop survey form, restaurant managers could make rounds among tables soliciting service evaluations. Finally, suppliers and intermediaries need formal and informal mechanisms for feedback. Logs should be kept and all groups' complaints analyzed periodically. Only when all angles are viewed can top managers get a clear perception of issues and problems. These feedback systems promote synergism among the channel members.

### Always Take Corrective Action

Although it seems intuitively legitimate to focus on only the greatest producing employees, or high-volume, profit-generating suppliers, intermediaries, or customers, this can be a destructive mentality. A mistreated customer or an agent who perceives unfair treatment and defects can represent boundless potential loss of business, which cannot be measured and therefore is unknown to the perpetrating organization. Relationship marketing moves beyond problem resolution. It requires analysis of how and why the problem occurred in the first place. It necessitates the development of a program for improvement to avoid recurrence.

### Conduct Business in a Socially Responsible Manner

Being a good citizen is part of the broadening of the marketing concept. Examples include using environmentally safe packaging, training employees to serve alcohol responsibly, and voluntarily banning smoking in restaurants. Sponsorships, fund-raisers, and donations are additional ways to practice good citizenship. Organizations can partner with employees, customers, and intermediaries in providing these kinds of societal contributions.

## *CONCLUSION*

Delivery of quality service in hospitality, tourism, and leisure organizations requires coordination and cooperation from employees, suppliers, intermediaries, and all other stakeholders of an organizaiton. This chapter presented deliberate strategies for the management and marketing of these internal and external relationships. Three major categories of relationships were reviewed: employees, suppliers and intermediaries, and customers. How these relationships narrow the gaps in service quality was then illustrated. Finally, several guidelines applicable to the development and maintenance of these relationships were suggested. Implementaiton of these strategic activities creates synergism in these markets and contributed to the overall quality of service.

## REFERENCES

Bateson, J.E.G. (1995). *Managing Services Marketing,* Third Edition (pp. 456-459). Fort Worth, TX: Dryden Press.

Berry, L.L. and Parasuraman, A. (1991). *Marketing Services: Competing Through Quality* (pp. 136-140). New York: Free Press.

Berry, L.L., Parasuraman, A., and Zeithaml, V.A. (1994). Improving Service Quality in America: Lessons Learned. *Academy of Management Executive.* 8 (2): 32-52.

Bitner, M.J., Booms, B.H., and Tetreault, M.S. (1990). The Service Encounter: Diagnosing Favorable and Unfavorable Incidents. *Journal of Marketing.* 54 (January): 71-84.

Bowen, J.T. and Shoemaker, S. (1998). Loyalty: A Strategic Commitment. *Cornell Hotel and Restaurant Administration Quarterly.* 39 (1):12-25.

Bruns, R. (1998). Hotel Companies Are Using Technology and Clever Marketing to Identify and Reward Their Most Valuable Guests. *Lodging.* June: 55-60.

Carlzon, J. (1987). Putting the Customer First: The Key to Service Strategy. *McKinsey Quarterly.* Summer. Reprinted in Lovelock, C.H. (1991). *Services Marketing* (Second Edition) (pp. 424-432). Englewood Cliffs, NJ: Prentice Hall.

Connolly, D.J., Olsen, M.D., and Moore, R.C. (1998). The Internet As a Distribution Channel. *The Cornell Hotel and Restaurant Administration Quarterly.* 39 (4): 42-54.

Gillette, B. (1998). Luxury Segment Players. *Lodging.* October: 55-59.

Kotler, P., Bowen, J., and Makens, J. (1999). *Marketing for Hospitality and Tourism* (Second Edition). Upper Saddle River, NJ: Prentice Hall.

Parasuraman, A., Zeithaml, V.A., and Berry, L.L. (1985). A Conceptual Model of Service Quality and Its Implications for Future Research. *Journal of Marketing.* 49 (Fall): 41-50.

Parets, R.T. (1998). Details, Details, Details. *Lodging.* June: 56.

Schulz, C. (1994). Hotels and Travel Agents: The New Partnership. *Cornell Hotel and Restaurant Administration Quarterly.* 35 (2): 45-50.

Shamir, B. (1980). Between Service and Servility: Role Conflict in Subordinate Service Roles. *Human Relations.* 33 (10): 741-756.

Vis, D. (1995) Best Western Is Latest Hotel to Market Properties on Internet. *Travel Weekly.* 54 (8): 53.

Zeithaml, V.A. and Bitner, M.J. (1996). *Services Marketing* (pp. 190-193; 342-354). New York: McGraw-Hill Companies, Inc.

# Chapter 15

# Cross-Cultural Issues in Service Quality

## Connie Mok

## *INTRODUCTION*

It was estimated that by the year 2000, multinational corporations (MNCs) would control approximately half of the world's assets (Dulek, Fielden, and Hill, 1991). Many companies that were identified as American, such as Kentucky Fried Chicken (KFC), Wendy's, McDonald's, Holiday Inn, and others, may saturate the U.S. market, but they are no longer domestic companies. KFC has been expanding in overseas markets such as Japan since 1970. In the 1990s the KFC store at the heart of the Forbidden City in Beijing attracted more Chinese tourists than the city itself. The McDonald's Corporation 1997 Annual Report reported that, in 1996, 50 percent of McDonald's Corporation's income came from operations outside the United States. In the hotel industry, globalization has also continued to grow. Holiday Inn, for example, entered the European market in 1969 and the Asian market in 1973. Slattery (1996) reported progressive international development of hotel chains from 1990 to 1995, most notably, Bass, Accor, Forte, New World, and Four Seasons. International expansion has many benefits; additional growth or expansion and added revenues or profits, which lead to improved return on investment, were reported as the greatest benefits (Go and Christensen, 1989). Other benefits included larger market penetration and thus more market share. In addition, greater name recognition and an international identity are also advantageous to the company. These benefits are undoubtedly most favorable; however, international expansion has exposed U.S. hospitality companies to groups of multicultural consumers. The rapid global development of the hospitality industry has made it important for MNCs to be able to function profitably in foreign markets. Global managers are expected to successfully interact with people from various cultures and, more important, to be able to understand more than the domestic market, both in managing their operations and in marketing their products and services.

Internationally, as competition and customer sensitivity intensifies, lodging providers are becoming increasingly concerned with the quality of their service offerings. Hotels with poor service have difficulty succeeding in the area of marketing, no matter how aggressive their advertising and sales promotion may be. Since there is general agreement that customer satisfaction has a direct relationship to profitability, the question remains as to how companies can best merge the goals of profit maximization and customer satisfaction so as to reap the benefits of an increasingly global market. On one hand, there is the trend toward standardization of services to compete on the international market with value-added products or services (Pizam, Jansen-Verbeke, and Steel, 1997). On the other hand, the hospitality industry has recognized the importance of differentiating product/service offerings to suit local tastes and preferences. Which way should we go?

## THE CONVERGENCE AND DIVERGENCE DEBATE

### Convergence

One of the ongoing debates fueled by globalization involves hypotheses of convergence and divergence. In 1983, T. Levitt published an article on global convergence of markets in *Harvard Business Review,* criticizing the practices of MNCs that manufacture products customized for each country at a high cost (Levitt, 1983). He refutes the effectiveness of these practices by claiming that only global companies will achieve long-term success by offering globally standardized products that are advanced, functional, reliable, and low priced. He claims that two vectors shape the world—technology and globalization. Technology is a powerful force driving the world toward an increasing similarity, which will result in global markets for standardized consumer products on a large scale. Global corporations can enjoy enormous economies of scale in production, distribution, marketing, and management as well as reduced world prices. Therefore companies must learn to operate as if the world were one large market—ignoring superficial regional and national differences.

Six years later, Kenichi Ohmae (1989) lamented that, as a consequence of the flow of information through satellite-broadcast television and the dominance of the English language, everyone receives the same information almost simultaneously and hence become global citizens. In Ohmae's view, it is not diversification or competition that exerts pressure toward globalization but the needs and preferences of customers who have become globalized. Proponents of the convergence process support the notion that global markets are converging and becoming more homogeneous and, therefore, customers of different cultural backgrounds will have common preferences. Convergence theorists contend that globalization will support homogeneity and thus consumers with different cultural backgrounds will accept a homogeneous product.

A more recent publication, *The McDonaldization of Society* (Ritzer, 1993) proposed McDonaldization as both a literal critique of food production and service arrangements and a metaphor for standardizing forces in the wider society. "This mass production is a process by which the principles of the fast-food restaurants are coming to dominate more and more sectors of American society as well as the rest of the world" (p. 1). Fast-food restaurants and other McDonaldized systems are mass-production systems, which are built upon the belief that in the world of mass production, consumers accept homogeneous products. Their acceptance facilitates market growth and the reduction of prices through economies of scale, which in turn leads to a greater price gap between mass-produced goods and customized goods. Low price encourages the clustering of demand around homogeneous products (Taylor and Lyon, 1995).

## Divergence

On the other hand, proponents of the divergence hypothesis such as Douglas and Wind (1987) agree that the growing integration of international markets implies that adoption of a global perspective has become increasingly imperative. However, they argue that to conclude that this mandates the adoption of a strategy of universal standardization appears naive and oversimplistic because it ignores the inherent complexity of operations in international markets. They explain that substantial evidence exists to suggest an increasing diversity of behavior within countries, and the emergence of idiosyncratic country-specific segments. Other proponents of the divergence hypothesis point to the barriers of standardization, and suggest that greater returns are to be obtained from adapting products and marketing strategies to the specific characteristics of individual markets (Fisher, 1984). Douglas and Wind (1987) give examples of how companies adapt lines to idiosyncratic country preferences and develop local brands or product variants targeted to local market segments. The Findus frozen food division of Nestlé markets fish cakes and fish fingers in the United Kingdom, but beef bourguignonne and coq au vin in France, and vitello con funghi and braviola in Italy. Similarly, in Asia, Coca-Cola markets products such as Georgia, cold coffee in a can, and Aquarius, a tonic drink, as well as Classic Coke and Hi-C.

Taylor and Lyon (1995) think that the mass producer has reached the limits of the old paradigm. With rising costs, price competition, shifting demographics, and changing eating habits, mass production for homogeneous markets is no longer enough for companies to survive. They proposed a new paradigm: mass customization. Variety and customization through flexibility and quick responsiveness are the focus of mass customization. The goal is to develop, produce, market, and deliver affordable goods and services with enough variety and customization that nearly everyone finds exactly what he or she wants. They believe mass customization becomes a self-reinforcing cycle: "meeting customer demands leads to higher profits, which in turn facilitates the organization's ability to increase its customization capability, which in turn stimulates further market fragmentation" (p. 65).

Proponents of both sides agreed that some adaptation is necessary for MNCs to operate successfully in global markets. While the end products are different, they share some common characteristics that may well be derived from technology and globalization. The real issues being debated are at what level is standardization appropriate and at what level is adaptation appropriate, and for which products.

## STANDARDIZATION AND ADAPTATION

In 1988, Don I. Smith postulated that menu and service are solely determined by customers rather than industry. This was then a bold statement but one that logically derived from the inherent service orientation of hospitality operators. An examination of the development of the fast-food industry will illustrate this point. The domestic U.S. fast-food market is saturated. Chain restaurants are gaining market share through concept evolution, marketing and promotion programs, nontraditional venues, and expansion in international markets. Two major driving forces of the success of the fast-food industry's global expansion are customer acceptance and frequency of use. A total of twenty fast-food chains operate internationally. McDonald's has operations in 106 countries which made it the biggest international fast-food chain as of 1998.

Standardization is still a characteristic of McDonald's operations. However, its menu has been adapted to local tastes and preferences. For example, in France the menu is written in three to five different languages, usually French, German, Italian, Belgian, and Japanese. Some menu items offered in France are not available in the United States, including bagels, seasoned red potato wedges with dipping sauce, cakes and pastries, scones, and croissants. The drinks offered are also different. Dr. Pepper and root beer are not offered while Orangina, an orange-flavored carbonated drink, beer, and wine are available for purchase. For the breakfast menu, McDonald's in France also offers a fruit salad and scones. McMarins, which are the fish version of chicken McNuggets, are not available in the United States. Salad and dessert choices are also varied. The chef salad is served with salmon and shrimp while eclairs, brownies, muffins, and beignets are on the dessert menu. Mass customization has incorporated local preferences and tastes into the process as this example demonstrates.

## PREVIOUS RESEARCH IN SERVICE QUALITY IN THE CROSS-CULTURAL CONTEXT

### Studies and Their Findings

Consumer preferences cannot be fully understood without considering their cultural context. The effects of culture on consumer behavior are both powerful and far-reaching, and this importance is sometimes difficult to grasp or appreciate (Solomon, 1999). For example, most people would think couples on their honeymoon would like as much privacy as possible. In Japan, however, many newlyweds spend their honeymoon by joining package tour groups. A consumer's culture determines the priorities and meanings he or she attaches to different services and products. It also mandates the success or failure of specific products and services. A product or service that provides the desired benefits to consumers in a particular culture at any point in time has a better chance of gaining acceptance in that market. For example, KFC first entered the Asian market in 1973 and failed because of lack of understanding of the market and proper control. In 1985, KFC did its homework and reentered the Asian market after careful market research and product modification.

To further understand the influence of culture on tourists' behavior, it is important to examine the research findings on hospitality and tourism service quality expectations and perceptions in the cross-cultural context. Most of the service quality research reported in the hospitality and tourism literature has been conducted in North America. Very little has been reported on service quality expectations or perception of consumers from other countries. With increasing globalization of the hospitality and tourism industry, it is important that differences in multicultural market needs, and the servicing of these needs, be understood (Patton, Stevens, and Knutson, 1994).

Luk and colleagues (1993) investigated international tourists' expectations of the quality of organized tour service and the influences of cultural values on quality expectations. They surveyed 311 tourists who were in Hong Kong as participants in organized tours. The sample included 201 tourists from Europe and America and 110 from the Asia-Pacific region. The Rokeach Value Survey (RVS) (Rokeach, 1973) was used to measure cultural values. The SERVQUAL instrument (Parasuraman, Berry, and Zeithaml, 1988) was used to measure the tourists' expectations of service on five service quality dimensions: assurance, reliability, empathy, tangibility, and responsiveness. Because of the generic nature of SERVQUAL, this study modified the SERVQUAL scale to include the distinctive components of organized tour service. Comparison of service quality expectations of organized tour service between tourists from the two regions found that the tourists from the Asia-Pacific region had much higher expectations on all of the five dimensions. Reliability was shown to be the most important factor to Asia-Pacific tourists, followed by assurance, while Europe-America tourists rated reliability and assurance as of equal importance. Empathy and responsiveness were considered less important by both groups. The study findings also showed that cultural values significantly affected service quality expectations of tourists. Differences in quality expectations of organized tour service were shown to be specifically influenced by tourists' value for sociability. Sociability refers to the values of being polite, helpful, obedient, forgiving, loving, honest, and clean. It was suggested that because of these differences in expectations, tourism marketers need to reexamine the basic assumptions that have traditionally dominated the design and the service of organized tours.

Mok and Armstrong (1998) examined hotel service quality expectations of international tourists using cross-cultural samples. Data were collected from hotel guests from different cultures in three Hong Kong hotels, which belonged to the same hotel segment—midprice. The expectation scale of the SERVQUAL instrument (Parasuraman, Berry, and Zeithaml, 1988) was adopted to measure service quality expectations. The wording of the scale was modified for the hotel setting. Three hundred and twenty-five hotel guests completed usable questionnaires. The sample was segmented by country of origin, which included Australia, Japan, Taiwan, the United Kingdom, and the United States. The findings of the study indicate that tourists from these five countries have different expectations in two of the five service quality dimensions, namely, tangibles and empathy. The Japanese guests have the lowest scores on all of the five dimensions. The researchers suggested that these findings could be attributed to the travel-related behavior of Japanese tourists. Japanese tourists could be described as "always traveling in groups," "not adventurous," "big spenders," and "love to shop." Their tour itineraries are usually packed with sightseeing and shopping activities prearranged by tour operators, which allow very little free time for individual activities. Japanese tourists spend relatively little time in hotels where they stay (except, of course, for rest); and rarely will you find them using the health club or other facilities in the hotels. Their preferred activities and travel behavior could partly explain their relatively lower expectations for hotel service quality.

It was also reported that both Japanese and Taiwanese tourists have significantly lower expectations for the empathy dimension than their Western counterparts. The empathy dimension refers to providing caring, individual attention to customers. In general, Asian tourists prefer to travel in groups by joining package tours. Accommodation is included in these package tours and usually members check in and out as a group rather than individually. Meals, sightseeing, and entertainment are also included in the package. All these activities are prearranged by tour guides. This type of arrangement might leave much less room for tourists to seek individual attention from hotel employees. Language barriers might be another reason for lower expectations for individual attention, since most hotel personnel in Hong Kong speak English and Cantonese. Japanese is not commonly spoken, and Taiwanese speak the Mandarin dialect.

Another study conducted by DeFranco and Mok (1998) measured tourists' expectations for hotel service quality in the cross-cultural context. A total of 594 North American tourists (200 from the United States and 394 from Mexico) participated in their survey. The LODGSERV instrument (Knutson et al., 1991) was used to measure hotel service expectations. Results from their study show that while tourist expectations for hotel service quality were high in general, Mexican tourists had significantly higher expectations on all service quality dimensions than the U.S. tourists. In search of an explanation for such differences, the researchers considered the hospitable characteristics of Mexicans. They might put more emphasis on whether hotel employees are caring, empathetic, and responsive. Besides, traveling and staying in a hotel may be a bigger event for Mexicans than for people from the United States who are known to be frequent travelers; the Mexicans, therefore, may have higher expectations.

Lim and Ha (1997) investigated how foreign tourists evaluate service quality of the restaurants in the Etaewon special tourist district of Seoul. They hypothesized that there were significant differences among different nationalities in terms of their perceptions of restaurant service factors.

Data were collected using Cadotte and Turgeon's (1988) twenty-six food service attributes. Questionnaires were administered to 180 Japanese, American, and Asian tourists. The results of their study showed significant perception differences among tourists from different nationalities in the following food service attributes: attitude of employees, employees' communication ability in a foreign language, availability of food on menu, convenience of location, and quality of advertising. In general, American tourists evaluated service quality more positively than Asian tourists did for most items. The researchers attributed these findings to the fact that most restaurants in Etaewon district are more Western culture oriented. They suggested that restaurant owners and employees should widen their service focus to better meet the needs of the Japanese and other Asian tourists who constitute nearly 70 percent of foreign tourists in the district.

## MAJOR METHODOLOGICAL ISSUES

A full discussion of the methodological issues in cross-cultural studies is beyond the scope of this chapter. Only two major issues, sample comparability and transferability of research instrument, are discussed.

One of the major difficulties in doing cross-cultural research is drawing samples that are comparable. Totally matched samples are hard to obtain in reality. Demographic variables such as income and education are often not comparable due to different standards of living and systems. Some researchers emphasize the need to match demographic variables in cross-cultural studies so that the only variable that is different is culture (Hofstede, 1980). However, the usefulness of demographics in segmentation and predicting consumer behavior is often questioned (Pizam and Calantone, 1987; Snepenger and Milner, 1990; Oh and Jeong, 1996; McCleary, Choi, and Weaver, 1998) because a significant relationship between demographic variables in segmentation and consumer behavior has not been consistently demonstrated in studies. Hofstede (1980) differentiated between the approaches used for comparison of total cultures and those used for subcultures. For comparing total cultures, a very broad sample may be appropriate so that differences due to subcultures are eliminated. If the purpose is to compare subcultures, narrow similar samples should be drawn from different countries. For example, compare Japanese leisure travelers with Australian leisure travelers. For those readers who wish to understand more about the issue of cross-cultural comparability, please refer to Berry's (1969) work.

The other major concern is the transferability of research instruments. The goals of methodology in cross-cultural research are not different from those of other research: reliability, validity, representativeness, generalizability, and so forth. A major problem is that researchers use instruments (without modification) in one culture that were designed, pretested, revised, and validated in another culture. The problem arises when the researcher tries to reach conclusions about a culture by scoring according to the norms derived in another culture. Brislin (1976) emphasized the importance of the emic-etic distinction as it applies to cross-cultural psychology. The distinction relates to two goals of cross-cultural research:

1. The first goal is to document valid principles that describe behavior in any one culture under study, taking into account what the people themselves value as meaningful and important. This is an emic analysis, which refers to meanings that hold only in one culture.
2. The second goal is to make generalizations across cultures that take into account all human behavior. This is an etic analysis.

For example, in a study aiming to internationalize a survey instrument, LODGSERV, that has been validated with American consumers (Patton, Stevens, and Knutson, 1994), an emic item was found in the translation process that is unique to American-English culture, the phrase "no red tape." The American-English version of LODGSERV was translated into Japanese, Chinese, Australian and British English. After several rounds of translation and back translation, the phase was reworded to read "should eliminate unnecessary bureaucracy."

## CONCLUSION

The need for greater cross-cultural understanding of consumer behavior has been proclaimed by both managers and researchers as essential for improving international marketing efforts (Wilkie, 1990; McCort and Malhotra, 1993). Nevertheless, limited cross-cultural research within service marketing on the effect of culture on consumers exists (Mok and Armstrong, 1998). Research findings reported previously indicate that tourists from different cultural backgrounds have different expectations and perceptions of service quality. To exceed customers' expectations, we need to understand these differences. For instance, Japanese travelers' overwhelming preference for traveling in groups by joining package tours might require special arrangements by hotels. Instead of catering to individual needs and requests, special arrangements for groups might be very much appreciated. Assigning rooms to tour group members on the same floor or preparing one or two special breakfast items just for the tour group are examples of how hotels can exceed customers' expectations.

In general, the lower the customer expectations, the higher the possibility that service quality will be better perceived and vice versa. Therefore, understanding the service preferences and differences in expectations of tourists from different cultural backgrounds can help a business provide the type of services they appreciate so that efforts and resources are not wasted. The strategy of "all things for all people" is outdated. To exemplify how one international chain caters to the needs of their guests from Japan, Four Seasons Hotels offer green tea service when Japanese guests arrive; serve authentic Japanese breakfast; provide Japanese slippers, bathrobes, and towels; and train their employees on Japanese protocol. Exported tourism services cater to a highly heterogeneous international market, with marketing activities that not only cross geographical boundaries but also transcend cultural differences. Meaningful market segmentation is a prerequisite for the formulation of an effective marketing strategy. Tourists' service quality expectations and preferences are important factors, which should be taken into consideration in the segmentation of the international market.

Despite the complexity and difficulties involved, it is hoped that more researchers will embark on cross-cultural research in the area of service quality management to enhance the understanding of international customers.

# REFERENCES

Berry, J.W. (1969). On cross-cultural comparability. *International Journal of Psychology,* 4(2), 119-128.

Brislin, R.W. (1976). Comparative research methodology: Cross-cultural studies. *International Journal of Psychology,* 11(3), 215-229.

Cadotte, E.R. and Turgeon, N. (1988). Key factors in guest satisfaction. *The Cornell Hotel and Restaurant Administration Quarterly,* 28(4), 44-51.

DeFranco, A.L. and Mok, C. (1998). Expectations for hotel service quality: A case of United States and Mexican tourists. *The Consortium Journal,* 2(1), 67-79.

Douglas, S.P. and Wind, Y. (1987). The myth of globalization. *Columbia Journal of World Business,* (Winter), 19-30.

Dulek, R.E., Fielden, J.S., and Hill, J.S. (1991). International communication: An executive primer. *Business Horizons,* (June), 20-25.

Fisher, A.B. (1984). The ad biz gloms onto global. *Fortune,* November 12, 77-80.

Go, F.M. and Christensen, J. (1989). Going global. *Cornell HRA Quarterly,* 30(3), 73-80.

Hofstede, G. (1980). *Culture's Consequences: International Differences in Work-Related Values.* Newbury Park, CA: Sage.

Knutson, K.B., Stevens, P., Wullaert, C., Patton, M., and Yokoyama, F. (1991). LODGSERV: A service quality index for the lodging industry. *Hospitality Research Journal,* 14(2), 277-284.

Levitt, T. (1983). The globalization of markets. *Harvard Business Review,* 83(3), 92-102.

Lim, S.T. and Ha, E.S. (1997). Evaluation of restaurant service quality in the Etaewon special tourist district of Seoul. *Asia Pacific Journal of Tourism Research,* 2(1), 51-63.

Luk, S.T.K., de Leon, C.T., Leong, F.W., and Li, E.L.Y. (1993). Value segmentation of tourists' expectations of service quality. *Journal of Travel and Tourism Marketing,* 2(4), 23-38.

McCleary, K.W., Choi, B.M., and Weaver, P.A. (1998). A comparison of hotel selection criteria between U.S. and Korean business travelers. *Journal of Hospitality and Tourism Research,* 22(1), 25-38.

McCort, D.J. and Malhotra, N.K. (1993). Culture and consumer behavior: Toward an understanding of cross-cultural consumer behavior in international marketing. *Journal of International Consumer Marketing,* 6(2), 91-127.

McDonald's Corporation (1997). *McDonald's Corporation 1997 Annual Report.* Author, pp. 1-2.

Mok, C. and Armstrong, R.W. (1998). Expectations for hotel services: Do they differ from culture to culture? *Journal of Vacation Marketing,* 4(4), 381-391.

Oh, H. and Jeong, M. (1996). Improving marketers' predictive power of customer satisfaction on expectation-based target market levels. *Hospitality Research Journal,* 19(4), 65-85.

Ohmae, K. (1989). Managing in a borderless world. *Harvard Business Review,* 67(3), 152-161.

Parasuraman, A., Berry, L.L., and Zeithaml, V.A. (1988). SERVQUAL: A multiple-item scale for measuring consumer perceptions of service quality. *Journal of Retailing,* 64(1), 12-40.

Patton, M., Stevens, P., and Knutson, B.J. (1994). Internationalizing LODGSERV as a measurement tool: A pilot study. *Journal of Hospitality and Leisure Marketing,* 2(2), 30-55.

Pizam, A. and Calantone, R. (1987). Neyong psychographics: Values as determinants of tourist behavior. *International Journal of Hospitality Management,* 6(3), 177-181.

Pizam, A., Jansen-Verbeke, M., and Steel, L. (1997). Are all tourists alike regardless of nationality? The perceptions of Dutch tour-guides. *Journal of International Hospitality, Leisure and Tourism Management,* 1(1), 19-39.

Ritzer, G. (1993). *The McDonaldization of Society: An Investigation into the Changing Character of Contemporary Social Life.* Newbury Park, CA: Pine Forge Press.

Rokeach, M. (1973). *The Nature of Human Value.* New York: The Free Press.

Slattery, P. (1996). International development of hotel chains. In R. Kotas, R. Teare, J. Logie, C. Jayawaedema, and J. Bowen (Eds.), *The International Hospitality Business*. London: Cassell Wellington House, pp. 30-37.

Smith, D.I. (1988). How to win in the chain game: Pay attention to the customer. *Nation's Restaurant News*, 22(4), 35.

Snepenger, D. and Milner, L. (1990). Demographic and situational correlates of business travel. *Journal of Travel Research*, 28(4), 27-32.

Solomon, M.R. (1999). *Consumer Behavior*, Fourth Edition. Englewood Cliffs, NJ: Prentice Hall.

Taylor, S. and Lyon, P. (1995). Paradigm lost: The rise and fall of McDonaldization. *International Journal of Contemporary Hospitality Management*, 7(2/3), 64-68.

Wilkie, W. (1990). *Consumer Behavior*, Second Edition. New York: John Wiley and Sons.

# Chapter 16

# Technology and Its Impact on Service Quality

Simon Milne
Jovo Ateljevic

## INTRODUCTION

There can be no doubt that information technology (IT) is changing the business of tourism. Studies of the significant intrafirm impacts of new technologies (Haywood, 1990; Peacock, 1995; Mutch, 1998) have been paralleled by broader analyses of IT's ability to alter distribution networks and industry structures (Bennett and Radburn, 1991; Reinders and Baker, 1998). Some commentators have even suggested that IT changes the very rules of tourism—with industry leaders adopting a new managerial and strategic "best practice" (Poon, 1993, pp. 12-13).

Although many benefits are attributed to IT, it is not always clear whether the "hype" matches reality. In this chapter we explore the degree to which IT is influencing one area of particular importance to tourism, hospitality, and leisure managers—service quality (SQ) (Coyne, 1993; Church and Lincoln, 1998). In an increasingly competitive environment it is SQ that provides a differentiation strategy for firms and a means to enhance customer relations and long-term profitability (Gamble and Jones, 1991; Johns, 1996, p. 254; Lewis and Gabrielsen, 1998, p. 64). Indeed, a 1995 survey of U.S. lodging managers' perceptions of the utility of technology use on their properties shows that the main perceived advantage is an improvement in guest satisfaction (Van Hoof et al., 1995). Over 80 percent of the 550 survey respondents felt that technology enhanced customer satisfaction. The figure is lower in companies with fewer than 100 rooms (70.2 percent) and higher in properties of more than 300 rooms.

Although it is clear that new technologies can influence SQ in profound ways, we still know relatively little about their specific impacts on measures of service quality, and even less about their impact on a key link in the service quality equation—the worker. This chapter examines some of the research that has been conducted on the relationships between SQ and the introduction of new technologies in the lodging industry. We focus on some of the key issues that face managers as they attempt to maximize the benefits of IT for service enhancement.

The chapter begins with an outline of some of the key information technologies being adopted by accommodation establishments. We then review the literature dealing with the impacts of technology use on SQ in the lodging industry. We draw on a range of empirical research that has been conducted around the world. Our review reveals that SQ and IT use are not always positively correlated. In particular, we argue that it is dangerous to ignore the human resource dimensions of IT introduction. We also stress that not all firms are equally able to turn IT to their advantage. Although our focus is on the lodging industry, the themes raised have a broad applicability for managers in all areas of tourism, leisure, and hospitality.

## LODGING AND INFORMATION TECHNOLOGY: AN OVERVIEW

The lodging industry is constantly adopting new information technologies, and the pace of adoption is quickening. Facing demanding clients, and under pressure from increasingly intense global competition, companies are turning to technology as a means to improve SQ, increase productivity, and lower labor costs (Olsen, Crawford-Welch, and Tse, 1991; Go and Pine, 1995).

Rather than conduct an exhaustive review of existing and emerging IT applications, we choose to focus on the dominant forms of technology. Our review is conducted at three scales: the room level, hotelwide, and beyond the hotel (including the growth of global communication networks).

### The Room

Hotel guests have become ever more demanding of in-room technology. This is particularly true for the business traveler whose laptop computer and hotel room often serve as a virtual office. Guests are used to multichannel and increasingly interactive TV in their own homes and therefore demand more from guest room televisions (Wolff, 1998b).

Technology-driven entertainment options for both business- and leisure-oriented guests will become increasingly linked to Internet access. Net access and intelligent rooms will become a part of guest service at full-service establishments in the not-too-distant future. For example, in March 1998, one of the first video (and information) on demand systems for the residential and hospitality markets was introduced at the Residence on Georgia condominium and hotel complex in Vancouver, British Columbia. The system lets the 500 residents and guests simultaneously access the Internet, video on demand, cable television, music channels, and security cameras (Raman and Cleary, 1998).

Personal data cards will also become more common. These will incorporate guests' Internet bookmarks and other customized information. Active badges will give guests automatic access to their rooms and ensure that room lighting, heating, and other functions instantly meet the guest's needs (Grimes, 1998). These cards may also be used to generate information that may enable market segmentation to be conducted. Current in-room checkout and ordering systems will continue to improve in sophistication and user friendliness, to the point where front desk checkout becomes the exception rather than the norm.

### The Hotel

The most common technologies used for hotel management purposes are telephones, faxes, and desktop or portable computers. User-friendly software enables managers and owners to master basic tasks without specific knowledge of accounting or computer techniques (see Milne and Pohlmann, 1998; Mutch, 1998).

In larger hotels, peripherals are usually connected to a central unit. The more advanced property management systems (PMS) provide seamless connections between different elements of a hotel's operations and create links to external communication networks (Chervenak, 1993; Wolff, 1998a). A typical PMS will cover several core elements of a hotel's operations:

- *Front-office functions:* Reservation, registration, checkout; individual, delegate, walk-in, and "house" account folios are all monitored and updated automatically
- *Guest history:* Tracks guest history status, records special requests, VIP services, and handles room preferences with an automatic link to reservations and sales modules

- *Software integration:* Upon checkout and after the night audit, guest information automatically updates the guest history, company history, city ledger, travel agent, and other modules
- *Housekeeping:* Tracks and maintains the physical status of rooms; energy management systems have also been built in current PMS
- *Yield management:* Provides immediate feedback on average daily rate and is integrated into the front-office system
- *Back-office accounting:* Front-office revenue update, back-office revenue journals; accounts payable is integrated with the general ledger

Local area networks (LAN) and intranets can enable greater levels of information flow within the firm. Databases on worker performance can be designed to provide management with greater knowledge about worker performance and how to allocate labor most effectively. Group decision support systems (GDSS) may also play a role in reducing the need for management meetings and in speeding up the decision-making process. With GDSS software and a LAN, real-time discussions and debates can be held from individual offices and computer screens. Idea generation and brainstorming are argued by some to be particularly well suited to this approach (see Davin, 1997).

### The Hotel and Beyond—Networking

Of the various tourism-related IT developments that have captured the imagination of researchers during the past two decades, computer reservation systems (CRS) have undoubtedly held center stage (Milne and Gill, 1998). These powerful travel distribution technologies are seen by many commentators to offer significant opportunities for companies to improve customer service and increase the efficiency and flexibility of product delivery (Go and Williams, 1993; Wolff, 1998a).

The costs inherent in the development of a hotel CRS are high, especially for independent operators. For this reason many enterprises do not develop their own systems, preferring instead to align themselves with a hotel consortium or hotel group representative. In 1996 the Utell consortium, the world's largest, brought together over 6,500 subscribing hotels from 160 countries, and processed over 2.8 million reservations a year through its forty-four international offices (Milne and Pohlmann, 1998).

It is important to link hotel PMS/CRS with airline global distribution systems (GDS) such as Sabre (Wolff, 1998a). Without such a link properties become largely invisible to the bulk of potential customers. For the vast majority of properties this connection is made possible via "switches" such as THISCO—a unified interface linking about twenty major hotel chain CRSs in the United States to airline GDSs (McGuffie, 1994).

The Internet is playing a growing role in the tourism industry as a sales and marketing force, and lodging is no exception to the trend. The American Hotel and Motel Association estimates that by 2001, e-commerce in the lodging arena will be worth $2.9 billion within the United States alone (Gatty and Blalock, 1998). Another technology just beginning to be implemented by larger enterprises is the data warehouse. Although similar in some respects to a corporate intranet system, a data warehouse utilizes complex software programs to read and interpret the data in other systems, while intranet information is largely built and maintained manually.

Data warehouse information is therefore "online, real-time," providing management with the most precise analytical and decision-support tools. The type of information a data warehouse provides is frequently marketing-related, with a focus on guest information. Other data applications might include accounting, employee records, vendor information, or any other information category of interest or useful to multiple departments or locations (Berry and Parasuraman, 1997; *The Economist,* 1999).

### Technology Diffusion

It is important to note that small tourism firms are generally less likely to implement IT than their larger counterparts (Van Hoof et al., 1995; Mutch, 1998; Buhalis, 1999). The consensus that emerges from the research is that small-accommodation managers often feel that computerization is relatively unimportant to their competitiveness and that they would rather focus attention on human contact dimensions (Milne and Pohlmann, 1998; Ateljevic et al., 1999). The managers of some smaller operations also complain that it is difficult to find affordable customized software to meet small-hotel needs. On other occasions, managers are simply "technophobes" (Milne and Gill, 1998).

It is interesting to note that larger, full-service hotels have a much bigger presence on the Internet than their small, limited-service counterparts. Studies in the United States show that managers in larger properties (greater than 300 rooms) attach significantly more importance to the Internet as a tool to make reservations and analyze the competition than their smaller counterparts. Similarly, they rated its importance as a means to communicate with colleagues, vendors, and corporate offices significantly higher (Van Hoof and Verbeeten, 1998).

## TECHNOLOGY AND SERVICE QUALITY

The outcome of service encounters is determined by the interactions between providers and customers, and is influenced by employee and customer characteristics, organizational culture, systems and procedures, enterprise structure, and technology (Solomon et al., 1985; Grove and Fisk, 1991). Lehtinen and Lehtinen (1991) view SQ as a function of interactive processes. This in turn requires organizations to manage and control their service encounters via technical control systems and procedures, human resource management, and the development of service-oriented culture. We now focus on the impacts of IT on two key areas that shape SQ in the lodging industry—sales and marketing, and labor performance/management.

### Marketing and Sales

The use of the Internet for marketing and sales purposes represents an effective and flexible way to bypass traditional distribution channels. Indeed, a recent survey of Internet use by hotels showed that two of the most important benefits identified were the exposure it can generate for the property, and the benefits it creates for marketing and advertising (Van Hoof and Verbeeten, 1998). Managers also value its communication capabilities and are relatively enthusiastic about the Internet as a means to check out the competition and to make reservations.

Of course, the most interactive Web site in the world will not create guest satisfaction unless information provision is prompt and the site is well maintained. It is certainly not uncommon to find Web sites and e-mail connections being established and then forgotten. In this case, the outcome will be visitor frustration (especially given the supposed promise of immediate response) and a negative impact on SQ. Clearly, the true potential of the Internet as a marketing tool has yet to be unleashed (Ghosh, 1998).

Small hotels around the world face very real problems in gaining access to the global travel distribution system. Large-scale computer reservation systems are usually prohibitively expensive and have some difficulty catering to nonstandardized types of tourist product. At the same time, small-scale traditional marketing approaches such as brochures have only limited effectiveness. As a result of these difficulties increasing numbers of small hotels are turning to the Internet as a marketing tool. The Internet has several key elements that make it an appealing alternative to traditional marketing approaches:

- Web sites are flexible; the images and text they present can be changed easily and presented cost effectively.
- Web sites have the potential to reflect community/business desires and information more effectively than many traditional marketing approaches.
- The number of Internet users is growing rapidly and the demographic profile of users (wealthy, well educated) is of interest to communities and businesses that wish to attract visitors at the higher end of the tourist spectrum.

However, a number of factors may also reduce the effectiveness of the Internet as a marketing and business development tool:

- Web sites are often poorly designed and slow to download.
- Many small hotel sites tend to be "virtual brochures" rather than actual booking tools. If the Internet is to be used to its full potential then it is essential that it facilitate bookings via e-mail or other approaches.
- Many small hotels fail to present the unique aspects of their enterprise and the place within which it is situated. The key issue here is to stand out from the crowd.

As hardware and software costs fall, more companies are gathering and manipulating visitor data (Bruns, 1998; *The Economist,* 1999). Innovative establishments are gathering as much information as possible firsthand from customers through frequent stay programs, smart cards, and sophisticated surveying methods. A key competitive advantage lies in effectively tracking customer needs and purchases, talking to the customer, and then tailoring services for the visitor (Albrecht and Bradford, 1990). In simple terms this involves setting up an ongoing learning relationship with core customers (see Berry and Parasuraman, 1997).

The development of customer databases need not be the preserve of larger hotel chains. It is now not uncommon to find boutique hotels that use a database to keep tabs on the needs and desires of important clients. The trick is to identify valuable customers and to concentrate on them. This information can be used to customize traditional marketing tools such as brochures.

In one example of this approach, a small boutique bed-and-breakfast based in New Zealand's capital city, Wellington, has successfully developed a detailed database that covers key return clients. The company focuses almost entirely on woman business travelers and has a database which provides information on the types of newspapers and refreshments that guests like and the sort of breakfasts they normally order. It also provides information on the special family needs of the travelers (for example, the special needs of children who may be accompanying their mothers. The company now has the ability to customize mailings to key clients, letting them know of special offers or simply wishing them a happy birthday.

## *Labor*

> The more that technology becomes a standard part of delivering services, the more important personal interactions are in satisfying customers and in differentiating competitors. (Schlesinger and Heskett, 1991, p. 74)

In his detailed survey of labor use in hotels, Wood (1992, pp. 133-137) points to two common misconceptions about the impact of technology on labor. The first is that technology can play only a limited role in improving labor productivity and reducing costs. The second is that where technology is introduced, it is inevitably associated with processes of de-skilling.

The labor management issues associated with IT introduction are complex, and it is important that management be aware of both the possible negative and positive impacts on staff. Technology cannot substitute for decisive strategies or for efficient employees; rather, it can complement them. Although technology can aid in furthering efficiency and quality, the true creators of SQ are happy, satisfied, and loyal employees (Peacock, 1995; Strebel, 1996; Lewis and Gabrielsen, 1998).

The lodging industry labor force has two broad categories: *frontline* workers are involved in direct contact with the consumer (waiters, front office staff), while *background* workers tend to perform behind-the-scenes tasks (making beds, preparing food, accounting, etc.) (Drucker, 1991; Yavas, Yasin, and Wafa, 1995). Service quality and performance in background jobs are largely measured in terms of quantity (how many bedrooms can be tidied during a shift) while quality is largely a matter of meeting externally imposed criteria. On the other hand, the performance of a frontline worker embodies both quantity and quality: with behavior toward customers often viewed as being just as important as the physical labor undertaken in performing the task (Drucker, 1991).

The links between empowerment, job satisfaction, and SQ have been analyzed by several researchers (Wood, 1992; Lewis and Gabrielsen, 1998). Motivated and satisfied employees will have positive impacts on external customer satisfaction, and also lead to increased employee retention rates. Lower levels of employee turnover will lead to a more experienced workforce and higher levels of consumer satisfaction. On the other hand, disgruntled or disempowered employees will clearly have a negative impact on overall SQ.

Technology can, for example, allow frontline workers to reduce time spent on certain functions, enabling them to focus more on the people-oriented activities that are so critical to service enterprise success (Quinn and Paquette, 1990, p. 70; Schlesinger and Heskett, 1991). Front office work has also become more comfortable and varied—stripped of many repetitive and often irksome tasks such as entering data in books and issuing bills manually. The introduction of sophisticated yield management systems gives greater responsibility for price bargaining to reservation/front office staff. In effect, they become sales managers rather than simply order takers (ILO, 1997, p. 54; Rodger and Vicar, 1996). On the other hand, night audits are now done effortlessly by PMS-based technology—as a result, many of the functions of the traditional night auditor have been made redundant and jobs have been lost or de-skilled.

Although the improvement of SQ is clearly a key reason for the introduction of IT, the decision is also often driven by a desire to improve productivity and reduce costs. In contrast to the U.S. case, a recent survey of Swiss-German hotels shows that the driving force behind technology implementation is "rationalization opportunities" (see ILO, 1997, p. 40). Even within the United States it is arguable that a sizable percentage of the reduction in the number of workers per 100 available rooms has been due to the introduction of IT. In their U.S. study of technology and SQ, Reid and Sandler (1992) note that the most popular forms of technology usually tend to produce the greatest labor-cost savings. In Europe, where computerization is less advanced than in the United States, there has been a less marked reduction in workers per room (Van Hoof, Verbeeten, and Combrink, 1996; ILO, 1997, p. 57).

Research into the impacts of technology on labor requirements is limited, but recent work conducted in Montreal and elsewhere reveals that job loss due to technological innovation is more likely to occur in larger properties. Indeed, 75 percent of nearly seventy Montreal large hotel managers interviewed in 1992 and 1995 felt that technology had been responsible for some job losses in recent times. On the other hand, 90 percent of small operators felt that technology had had no discernable impact on labor needs (Milne and Pohlmann, 1998; Milne and Gill, 1998).

IT is also playing a role in changing the way in which SQ is monitored. Some companies focus on management by objective approaches—with an emphasis on setting targets to be met during the year. In other cases hotels may take the approach of viewing the monitoring of SQ as everyone's job.

In larger hotels a transparent computer database can register customer preferences and complaints and quantify staff activities so that labor use can be more effectively matched to demand. This in turn leads to tighter scheduling of work, with employees having fewer busy periods interspersed with lulls.

New forms of evaluation also lead to new reward structures. For example, the French group Novotel recently introduced a competency-based reward system for all levels of staff. The key competencies of employees are evaluated continuously. As employees improve, they receive a centrally set percentage increase in pay. This approach replaces annual performance evaluations—improving objectivity and transparency. As IT aids in the breakdown of traditional barriers between different aspects of accommodation operations, availability to work in teams, attitude, and personal behavior become more important. Several large chains, including Accor, are highlighting the added social values of staff as part of a major endeavor to improve service levels and worker retention.

A key question here is to what extent workers will feel that technological changes have affected their jobs and workplace environment—either positively or negatively (Peacock, 1995; Ledgerwood, Crotts, and Everett, 1998). Some commentators argue that the introduction of IT is often linked with a feeling of weakening the employee's position (ILO, 1997, p. 56). To minimize the negative impacts of IT introduction, workers and, where applicable, unions should be consulted before new technologies are introduced (Strebel, 1996, p. 87). Negotiations and discussions should cover the following items (ILO, 1997, p. 73):

- Workers' participation in the identification and introduction of new technologies
- Training on new equipment and related safety/health issues
- Job security, work organization, and working time
- Modalities for the participation of unions concerning new management methods
- Details (where applicable) on expected productivity and profitability increases

Internal marketing of enterprise SQ (and IT) philosophy to employees is vital (Scheuing, 1996), while training is a key feature in the successful implementation of new technologies (Larkin and Larkin, 1996; Lashley, 1998). IT offers a range of opportunities to improve the training and communications environment within a hotel. New interfaces, simulation of real-life situations, and access to networked training software all offer management the chance to maximize effective interaction with employees.

Unfortunately, we have some distance to go before emerging IT, such as the Internet, can really lead to improved training procedures and communication within the firm. A recent study of perceptions of the value of Internet use in the U.S. lodging industry reveals, for example, that managers have a very low opinion of the Internet as a training tool and do not view its internal communications capabilities much more highly (Van Hoof and Verbeeten, 1998). Managers in larger, full-service hotels rated the importance of the Internet as a potential training tool more highly than their counterparts in smaller, limited-service properties.

It must also be remembered that the introduction of IT influences management as well as staff. A manager in an IT-rich work environment needs knowledge of computer systems to select the required equipment and use it effectively; ability to make rapid judgments based on the information provided by systems, and a high degree of interpersonal skills.

The use of technology may save some time by reducing more mundane tasks and opening up opportunities for managers to have more involvement with guests and staff. However, not all IT introductions will bring positive outcomes for management. Davin (1997) has shown that the benefits of GDSS may, for example, not be as apparent as some commentators point out. Her research reveals that GDSS does not offer benefits in decision time or participation quantity, with face-to-face meetings being more efficient. Donaghy and McMahon-Beattie (1998) show that the introduction of yield management (with related IT) can lead to a marked change in the time and importance that managers attach to their job components and roles. Although yield management was found to facilitate and enhance teamwork, its use did tend to overshadow employee recruitment and development within the establishments studied.

## CONCLUSION

The lodging industry will be called upon to spend increasing sums of money on IT. This investment will be crucial to improve efficiency and reduce costs, and, perhaps most important, to facilitate the provision and monitoring of SQ.

IT has great potential to improve the quality of service provided by lodging establishments. The integration of computing and telecommunications will create global information networks based most probably on the Internet. As the Internet evolves into a single, powerful "information highway" supported by diverse technology applications, there will be many opportunities for more flexible and efficient sales processes, data warehousing, customized service provision, and labor monitoring. At the same time, the hospitality industry will benefit from the continued development of intranet/PMS software and technologies.

Hotels vary widely in their ability and willingness to adopt IT (Van Hoof et al., 1995; Van Hoof, Verbeeten, and Combrink, 1996; Milne and Pohlmann, 1998). Some organizations are on the cutting edge, while others embrace advances long after they have been adopted by competitors (Cline, 1997). Technology influences SQ in small independent hotels as well as large chain operations, in both the developed and the developing world. The real differences lie in the cost and degree of sophistication of the equipment installed—and the infrastructural base to support it.

This chapter has shown that the task of improving service in organizations is complex. It involves knowing what to do on multiple fronts. The implementation of technology may very well assist in improving SQ, but research shows quite clearly that technology and information alone do not confer competitive advantage (Cline, 1997). If managers want to convert IT investments into real service quality improvements they must understand its links to, and impacts on, workers, managers, and suppliers.

A central issue is the fact that not all of the impacts of IT on service quality can be expected to be positive. In particular, managers need to work closely with workers to maximize the benefits of IT introduction (Strebel, 1996, p. 87). If managers are willing to grapple with the complexities of IT adoption, and are prepared to manage its myriad impacts effectively, then there appears to be little doubt that technology will facilitate ongoing improvements in service quality in the lodging industry and throughout the tourism, hospitality, and leisure arena.

## REFERENCES

Albrecht, K. and Bradford, L.J. (1990). *The Service Advantage.* Homewood, IL: Dow Jones-Irwin.

Ateljevic, J., Milne, S., Doorne, S., and Ateljevic, I. (1999). Tourism Micro-Firms in New Zealand: Key Issues for the Coming Millennium. Victoria University Tourism Group, Centre Stage Report No. 7, School of Business and Public Management, Victoria University, Wellington.

Bennett, M. and Radburn, M. (1991). Information Technology in Tourism: The Impact on the Industry and Supply of Holidays. In Sinclair, M.T. and Stabler, M.J. (Eds.), *The Tourism Industry: An International Analysis* (pp. 45-65). Wellingford, U.K.: C.A.B. International.

Berry, L. and Parasuraman, A. (1997). Listening to the Customer—The Concept of the Service Quality Information System. *Sloan Management Review.* 38(3): 65-76.

Bruns, R. (1998). Know Thy Guest. *Lodging.* June: 55-60.

Buhalis, D. (1999). The Cost and Benefits of Information Technology and the Internet for Small and Medium-Sized Tourism Enterprises. In Buhalis, D. and Schertler, W. (Eds.), *Information and Communication Technologies in Tourism, Proceedings of the ENTER 1999 Conference* (pp. 218-227). New York: Springer-Verlag Wein.

Chervenak, L. (1993). Hotel Technology at the Start of the New Millennium. *Hospitality Research Journal.* 17(1): 113-120.

Church, I. and Lincoln, G. (1998). Quality Management. In Thomas, R. (Ed.), *The Management of Small Tourism and Hospitality Firms* (pp. 138-155). London: Cassell.

Cline, R.S. (1997). Investing in Technology. *Lodging Hospitality.* 53(12): 59-61.

Coyne, K. (1993). Achieving Sustainable Service Advantage. *Journal of Business Strategy.* 14(1): 3-10.

Davin, K. (1997). Effects of Computer Support on Group Decisions. *Journal of Hospitality and Tourism Research.* 21(2): 44-57.

Donaghy, K. and McMahon-Beattie, U. (1998). The Impact of Yield Management on the Role of the Hotel General Manager. *Progress in Tourism and Hospitality Research.* 4(3): 217-228.

Drucker, P.F. (1991). The New Productivity Challenge. *Harvard Business Review.* 69(6): 69-79.

Gamble, P. and Jones, P. (1991). Quality as a Strategic Issue. In Teare, R. and Boer, A. (Eds.), *Strategic Hospitality Management* (pp. 72-82). London: Cassell.

Gatty, B. and Blalock, C. 1998. E-Commerce Gives Lodging Industry Edge. *Hotel and Motel Management.* 213(7): 12, 24.

Ghosh, S. (1998). Making Business Sense of the Internet. *Harvard Business Review.* March-April: 127-135.

Go, F.G. and Pine, R. (1995). *Globalization Strategy in the Hotel Industry.* London: Routledge.

Go, F.G. and Williams, A.P. (1993). Competing and Cooperating in the Changing Tourism Channel System. *Journal of Travel and Tourism Marketing.* 2(2/3): 229-248.

Grimes, R. (1998). Smart Cards Help Operators Build Better Customer Relations. *Nation's Restaurant News.* 32(13): 54.

Grove, S.J. and Fisk, R.P. (1991). The Dramaturgy of Service Exchange: An Analytical Framework for Services Marketing. In C.H. Lovelock (Ed.), *Services Marketing* (pp. 59-68). London: Prentice Hall.

Haywood, M. (1990). A Strategic Approach to Managing Technology. *Cornell Hotel and Restaurant Administration Quarterly.* 31(3): 39-45.

ILO (1997). *New Technologies and Working Conditions in the Hotel, Catering and Tourism Sector.* Geneva: International Labour Organisation.

Johns, N. (1996). The Developing Role of Quality in the Hospitality Industry. In Olsen, M.D., Teare, R., and Gummesson, E. (Eds.), *Service Quality in Hospitality Organisations* (pp. 9-26). London: Cassell.

Larkin, S. and Larkin, T.J. (1996). Reaching and Changing Frontline Employees. *Harvard Business Review.* May-June: 95-104.

Lashley, C. (1998). Research Issues for Employee Empowerment in Hospitality Organisations. *International Journal of Hospitality Management.* 15(4): 333-346.

Ledgerwood, C.E., Crotts, J.C., and Everett, A.M. (1998). Antecedents of Employee Burnout in the Hotel Industry. *Progress in Tourism and Hospitality Research.* 4(1): 31-44.

Lehtinen, U. and Lehtinen, J.R. (1991). Two Approaches to Service Quality Dimensions. *Service Industries Journal.* 11(3): 287-303.

Lewis, B.R. and Gabrielsen, G. (1998). Intra-Organisational Aspects of Service Quality Management: The Employees' Perspective. *Service Industries Journal.* 18(2): 64-89.

McGuffie, J. (1994). CRS Development and the Hotel Sector. *EIU Travel and Tourism Analyst.* (2): 53-68.

Milne, S. and Gill, K. (1998). Distribution Technologies and Destination Development: Myths and Realities. In Iaonnides, D. and Debbage, K.G. (Eds.), *The Economic Geography of the Tourist Industry: A Supply-Side Analysis* (pp. 123-138). London: Routledge.

Milne, S. and Pohlmann, C. (1998). Continuity and Change in the Hotel Sector: Some Evidence from Montreal. In Iaonnides, D. and Debbage, K.G. (Eds.), *The Economic Geography of the Tourist Industry: A Supply-Side Analysis* (pp. 180-196). London: Routledge.

Mutch, A. (1998). Using Information Technology. In Thomas, R. (Ed.), *The Management of Small Tourism and Hospitality Firms* (pp. 192-206). London: Cassell.

Olsen, M., Crawford-Welch, S., and Tse, E. (1991). The Global Hospitality Industry of the 1990s. In Teare, R. and Boer, A. (Eds.), *Strategic Hospitality Management* (pp. 213-226). London: Cassell.

Peacock, M. (1995). *Information Technology in the Hospitality Industry.* London: Cassell.

Poon, A. (1993). *Tourism, Technology and Competitive Strategies.* Wellingford, U.K.: CAB International.

Quinn, J.R. and Paquette, P.C. (1990). Technology in Services: Creating Organizational Revolutions. *Sloan Management Review.* 31(2): 67-78.

Raman, N.V. and Cleary, K.P. (1998). House Intelligent. *Telephony.* 234(17): 74-76.

Reid, R. and Sandler, M. (1992). The Use of Technology to Improve Service Quality. *Cornell Hotel and Restaurant Administration Quarterly.* 33(3): 12-16.

Reinders, J. and Baker, M. (1998). The Future for Direct Retailing of Travel and Tourism Products: The Influence of Information Technology. *Progress in Tourism and Hospitality Research.* 4(1): 1-15.

Rodger, J. and Vicar, A.M. (1996). Computerised Yield Management Systems: A Comparative Analysis of the Human Rescue Management Implication. *International Journal of Hospitality Management.* 15(4): 325-332.

Scheslinger, L. and Heskett, J. (1991). The Service-Driven Service Company. *Harvard Business Review.* 69(5): 71-82.

Scheuing, E.E. (1996). Delighting Internal Customers. In Olsen, M.D., Teare, R., and Gummesson, E. (Eds.), *Service Quality in Hospitality Organisation* (pp. 41-47). London: Cassell.

Solomon, M.R., Surprenant, C., Czepiel, J.A., and Gutman, E.G. (1985). A Role Theory Perspective on Dyadic Interactions: The Service Encounter. *Journal of Marketing.* 49(1): 99-111.

Strebel, P. (1996). Why Do Employees Resist Change? *Harvard Business Review.* May-June: 86-92.

*The Economist* (1999). Direct Hit. Business Section, January 9: 57-59.

Van Hoof, H., Collins, R., Combrink, E., and Verbeeten, M. (1995). Technology Needs and Perceptions: An Assessment of the US Lodging Industry. *Cornell Hotel and Restaurant Administration Quarterly,* 36(5): 64-69.

Van Hoof, H.B. and Verbeeten, M.J. (1998). HITA Survey Shows Managers Hesitant to Jump on Internet Speedway. *Hotel and Motel Management.* 213(4): 43-52.

Van Hoof, H., Verbeeten, M.J., and Combrink T.E. (1996). Information Technology Re-Visited—International Lodging Industry Technology Needs and Perceptions: A Comparative Study. *Cornell Hotel and Restaurant Administration Quarterly.* 37(6): 86-91.

Wolff, C. (1998a). Microsoft Sees Integration Changing Face of PMS. *Lodging Hospitality.* 54(3): 41.

Wolff, C. (1998b). Making the Guestroom "Information Central." *Lodging Hospitality.* 54(4): 35-36.

Wood, R.C. (1992). *Working in Hotels and Catering.* London: Routledge.

Yavas, U., Yasin, M.M., and Wafa, M. (1995). Front and Back-Stage Strategies in Service Delivery in the Hospitality Industry: A Conceptual Framework. *Marketing Intelligence and Planning.* 13(11): 22-26.

Chapter 17

# Delivering on Service:
# What Are the Questions and Challenges
# for Tomorrow's "Virtual University"?

Richard Teare

## *CHANGE FACTORS:*
## *HOW CAN INFORMATION NEEDS*
## *AND EXTERNAL CHANGE BE ASSESSED?*

Teare and Bowen (1997) examine the managerial activity of learning about events and trends in the organization's environment by profiling the top thirty hospitality industry issues as reflected by U.K.-based and North American hospitality management journals.

Figure 17.1 portrays a thematic picture of the clusters of research-based articles that reflect patterns in management, service improvement, and business performance issues. These themes sit at the center of organizational purpose and form a logical starting position for framing a learning agenda.

In seminar discussions with a group of twenty-five experienced U.K. hotel general managers during 1997, the Worldwide Hospitality and Tourism Trends (WHATT online) research team sought to draw together the participants' own top ten priority ranking. Industry priorities reflected a very real sense of concern about both customer and employee retention and development as well as the means of enabling these goals to be achieved. A summary of the key issues and priorities is included here.

### *People*

The problem of retaining high-caliber employees in the United Kingdom is related to the industry's inability to attract the right people (manag-

FIGURE 17.1. Patterns in Management, Service Improvement, and Business Performance

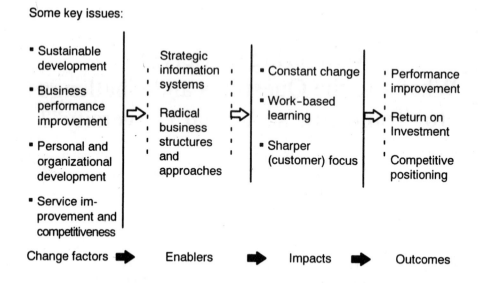

ers claimed that entrants have unrealistic expectations about hours of work and wages). The highest level of turnover occurs if expectations are not met during the first few weeks of employment.

High turnover is also attributed to inadequate training and lack of on-going development for employees—a need exists for initial management training and continuous, self-directed learning for all. The "Investors in People" scheme is seen as a positive step (especially for managing frontline employees), but other areas were viewed as equally important—e.g., leadership training, "adaptive (adaptable) manager" techniques, information management skills, and responding effectively to challenging financial targets (among many others). Maximizing effectiveness, both individually and in team performance, is seen as the prime means of delivering better results—financial, customers, employees, and systems.

## Business

Participants were eager to see industrywide improvements in strategic systems, especially relating to information and yield performance. In turn, it was thought that this would help industry to focus more attention on organizational indicators that are harder to monitor and measure but are potentially important measures of success (e.g., effectiveness of communications, morale, "best practice breakthroughs" or "best in class" innovations).

Branding and brand awareness coupled with operational consistency and perceptions of quality were seen as key issues then and in the future, especially in relation to the U.K. trend toward the "outsourcing" of hotel restaurants (using external providers).

### The Top Priorities

Overall, the discussion groups felt that the most pressing priorities for the U.K. hotel sector were: (a) customer retention and being customer focused, (b) motivating employees with a vision of the long term, and (c) personal development so that employees are equipped with the skills necessary to make things happen. Other key benefits will include improved retention rates among the pool of "good" managers and operatives, which is linked to development initiatives to lead, motivate, inspire, recognize, and reward the workforce.

### ENABLERS:
### HOW ARE STRATEGY, STRUCTURE, AND PERFORMANCE RELATED?

In reviewing the interrelationships between the external environment, strategy, structure, and performance, it is possible to discover a number of challenges for business learning (Teare, Costa, and Eccles, 1998). In summary form, they are described as follows.

### Strategy and External Analysis

- How might the organization assign environmental scanning tasks to detect and interpret the likely impact of external events?
- Who should be involved in "inside out" environmental scanning (reviewing the competitive environment)? Who will identify information needs and sources and assign scanning tasks? How will information be stored, processed, and disseminated so that it provides timely, well-focused, and meaningful inputs to organizational learning and updating?

### Strategy and Structure

- How should the organization seek to develop and sustain forms of competitive advantage now and in the future?

- Should unit managers adopt an enhanced role in the ongoing task of maintaining alignment between the strategic variables of structure, strategy, and environment? What additional contributions could they make to organizational efforts to improve processes, embed a customer-focused culture, and maintain "open" internal communication networks?
- How might workplace learning programs be used to optimize: flexibility (e.g., employee participation in idea generation and decision making); adaptability (e.g., responding quickly to changing market conditions); empowerment (e.g., giving employees the scope to be creative and to experiment); innovation (e.g., allowing employees to reinvent processes and procedures); and team support (encouraging, sharing, and providing mutual support)?

### Strategy and Performance

- To what extent should financial, functional, asset, and investment performance influence the organization's strategic direction?

Although these challenges have the appearance of strategy-level complexity, they provide meaningful categories for organizational learning that can be subdivided and "cascaded" (disseminated) as project assignments to an operational level.

## IMPACTS: HOW CAN LEARNING BE LINKED TO INTERPRETING AND RESPONDING TO CUSTOMER NEEDS?

If managers have discerned the main business issues, then how should they interpret and respond to their customers? How can they close the loop on managerial learning by relating industry issues and imperatives to customers and customer-led processes for delivering and assuring customer service? These challenges give rise to a number of questions for workplace learning initiatives related to customers (Teare, 1998).

### Understanding Customers

- Which services might be standardized and which should be customized (or personalized)? What are the design and delivery implications of these approaches for hospitality services?

- In what circumstances are customers likely to attribute more credibility to internal information than external information sources (and vice versa)?
- How does prior experience and familiarity with the product affect the customer's preference structure (preferences) and the formation of expectations, assessment criteria, and reference point experiences as key performance indicators?
- To what extent does role specialization in family purchase situations influence choice? What are the implications for the marketing of hospitality services?
- When are customers likely to use a decision rule (predetermined choice criteria)? How does this approach help to confirm the appropriateness of the decision?
- How does a customer's personal rating system operate and vary between different customer groups and across different hospitality settings?
- In what circumstances might customers be willing to compensate for a feeling of dissatisfaction with hospitality services? How might a feeling of dissatisfaction affect the approach to a repurchase situation?
- What practical steps might the organization take to minimize the potential impact of dissonance?
- How might the experiences of customers and employees be used to monitor and improve customer satisfaction levels?

### Designing and Delivering Services

- How should the organization integrate or at least coordinate its customer service, quality assurance, and marketing effort throughout the value chain?
- How might the organization refocus its internal service culture so that it is customer led? What practical steps does this involve and how should they be reinforced?
- To what extent could the organization benefit from service branding?
- How might the organization interrelate its efforts to maintain customer loyalty and product consistency?
- How might the organization localize its operations to adapt and respond to culturally and geographically different customer needs and expectations?

## Assuring Total Quality Services

- How might customer-perceived quality measures be used to identify and rectify quality gaps in the organization?
- What practical steps does the organization need to take in order to design and implement its own program for service quality benchmarking? To what extent might this activity drive organizational learning, both internally and in partnership with other service providers?
- How might the organization ensure that its quality and performance improvement efforts are customer focused?

The answers to what seem to be technical questions can in the main be addressed by attaining and sustaining a service leadership position. Whatever else this might mean, the overriding task is to learn from mistakes and to find ways of embedding a habit of active learning. To underline this, it is helpful to note one of the main findings of an Anglo-U.S. benchmark comparison of service practice and performance report on the competitiveness of U.K. service. The report observes that *training alone is insufficient—a concerted effort is needed to retain employees and develop their potential to its fullest extent* (London Business School, 1996).

If those who deliver service are themselves capturing the best ways of improving it (given that those in the front line are truly the eyes and ears of service leadership) then work-based learning might well be the key that unlocks the full potential for learning from customers.

### FROM IMPACTS TO OUTCOMES:
### THE VIRTUAL UNIVERSITY—
### TOMORROW'S LEARNING ORGANIZATION?

Although a great deal was written during the 1990s about the learning organization, there is no magic formula for embedding better ways of working and, in turn, learning from work. At its simplest level, individuals have a capacity to learn and to share their experiences with others. If team or shared learning can be nurtured with imagination and courageous leadership, it can, it seems, be cross-pollinated. But what are the consequences? If the organization is too rigid or hierarchical, then the good ideas will live with the enthusiasts and perish with the diehards who refuse to renew their learning regularly. How can managers embed a culture of learning and, most significantly, how can they make it "catch fire" so that it becomes infectious and quickens the pace and increases the competence of the people who make an organization what it is?

## Step 1: How Can Organizations Support Managerial Learning in the Workplace?

A thematic review of four areas (managerial learning and work; coaching, mentoring, and team development; competencies, managerial learning and the curriculum; and work-based action learning) (Teare, 1997a) reveals a number of key questions for embedding managerial learning:

- How are the participants' roles defined (scope, tasks, responsibilities, relationships); how do they currently enact their roles (gather information, take decisions and action, contribute to key activities such as planning, organizing, staffing, leading, and controlling); and what improvements would participants like to achieve for themselves, their work group and the wider organization?
- What are the external variables affecting managerial work (e.g., related to sources of discontinuity, uncertainty, ambiguity, complexity) and how might the program enable parallel, ongoing learning to occur so that managerial skills and knowledge keep pace?
- How can the program encourage participants to enhance their capacity to learn from work by using a variety of ways of analyzing experiences (e.g., intuitive, incidental, retrospective, prospective approaches) so that learning becomes self-sustaining?
- What forms of learner support should be used (e.g., coaching, mentoring, team development) so as to help people to learn, widen, and strengthen organizational participation, and embed a culture of learning?
- Who will coach and mentor and what are the resource and development implications?
- What are the core and specialist levels of competency, and how will these be built into the program and measured for attainment? How will these considerations affect the forms of learning and the methods of delivery?
- How will the efforts of participants be recognized—formally (e.g., accredited learning and the completion of an academic award), informally (e.g., support, encouragement, study time), and professionally (e.g., enhanced career prospects)?
- How will program outcomes add value for participants and the organization as a whole? How can the program encourage others to take

responsibility for recognizing and responding to their own development needs?
- How can the benefits of workplace learning be readily identified and sold to participants, their superiors, and subordinates? How can the reactions of skeptics and opponents be anticipated and effectively dealt with?
- How might return on investment (time, resources, individual and organizational effort) be measured and monitored?

### Step 2: What Is Needed to Enable Organizational Learning?

A thematic review of the literature relating to organizational vision, leadership and motivation, and organizational change and performance (Teare, 1997b) reveals that for both formal, programmed learning and informal self-reflection, it is helpful to consider the following:

- How can the organization equip itself to detect and respond appropriately to market trends? What processes and procedures are needed to isolate any given pattern of external events, devise suitable responses, and ensure that the implications for realigning resources and competencies are addressed? How should the organization assimilate the new knowledge that it acquires from this continuous cycle of adjustment and realignment?
- Should the organization make a deliberate attempt to connect its analysis of the internal and external change factors to cultural change? If so, how might the concept of an evolutionary organization (EVO) be launched? What are the organization's ideals or vision for an EVO? How can organizational members be encouraged to think and act responsively and without unnecessary constraint so that natural curiosity drives workplace learning?
- What kind of organizational structure is appropriate now and in the future? To what extent could and should the organization move toward facilitated self-organized learning networks so that budgets, resources, targets, and goals for learning are released to groups of employees, each managing enterprise activities? How will the differing roles of knowledge workers and generalists be reconciled if this approach is adopted?
- How should the organization adjust its information flows to take advantage of real-time communications (virtual office, global networking via Internet and intranet) for transacting its business? How could communications technologies be used to create a searchable knowledge network within the organization to support the learning effort?

- What action is needed to ensure that learning from experience is captured and that opportunities for organizational learning from self-reflection (individual and shared learning) and from studying other organizations are acted upon?
- How might learning partnerships with external catalysts be used to organize joint discovery and research projects, workshop and benchmarking activities, in-company tailored partnership programs, and organizational network activity assessments?
- What performance measures does the organization currently use most often, and why?
- Should "soft" employee-related performance measures (e.g., commitment, employee satisfaction, self-development, morale) be given more emphasis? How might the full range of organizational performance measures be related to improvements arising from the organizational learning effort?

### Step 3: How Can Managers Combine Managerial and Organizational Learning?

To "ground" some of the key learning organization concepts, several themes were explored concurrently during an Internet conference with managers from airport owner and operator BAA plc (Teare and Dealtry, 1998). The aim was to identify ways of creating a supportive learning environment and to relate this to an agenda for organizational learning and renewal. A summary of the main recommendations is given in Table 17.1.

Having created the information and communications infrastructure, what should the syllabus be if we are to support learning organization environments? Peters (1996) proposes a syllabus-driven approach for the aspiring learning organization, interlinking six areas that can be addressed by designing interventions for individuals, groups, and organizational systems:

- Learning about the participant's own job in the organization and how to do it better
- Learning how to create alignment between culture and strategy in the organization so that initiatives fit the context from inception to implementation
- Learning about the future by exploring the value of techniques for scenario planning and anticipating the likely implications for personal and organizational competency development
- Learning about the operating environment and the supply chain—essentially, systems thinking

- Learning how to challenge existing schools of thinking and avoid myopia so that personal and organizational mind-sets are open to change and to new ideas
- Developing an organizational memory for the purpose of capturing, storing, and retrieving knowledge and expertise

TABLE 17.1. The Learning Organization: Some Recommendations

| Themes | Recommendations |
|---|---|
| Modeling the learning process in organizations | • Use internal communications to explain and encourage personal learning and to promote its application to ongoing business improvement. "Sell the benefits" as often and in as many different ways as possible, throughout the organization. |
| | • Aim to recruit and retain people with different cognitive styles and skills to avoid "organizational cloning." |
| | • Aim to use taught and discovery methods, and where appropriate, a combination of both. |
| | • Encourage creative thinking and its application to opportunities for learning. |
| Organizational readiness | • Seek to enact change through individuals rather than overlaying an agenda for organizational change on the workforce as a whole. Use workplace learning founded on core values of trust, honesty, and integrity to encourage personal development. |
| | • Establish one or more independent action research sets to examine future scenarios and implications. Draw the set membership from people with different learning styles, skills, and from a variety of organizational functions. |
| Teamwork and learning | • Communicate the benefits of teamwork as widely as possible and link individual inputs to team outputs via the appraisal process. Use a learning journal to enable team members to reflect on the effectiveness of their own inputs. Establish targets for team participation (ongoing and different teams) and encourage shared learning. |
| Networked learning | • Seek to embed a culture of learning by devoting time and resources to developing a wider and deeper understanding of the concept of empowerment. Link this to on-the-job training and development, explain and communicate the benefits at all levels of the organization, and emphasize the benefits to individuals as well as the organization. |

The syllabus is for the organization as a whole and its members, who should participate according to their personal learning agenda and the organizational imperative. However, the sequence of its implementation is of some significance. Peters (1996) suggests that the learner's own job should be the starting point, as improvements here will yield organizational benefits from the outset. After this, longer-term debates should be established about future competencies and how to network learning throughout the organization's supply chain. The framework also provides a basis for monitoring the kind of organizational adjustments needed to maintain creativity and productivity and for routinizing improvements by creating and drawing upon a knowledge base that constitutes the organization's bank of knowledge capital.

The issues raised in steps 1 through 3 can be described as the ingredients of a learning organization, and they are depicted in Figure 17.2. But how can managers make this happen and integrate learning and work?

FIGURE 17.2. Systemized Organizational Learning

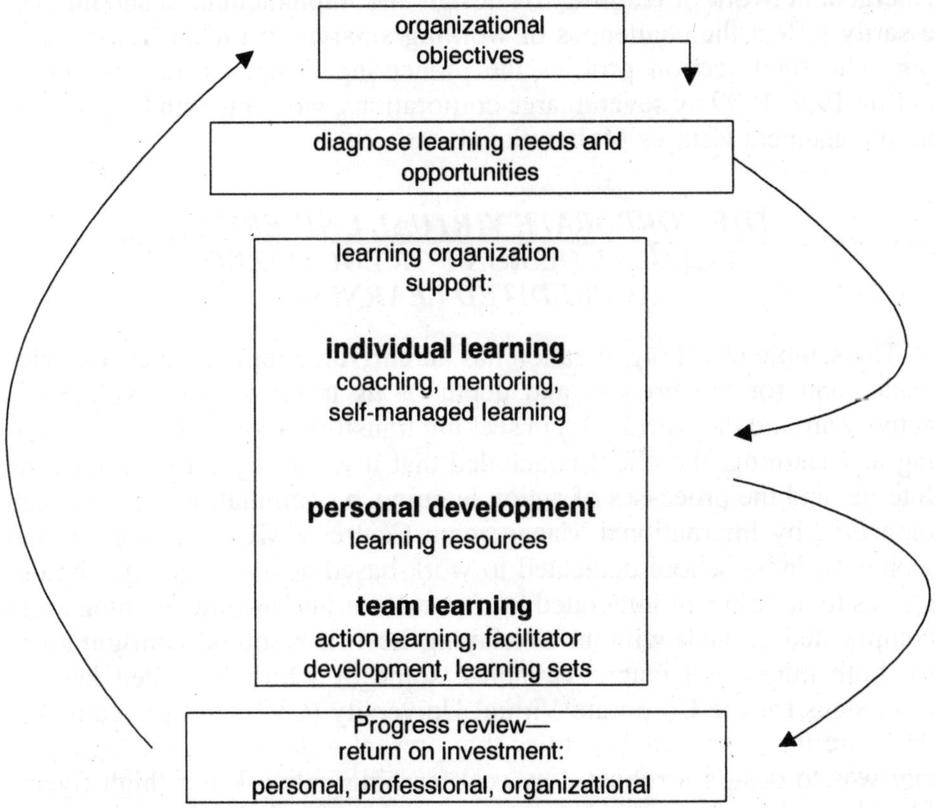

organizational
objectives

diagnose learning needs and
opportunities

learning organization
support:

**individual learning**
coaching, mentoring,
self-managed learning

**personal development**
learning resources

**team learning**
action learning, facilitator
development, learning sets

Progress review—
return on investment:
personal, professional, organizational

*Source:* Adapted from Buckler (1996), p. 37.

### Step 4: How Will Workplace Learning Evolve
### in the Information Age?

Work-based, career-long learning is increasingly seen as the route to personal effectiveness, and the new communications technologies are revolutionizing the delivery of learning experiences. Access to global domains of knowledge is now a reality, and the Internet brings the generators, brokers, and users of knowledge closer together than ever before. The Internet provides the means of interacting with communities of interest wherever they exist and of accessing, searching, and using learning resources linked to the Current Awareness database and other databases of articles and archive material. This capability offers the means of enabling a new form of online business learning and providing real-time links between the knowledge stakeholders—authors, editors, publishers, readers, learners, tutors, industry sponsors, and educationalists.

The virtual university represents the most advanced form, so far, of this emergent network of learning. Its design and implementation should necessarily reflect the challenges of working smarter and team-based learning. The final section profiles the pioneering design work undertaken during 1998-1999 by several large corporations, working with International Management Centres Multinational.

## THE CORPORATE VIRTUAL UNIVERSITY:
## A GLOBAL DESIGN FOR LOCALIZED,
## ACCREDITED LEARNING

The sample client organization has an unrivaled reputation as a service leader and for the breadth and depth of its training and development activity around the world. Yet, in seeking transformational change in training and learning, the client concluded that it would need to embrace the Internet and the processes of action learning, a combination that has been pioneered by International Management Centres (IMC), the world's first global business school dedicated to work-based action learning. The obstacles to building an integrated framework for just-in-time learning seem complicated enough without overlaying best-fit resource configurations for both micro and macro variables, some of which are cited later as challenges for the Corporate Virtual University (CVU) design team. But these are the operational realities that present a daunting challenge. Our aim was to design a robust, low-cost learning network for "high flyers" (people who are performing above expectations for their job role) at every organizational level, regardless of their prior academic background, that is capable of supporting a large organization working in every world region.

## International Challenges for the Client CVU

| Micro level | Macro level | Best configurations? |
|---|---|---|
| Owner involvement | Six-continent scope | Communications |
| Legal variance | Multiple languages | Multiple brands |
| Cross-cultural differences | Business in 52 currencies | Systems integration |
| Franchise integration | Political impacts to balance | Technical expertise |
| Casino operations | High-risk environments | Policy adaptation |

The client set itself the task of constructing a framework for accelerated, active learning so that it could build the competence levels of its managers as quickly and cost effectively as possible.

## Human Resource Challenges

- Generate and retain competence
- Leverage technology (fully utilize the potential of its technological investment)
- Develop future leadership performance capabilities
- Create rapid development routes for managers
- Accelerate paths for competency

Put simply, the goals are to work smarter and add value to the business by helping employees (called associates) to learn at work.

## Human Resource Goals

- Maintain a high-performance work environment
- Demonstrate added-value services
- See that continuous learning is the key to being a world-class organization
- Continually raise the "performance bar" (performance potential of the workforce) and accelerate development
- Build expertise in the knowledge of the business

To do this, it is necessary to speculate on the challenges that future service leadership organizations will need to embrace. The priorities are as follows:

- Learning at work, with minimal "time out" (time away from the workplace), using Internet resourcing to deliver "learnerware" (learning resources) to the work environment and engaging high-potential employees on the projects that frame the organization's own learning agenda.

- True partnerships between industry and education, with localized university support around the world—based on the client organization's learning agenda rather than a more traditional "static" learning agenda.
- A seamless (close) connection between accredited training and learning for career-long, just-in-time career development in the workplace. This should recognize the importance of learning outcomes (and the evidence of achievement) as the means of aligning training and other forms of accredited workplace learning via a process of "credit mapping" training and learning outcomes.
- Parity of status for nontraditional forms of learning achievement, using practitioner-oriented mechanisms for accrediting prior experiential learning so that no associate is discouraged or impeded from learning at work and gaining formal recognition for the outcomes of their study.
- Accelerated learning that is no longer bounded by traditional academic structures, yet is recognized as equivalent to conventional degree award frameworks—at all levels.

### The Process of Action Learning

If this process was to work, it would need to be a well-resourced, highly supportive learning process with opportunities for associates to customize their own learning and to share their learning with the "learning sets" both face-to-face and via the Internet (see Figure 17.3).

FIGURE 17.3. The Process of Action Learning

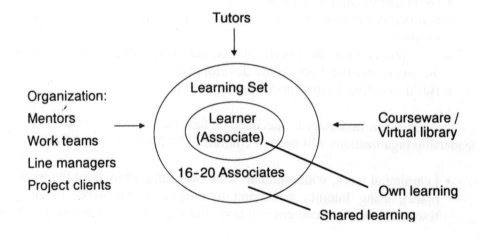

In promoting this radical agenda for learning at work to busy, successful associates, it is essential to set out the benefits and opportunities for personal development and for the company as a whole. In practical terms, this means stating how and by whom the learning process is directed.

## How Is the Learning Process Organized?

- It uses computers and the Internet to deliver a total learning infrastructure at low cost, nationally and internationally.
- A single Internet access point in any given work location provides complete access to all learning resources. A hands-on induction to Internet-resourced learning is provided so that those with no prior experience of computers or the Internet are not disadvantaged. This Internet resourcing is easy to access, navigate, and print at the point of use—with no time wasted and minimum fuss. The resources are constantly updated and used internationally to ensure that they are relevant to industry needs.
- Associates can access their "learnerware" at work so that they can relate it to the world of work—with minimal travel costs or time out for formal classroom study.
- CVU courses integrate with all existing in-company training courses —they do not replace them.

## By Whom Is the Learning Process Directed?

- The learning process is aligned with the change agenda and is built to the organization's specification.
- The learning process is professionally accredited and university validated: a consortium of universities around the world support the process—but do not control it. CVU's business objectives and the needs of learner-associates come first and drive the curriculum.
- The learning process is designed for busy managers—its purpose is to help them to function more effectively in their current jobs and to prepare them for the next job and/or promotion—not to create academically oriented managers for the sake of it.
- The learning process delivers return on investment as associates work on the company's key issues and in this sense, the value added is trackable and quantifiable.
- Evidence shows that action learning actually increases commitment (and employee retention). Associates can see the relevance and value of what they are doing by working on the projects that really matter to them and to the company.

### How Can Managers Make It Happen?

The international scale and scope of the client CVU required the maximum possible engagement of the senior training team in the phased design, internalization, implementation, and evaluation of the "first wave" of action learning sets. To embed the Internet-based quality assurance protocols and procedures used for managing all aspects of the courses offered at certificate, diploma, bachelor, and master's degree levels, a prototyping process was established. In essence, this meant that all trainer team members who were engaged in the architecture/design process undertook projects aligned with the CVU's training and learning strategy. The total project sought to explore, test, review, and refine all aspects of the CVU model prior to its launch. The model was designed to include:

- Internet resourcing (such as forum design, courseware design, Internet communications and learning, use of online publishing resources, learning sets, and learning dynamics for workplace learning—nationally and/or globally).
- Accreditation of prior experiential learning (APEL). This would enable the senior training team to mentor and undertake or supervise the learning portfolio assessments of its associates. The purpose is to recognize workplace learning achievement as a basis for entering CVU courses as a "proxy" for possessing conventional qualifications.
- Aspects of credit mapping. This enables the senior training team to "credit rate" the organization's existing training resources by mapping the learning outcomes against IMC's accredited and validated courses. Where outcomes are equivalent, academic credit can be given and the length and content of CVU courses can be customized to reflect this. In effect, this provides an integrated approach to training and accredited learning, by creating a career-long framework for "just-in-time" personal and professional development. It also means that the CVU team learns how to build in learning outcomes to achieve the maximum possible quantity of academic credit, when designing future training materials and courses.
- A fully customized and prototyped course for frontline, operational staff—using the full extent of IMC's courseware with individual organization contextualization.
- The transfer of expertise in tutoring; inducting tutors (who are members of both the CVU and IMC's global faculty); running Internet forums as meeting places for virtual learning; managing all aspects of dynamic quality assurance (ISO9000 certified); and equipping the

team to run their own evaluative research programs for training and learning.
- The transfer of expertise in capturing the learning outcomes of projects and formalizing this as internal systems, procedures, and routines so as to build on and fully utilize the intellectual capital of the organization as a whole.

In essence, these components are reflected in four strands of concurrent activity over a two- to three-year period of design, prototyping, implementation, evaluation, and incremental improvement (see Figure 17.4). Beyond the initial design phase, the CVU trainer team is organized to make rapid progress in three main areas of course-related activity, described in the following sections.

## Pilot Course Delivery Teams

A CVU trainer team responsible for organizing the support functions for the pilot courses (each with sixteen course members or associates per learning set) exists in every CVU world location. Additionally, each associate has his or her own mentor and a "client" for the main dissertation project and/or other assignments as appropriate. The main challenge here is to "cascade" the early successes of the initial U.K. prototype course and to build the CVU's mentor network so that every single learner has a helper close at hand.

FIGURE 17.4. Designing the Corporate Virtual University

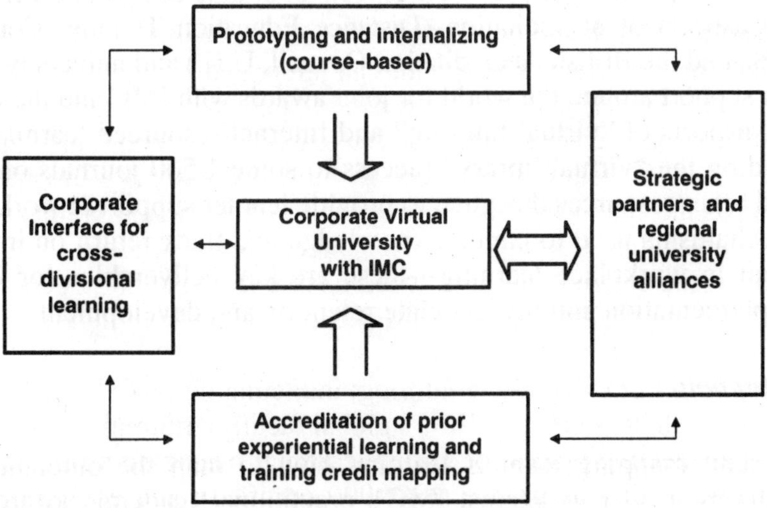

The key hands-on experiences for these teams are as follows:

- The course start-up process (when individual and team learning mechanisms are established)
- Taking action to ensure the "organizational fit" of the course, linked to the associates' own work
- Project assignment specification and marking (all based on real workplace challenges)
- Maintaining momentum in course set and subset working (face-to-face and Internet subset interactions) as well as organizing and facilitating both academic and company-specific inputs
- Operating the program management functions—including registry and quality assurance

### Partnership

The main role of the partnership trainer team is to internalize the IMC partnership framework so that the CVU could run its own accredited and validated courses. This framework should necessarily be built around the client's ways of working, and so the team must interpret the CVU design framework from their own experiences and knowledge of "how things are done." The team reports on all aspects of organizing and customizing CVU Internet-resourced workplace learning. The infrastructure includes the following:

- All courseware, and ISO9000-accredited quality assurance with full hands-on guides relating to all aspects of course design and delivery
- All aspects of accreditation (Distance Education Training Council, U.S., and the British Accreditation Council, U.K.) and university partner support around the world for joint awards with IMC and the CVU
- All aspects of "virtual tutoring" and Internet-resourced learning including the "virtual library" (access to some 1,500 journals online) and other resources designed to provide learner support at work
- Mechanisms used to capture knowledge and track return on investment in workplace learning—these are key deliverables for CVU implementation and for associate retention and development

### Credit Mapping

The credit mapping team is learning how to map the outcomes of internal training courses against IMC's practitioner/academic awards so that a seamless pathway between training and learning can be created. The hands-on work includes:

- Prototype mapping of existing company training courses (if the academic value is known, then associates can progress directly from internal training courses to certificate or bachelor's-level awards and obtain a "fast track" qualification at work).
- APEL portfolio building. The credit mapping team is also learning how to coach and counsel potential associates with nonstandard or no qualifications. The aim is to help applicants complete the APEL workbook so that it can be successfully verified and entitle them to CVU awards at the appropriate level.

### Have We Addressed the Challenges for Industry-Led Learning?

The development of the corporate university concept was a feature of the 1990s—there are many examples in the United States and elsewhere, and this phenomenon quite probably reflects a sense of frustration with the perceived narrowness of conventional management education in a business world that is obliged to work at a much faster pace (Teare, Davies, and Sandelands, 1998). The Corporate Virtual University represents a significant step forward in that it quite deliberately leverages the best that the world of education has to offer to apply it to learning at work. In effect, it is both a corporate university and a real university, with some ten university alliance partners supporting the CVU's agenda in their respective world regions and languages. The role played by IMC is key—it provides all the resourcing, quality assurance, and accreditation mechanisms and experience to enable learning to flourish in a sophisticated business context and on an international and multicultural basis. IMC also acts as a broker with the CVU of university relationships for joint awards and seeks to ensure that academic inputs are both meaningful and relevant. This is a challenging and difficult task, but the goal is worthwhile as it aligns university support with the company's global enterprise. In this way, the global network, orchestrated by the CVU and IMC, adds value to a global firm's enterprise rather than seeking to control the learning process and the curriculum as in the past. At last it is possible to say that we have applied a commercial mind-set to business learning that achieves global scope in resourcing terms and local attention to the issues and challenges that matter to individual learners, their business units and, in virtual university terms, to the company's business as a whole.

In summary, the CVU concept reflects a radical industry-based response to the issues and challenges of retaining service leadership. It has blazed the trail by:

- Promoting the workplace as a valid site of learning and giving prominence to continuous, lifelong learning with a truly open system of access and entry.
- Designing an organizationwide framework of action learning with industry-themed resourcing and accredited awards, supported by an Internet-rich learning environment with a single access point for all associates anywhere in the world.
- Aligning an array of university alliance partners with IMC and the CVU so that they deliver a meaningful support service with a curriculum that is rigorous, vibrant, and dynamic, within a framework designed to the client's specifications.
- Enabling the CVU's own trainer teams to run the courses with external tutors and examiners to "triangulate" a multidimensional view of quality assurance, characterized by fitness for purpose and evidenced by the attainment of learning outcomes that are derived from implementable solutions to real work projects with tangible benefits for the learner, his or her work teams, and for the client organization.

## REFERENCES

Buckler, B. (1996). "A learning process model to achieve continuous improvement and innovation." *The Learning Organization,* 3(3): 31-39.
International Management Centres <http://www.imc.org.uk/imc/>.
London Business School (1996). "Competitiveness of UK service: An Anglo-US benchmark comparison of service practice and performance." Occasional Paper, Centre for Operations Management, November.
Peters, J. (1996). "A learning organization's syllabus." *The Learning Organization,* 3(1): 4-10.
Teare, R. (1997a). "Supporting managerial learning in the workplace." *International Journal of Contemporary Hospitality Management,* 9(7): 304-314.
Teare, R. (1997b). "Enabling organizational learning." *International Journal of Contemporary Hospitality Management,* 9(7): 315-324.
Teare, R. (1998). "Interpreting and responding to customer needs." *The Journal of Workplace Learning,* 10(2): 76-94.
Teare, R. and Bowen, J.T. (1997). "Assessing information needs and external change." *International Journal of Contemporary Hospitality Management,* 9(7): 274-284.
Teare, R., Costa, J., and Eccles, J. (1998). "Relating strategy, structure and performance." *The Journal of Workplace Learning,* 10(2): 58-75.

Teare, R., Davies, D., and Sandelands, E. (1998). *The Virtual University: An Action Paradigm and Process for Workplace Learning.* London and New York: Cassell, p. 315.

Teare, R. and Dealtry, R. (1998). "Building and sustaining a learning organization." *The Learning Organization Journal,* 5(1): 47-60.

WHATT. Worldwide Hospitality and Tourism Trends Forum <http://www.mcb.co.uk/htgf/whatt/> or <http://www.whatt.net>.

# Index

Page numbers followed by the letter "e" indicate examples; those followed by the letter "f" indicate figures; and those followed by the letter "t" indicate tables.